ME
623.8
Mar
FREEPORT COMMUNITY LIBRARY

D1708849

Patriarch of Maine Shipbuilding

THE LIFE AND SHIPS OF GARDINER G. DEERING

Patriarch of Maine Shipbuilding

THE LIFE AND SHIPS OF GARDINER G. DEERING

By Kenneth R. Martin

Published by Jackson A. Parker
Woolwich, Maine

Distributed by
Tilbury House, Publishers
2 Mechanic Street
Gardiner, Maine 04345
800-582-1899
www.tilburyhouse.com

First Edition: April 2008

Designed by Michael Steere

ISBN: 978-0-88448-307-6

5 4 3 2 1

Printed in China

"The patriarch of Maine shipbuilding:" Gardiner G. Deering (1833–1921), builder of ninety-nine schooners. F. V. Moody photograph, courtesy Maine Maritime Museum.

Table of Contents

Foreword

No one ever really gets to know one's great-great grandfather. A life's story is extinguished with the passing of generations and lost forever unless it is recorded. In some cases the historical record can be merged with family documents to reconstruct an interesting or noteworthy life. Sometimes.

In the case of my great-great grandfather, Gardiner G. Deering, the trail had long since gone cold. I remember hearing my grandfather, Gardiner R. Deering, tell stories of growing up in a shipbuilding family but they were anecdotal and I never gained an understanding of the complete man or his life's work. I always wanted to know more, but the once-large family had dwindled over time and as a result of a 1920s court case involving the disposition of G. G. Deering's once substantial estate, remaining family members avoided one another.

I knew there had to be a story worth telling of a man who built ninety-nine ships in the City of Ships, but I did not know how to find it. Enter Ken Martin, maritime historian, author, friend and neighbor. Ken eagerly accepted my challenge to research and write about Gardiner G. Deering, even though neither of us knew where the effort would lead. We embarked on the project with no preconceived notions. Let the record unfold and tell the story, I said. Well, here it is and I hope you enjoy it as much as I do.

Ken has written this historical account in narrative form. At my request, he included details of commercial transactions, seafaring stories, family intrigue, local historical perspectives and just about anything else that was part of the story. You will see perhaps an excess of schooner photographs but I believe the beauty and majesty of these vessels justifies including as many as possible.

In the end, this book is more than I had hoped for and I am indebted to Ken Martin. It tells the story of a man of great skill and determination, strong instincts, an innovative nature, and a risk taker but frankly, someone who was not always lucky. But that is Gardiner G. Deering, the man who built ships for more than half a century on the banks of the Kennebec. When he died in 1921 at the age of eighty-eight, the *Boston Globe* eulogized him as the "Patriarch of Maine Shipbuilding." After reading the manuscript of this book I thought that title was fitting and well deserved for the man and for the book.

Jackson A. Parker
Days Ferry
Woolwich, Maine

Preface

If you enjoy surprises, envy me. From its very inception, this project has been a succession of unexpected developments, all of them pleasant.

The first surprise came when, out of the blue, my neighbor Jackson Parker proposed that I write a monograph about his great-great-grandfather, Gardiner G. Deering. It sounded good to me. "That's the sort of thing you do," he said, "Right?"

Right. Deering, an old-school Yankee shipbuilder even in his own time, enjoyed an eventful, successful career but had since largely slipped from historical memory. Accordingly, we supposed that a Deering project would lash up modest bits of information into a small commemorative.

Wrong. A quick look into local archives revealed enough source material perhaps to write a coherent biography. That was the second surprise, but perhaps it should not have been. Although he had somehow eluded posterity's attention, Gardiner Deering's career was substantial enough to have left a visible paper trail.

With slightly higher expectations, I went ahead with the project, research and writing to be completed within five months. Mission accomplished. But it was a bit of a stretch because (surprise!) the sources on Gard Deering turned out to be not just more numerous but better than expected. There were not enough to make the job easy; there never are. There were just enough to force me to think hard about what they did and didn't reveal. Making sense of those disparate, incomplete records has been my most challenging book assignment—not exactly fun, but fascinating.

The generous assistance I received from archivists was no surprise although their enthusiasm for the project took me unawares. At the Maine Maritime Museum, librarian Nathan

Lipfert, my onetime co-author and longtime esteemed colleague, answered big and small questions with admirable patience and good cheer. Every chat with Nathan left me with a few more clues and ideas. I was also given the run of the museum's well-organized photograph collection, which provided crucial illustrations for this work. Nathan's library assistant Kelly Page, a whiz with the computerized catalogue and a creative thinker to boot, made important suggestions about useful material that might be hiding in unlikely files. At the Patten Free Library in Bath, Peter Goodwin and Robin Haynes seemed to have the entire history of Bath between their ears, to say nothing of the Sagadahoc History and Genealogy Room's collections, which they enthusiastically shared with me. Having encountered my share of crypt keepers over the years, I found working with Nathan, Kelly, Peter, and Robin sheer delight. Thank you all.

Once during a conversation at the Maine Maritime Museum, Nathan let it slip to Capt. Doug Lee that I was doing a book on Deering. And thereby hangs another surprise. Capts. Doug and Linda Lee, skippers of the beautiful schooner *Heritage* of Rockland, deserve a book of their own because, among other accomplishments, they have proven it is still possible to make a living in schooners. They are also prodigious collectors of schooner history. I had been casually friendly with the Lees for years, but until I got a close look at their private archive I had underestimated their passion and expertise. During two brief visits to Rockland, Doug Lee guided me through his vast photograph files, provided a priceless, wildly enthusiastic, running tutorial on the subject, and loaned me seldom-seen and never-published images for the good of the cause. If a picture is worth a thousand words, and if you read on, you will soon appreciate the exponential importance of that generosity. Thank you, Doug and Linda.

Every week for twenty years, Ralph Linwood Snow and I have lunched together, solving the world's latest problems and sharing our mutual interest in maritime history. Lin and I have collaborated on three books, but his greatest work is *A Shipyard in Maine: Percy & Small and the Great Schooners* (2000), written with Capt. Doug Lee. Years of research on that book gave Lin, like Doug, comprehensive understanding of the shipyards, commerce, conventions, and problems of the Yankee schooner trade—the sort of work Gard Deering devoted his entire life to. Never at a loss for words on any topic, Lin was delighted to share anything and everything he thought might be of help—another private tutorial and an invaluable shortcut in my own work. The best part was that he, like Doug Lee, had a good time doing it. Thank you, Lin.

Thanks also to W. H. Bunting, another author and friend, who was always ready with quick answers to esoteric questions, and who made some creative suggestions of his own. Nancy Burden, a punctilious proofreader and a stickler for style, found glitches in the manuscript that I couldn't see for looking. Abbie McEwen, one of Gard Deering's descendants, lent an invaluable hand scanning and culling dozens of photographs. Two more pleasant surprises will end the list. Kathy Jensen, a descendant of Capt. William Merritt and a zealous keeper of family history, popped up on the Internet and generously contributed key photographs and facts about her ancestor. Another virtual kindred spirit, Joe Hartwell, provided photographs and information on the German submarine that sank Capt. Merritt's schooner. Small world.

A word on style. I have quoted original documents as they were written, believing that readers prefer eccentricity to grammatical makeovers. In the case of typographical errors, wherever possible I have inserted corrections between brackets [like this] rather than reprint a longstanding mistake followed by the conventional [sic], which I find editorially distracting and, often, a cop-out. In keeping with modern usage I have eliminated possessives in geographical names. In the text, for example, the small Maine village on the Kennebec is Days Ferry, not Day's Ferry.

All in all, I have to admit, with gratitude, that Jack Parker had a very good idea when he suggested a book about Gard Deering. Despite his guarded personal modesty, Deering's maritime career turns out to have been an open book. I hope readers will share some of my pleasure in reading it.

Ken Martin
Days Ferry, Maine
2 July 2007

CHAPTER ONE

The Call of the Shipyard

He would never forget what he saw that September day in 1813, standing on the rocky shore and looking out over the ocean. The guns booming off Monhegan Island had been heard in Edgecomb, several miles inland. Everyone knew what that meant: The HMS *Boxer*, a wartime nuisance on the Maine coast, had been found by the USS *Enterprise*, and a sea fight was under way.

Fourteen-year-old David Deering and his neighbors hightailed it to the oceanfront at Boothbay to watch the action. Without a spyglass it was hard to make out the two miniature warships as, almost becalmed, each maneuvered to gain an advantage. These preliminaries continued for hours, but eventually the *Enterprise* got to windward of the *Boxer* and thus could control the action. A raking volley from the American vessel damaged the *Boxer's* rigging, making her unmanageable. After less than an hour of fighting, she struck her colors—a thrilling moment for the watchers on shore, most of whom dearly longed for the enemy to get such a comeuppance. Later, young Deering and his friends would learn that during the engagement both commanders, still in their twenties, had been killed. Their bodies would be buried side by side in a Portland cemetery.

Off Monhegan, the victorious USS Enterprise *(left) escorts the beaten HMS* Boxer *toward Portland, where the warships' commanders—both killed in the action—will be buried side by side. Teenager David Deering watched this memorable fight from the distant shore on 5 September 1813. From Barber Badger's* Naval Temple *(1816). Courtesy: Private Collection.*

There would be other, more celebrated ship-to-ship engagements during the pointless War of 1812; but the *Enterprise* victory was a huge psychological boost to Maine people in general and David Deering in particular. Seventy-five years later he still enjoyed relating the story.[1] Mainers had suffered economically in the painful years before 1812, when Washington had curtailed trade because of high-handed British depredations. Unexportable Maine goods piled up uselessly while the ships that carried them idled along the coast. Then came the war, and things had gotten worse. To someone like David Deering, who planned to spend his life building vessels, it was a time of enormous frustration. After peace broke out in 1815, there was no quick recovery. Overcoming Britain's trade restrictions in the once lucrative West Indies, for example, would take years. The sluggish U.S. economy was tough on shipbuilding; so one might think twice before planning such a career. These drawbacks did not stop David Deering.

David was the second son of his namesake, an Edgecomb farmer and landowner who fathered twelve children by two wives. The younger David owned a bit of land in Edgecomb but farming was not for him. Shipbuilding was. He began in Boothbay and Edgecomb yards. Like all would-be ship carpenters, he started as a helper, working on small schooners, the two-masted, fore-and-aft-rigged vessels that were mainstays of the fishing and coastwise trades. And he stayed with it. Tradition has it that in early adulthood he was a "builder" of such vessels, but whether that means he constructed schooners on his own ticket or as a shipyard employee is not clear. In any event, over years he mastered ship carpentry through the customary system of commencing at the bottom and moving slowly upward through experience.

Meanwhile, he had married Catherine Sherman of Edgecomb and started a family. In 1820, his son George was born, the first of nine children: six boys and three girls. George too would become a carpenter. Two other sons will be important to our story: John (born in 1827), and Gardiner (1833). These siblings likewise followed in their father's footsteps. David Deering was a Freewill Baptist, a hardshell fundamentalist who instilled traditional values in his children. Hard work was a virtue to him, and during a lifetime of shipyard work he got what he probably expected: years of hard, honest toil with a few lucky breaks here and there, and—this is important—the satisfaction that comes when large, beautiful objects take shape under one's hands. But times were changing. The American economy had rebounded in the latter 1820s, a rising tide that floated Maine shipyards' boats. In growing numbers, Maine people prospered in coastal, Caribbean, and transatlantic commerce. In 1837, with a growing family to support, Deering sold his patch of land to his father and moved to Bath, a town on the Kennebec River that was fast becoming a shipbuilding center of worldwide importance.[2] Here was challenge as well as financial stability. Bath yards were building ever larger, more sophisticated vessels. It was an exciting place to be, and the Deering craftsmen would stay there the rest of their lives.

Bath in 1837 had just established ferry service across the Kennebec River, so it is possible that the Deerings came to town that way. They beheld a spot ideal for wooden shipbuilding. Stretched out narrowly on the Kennebec's western shore, twelve miles from the sea, Bath hugged a gently sloping bank that seemed custom-made for launching ships. The Kennebec, conveniently wide at this spot, obliged shipbuilders further by providing a long, straight, north-south anchorage known as Long Reach. Lumber from Maine's hinterland was handy, as were local sawmills, although large, prime cuts were becoming scarce, necessitating imports from southern forests. Bath's chief commercial disadvantage was that Maine's backwoods resources and infrastructure were too weak to support her growth as a seaport. These points were well understood by local entrepreneurs, who invested and reinvested in ships and shipping, thus providing livelihoods for hundreds of workers. At the time the Deerings arrived, Bath was the fastest-growing community in Maine and one of the fastest growing in the nation. Between 1830 and 1840, Bath yards built more than 100 vessels, 84 of them full-rigged ships. Local families such as the Houghtons, Sewalls, and Pattens were growing dynastically wealthy, building and then managing vessels in the sugar, lumber, cotton, and passenger trades. Bath was a world away from snoozy, rural Edgecomb.

Bath, Maine, in 1844, as portrayed from the Woolwich side of the Kennebec River by folk artist H.A. Hilling. The artist has captured the city's busy atmosphere and its genteel residential district. Courtesy: Maine Maritime Museum.

The arriving Deerings would have noticed the charred remnants of a serious fire that had damaged Bath's business section. An even worse fire would occur the next year. Nonetheless, their new home had an atmosphere of substance about it. Bath's population was approaching 5,000. A local press, banking and shopping facilities, and handsome upscale buildings gave it a touch of elegance, and community-conscious citizens were systematically improving civic amenities as well. But along with all that came some drawbacks. For example, rents were high. David Deering tackled that problem quickly. Shortly after his arrival, and probably using the nest egg from his Edgecomb land sale, he purchased a building known as the Jewell house in Bath's South End and moved it to the corner of Middle and Pine streets, into a closely packed neighborhood of clapboard homes half a mile below the business district and a block uphill from the bustling riverfront. Moving large structures was by no means uncommon in those times; and of course David Deering had plenty of family help with the carpentry. When completed, the house at 476 Middle Street became home for two generations of Deerings.[3]

The rest of David Deering's story can be briefly told. In fact it must be briefly told because of the shortage of biographical information. He spent most of his long career as a carpenter in various Bath yards, keeping busy during good times and riding out the recurring slumps that were a part of America's gyrating economy. He built at least one entire vessel himself, the 41-ton fishing schooner *Orville*, in 1856, constructed at the foot of Pine Street, a short walk from his home. He managed to keep bodies and souls together during Bath's periodic lean times. As the local press later noted, "Mr. Deering was a remarkably industrious man, and when shipbuilding was dull always found other occupation. He had fitted up a decked scow with grappling irons, and often made the depths of the Kennebec yield up lost anchors, timber, and the like. He also followed the sea a little."[4] He kept busy until the age of eighty-five and then enjoyed five more years of retirement in the company of his shipbuilding children, who had made him very proud.

David's sons George, John, and Gardiner all became master builders, earning their expertise along the Bath riverfront, sometimes working together. They would have lots of company, for Bath's population reached 11,000 by 1853. Of the Deering brothers, Gardiner's career is best known, and we shall follow it closely, for he was in for a very eventful life.

After arriving in Bath with his family at age fourteen, Gardiner briefly attended High Street Academy and then went to work at his father's trade. There was nowhere to go but up, and up he went. As the *Bath Daily Times* later put it, Gardiner Deering "came to Bath as a poor boy and by careful saving and close attention to business was able to venture on a business career when scarcely more than a boy."[5]

It is easy to imagine the youngster working under the protective eye of his two older brothers. Regardless of age, Bath shipwrights worked six days a week, rain or shine, from dawn until dusk in the summertime and ten hours per day in other seasons. Gard Deering refined his ship carpenter's skills by working in more than one yard, moving here and there as needed when a vessel was completed and another started. There was usually work somewhere. One report, possibly exaggerated, set the number of working shipyards in Bath at twenty-two. Much of Deering's time was spent in the Hitchcock shipyard, about half a mile downriver from home, working on ever larger ships (three-masted square-riggers) that were a far cry from the little vessels his father had cut his teeth on, and which were now Bath's stock in trade. An efficient yard could build a ship from scratch to launch in about six months, with another month for rigging and finishing touches. Between projects, repair work often kept crews busy. Bath was small enough to nurture communal spirit in the yards between workers and owners. People worked at close quarters, lived out of each other's pockets and in each other's neighborhoods, and pulled together through good times and bad. The so-called learning curve worked for all: With repetition came improved performance and reduced cycle time. Bath ships were esteemed the world over for their quality, a reputation that survives to this day.

In 1857, Gard Deering, now a young man, made a break with all this, signing on board the Bath ship *Union*, a cotton freighter. He was probably motivated to go to sea by the national financial panic of 1857, which stopped shipbuilding cold along with the jobs it had provided. Cotton freight rates were also down because of the panic, so the *Union* instead hauled good old Maine hay to Mobile, returned to Quebec for a cargo of deals (rough lumber), and carried that to the West Indies. Deering earned $45.00 a month on these voyages, about the going rate for carpenters in Bath yards at the time. Of course, he received room and board, such as it was, on the *Union*. He left that vessel somewhere in the West Indies and returned home aboard the bark *Howland* of Boston. Although going to sea may have been a last resort, those deepwater voyages were valuable practical lessons, affording Deering a first-hand look at the structural stresses sailing vessels underwent at sea. The year 1860 found him at work for E. & A. Sewall (among others, no doubt), for which he received $1.50 a day.

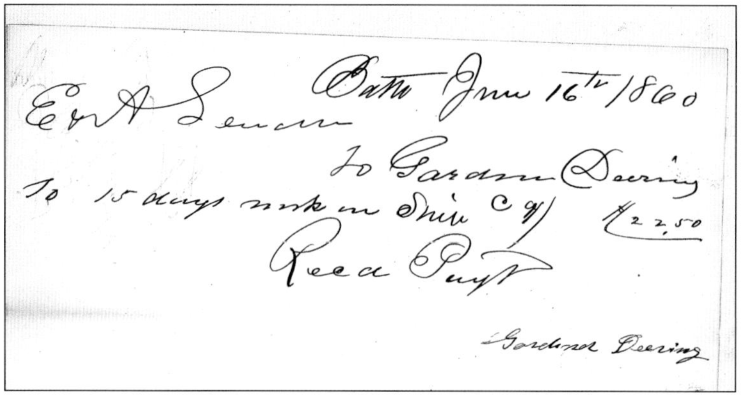

Bath June 16th/1860
E & A Sewall
To Gardiner Deering
To 15 days work on Ship @ $1.50 $22.50
Recd Payt
Gardiner Deering

A pay receipt for Gardiner Deering, carpenter, who worked briefly at E. & A. Sewall's Bath shipyard for $1.50 per day in 1860. Courtesy: Parker Family Collection.

But man does not live on money alone. In 1859, Gard Deering married the girl next door—or close to it. His bride was Lydia Robbins, twenty-three, who grew up at 36 Pine Street, a few doors away from the Deering household. Lydia was a daughter of Chaney Robbins, a shipyard caulker and real estate speculator who had become land-poor in his own neighborhood. The newlyweds were able to purchase a clapboard home at 62 Pine Street from Chaney's insolvent estate.

The young couple's family life, however, got off to a difficult start. Their first child, Emma, born in 1860, lived less than two years. Their second child, Susan, born in 1862, lived less than one. The sorrow this caused can only be imagined, although there would be more children in a few years. The loss may partially explain Lydia Deering's obscurity in this narrative. Evidence indicates that she remained a homebody, rather retiring although not an introvert. We know little else about her, which is a pity, for she surely played a vital supporting role in events that were to come.

If you had decided to visit Bath in the 1850s, you could arrive by train, thanks to the shipping magnates George and John Patten and William Sewell, whose influence and cash had brought the Portland and Kennebec Railroad to town in 1849. You would also be arriving in a city, for Bath had adopted a charter to that effect in 1847. Hungry? Good meals were available at the new Sagadahoc House in the downtown—a conspicuous symbol of the new city's growth. You could do worse than book a room there. Thirsty? That might be a problem. Maine had lately become a prohibitionist state, resolving, it was hoped, decades of organizational pressures and social debates. Bath, however, was still a waterfront community; so if you wished to wink at the new law, there were many joints in the city that unofficially offered a taste of "striped pig." Just ask anyone on Front Street.

During your stay, you would probably have been impressed, as many were, by the community's prosperous appearance and its citizens' air of satisfaction. As one traveler put it in 1853, "the stranger sees, on all sides, that he is in a city where the people are not only alive, but where they put forth their energies in the most intelligent, tasteful and productive manner."[6] The source of all that energy, of course, was shipping. By 1860, 500 commercial vessels were registered in the Bath customs district. You would soon discern that the Bath's uniquely "productive manner" literally emanated from the many shipyards extending from the business district and ferry terminal north and south along the waterfront. Accordingly, your visit would be incomplete without a personal look at these yards.

If you headed for the South End along Washington Street, and got as far as Pine, you would start to notice the contrast between the rough-and-tumble riverside shipyards on the left and the more sedate, often residential buildings on the right, a few yards inland. Chances are your attention would be to the left, for you could easily look into the yards that lay cheek-by-jowl between Washington Street and the river. Depending on the season, you would have to contend with dust, snow, slush, or mud, and you would of course need to watch where you stepped. You would quickly be struck by the noise, especially if the economy was in a periodic surge and the yards were extra busy. Bath people were accustomed to ambient noise along the waterfront: banging, clanging, pounding, and rasping of caulking mallets, adzes, pit saws, and mauls, accompanied by the shouts of shipwrights and the rumble of teamsters' rigs. But it took some getting used to for a stranger.

The objects of everyone's affection dominated each yard: wooden hulls in various stages of construction, propped at an incline, stern toward the river, and surrounded by rickety staging. When planked, finished, and painted, and with some fanfare, these hulls, freed of their restraints, would slide majestically into the Kennebec to begin their commercial careers. Here and there in each yard there might be a few seedy-looking buildings that supported all of this activity. And everywhere there was clutter: wood chips, idle tools, junk, puddles, and random-looking piles of shaped timber, some of it enormous. If you knew ships you might see a plan in all that disorder.

Then there was the smell, a pungent mixture, not unpleasant, of oakum, sawn timber;

Stockholm tar, hot metal, fresh paint, manure, and sweat. All in all, an environment that was unforgettable. And fascinating. And subject to change.

As happened everywhere in the nation, the American Civil War forever changed Bath. The city had rebounded from the Panic of '57. Production gradually resumed and Bath was humming again by 1860. But not for long. The onset of hostilities in 1861 disrupted commerce, inflated insurance rates to intolerable levels, and denied the lucrative cotton trade to Yankee vessels. It also cut off the supply of southern timber, upon which Bath yards now depended. As hostilities deepened, foreign vessels, mostly British and Canadian, moved in to fill the shipping gap. Many U.S. vessels were sold to foreign interests, many hid under foreign flags of convenience, and others became casualties of war. When the long ordeal was over in the States, America's maritime power was severely and permanently reduced. Meanwhile, the growing importance of steam-powered vessels and iron square-riggers was putting Maine's wooden shipbuilding on the defensive. Adapting to these changes would be the big story in Bath for the next generation. As we shall see, the City of Ships met this challenge remarkably well. And Gardiner Deering became one of the key players in meeting that challenge.

What did Deering and his brothers do during the Civil War? There is no clear answer, although later events suggest that Gard spent those years as a carpenter in the South End yard of Rufus and Henry Hitchcock. He must have been busy during the war years, because clearly he managed to save some investment capital. Unlike his brothers George and John, Gard was prepared to make a career jump from shipyard employee to shipyard employer, and that took cash. A year after the war ended he formed a partnership with William T. Donnell. The two had known each other since boyhood and, later, had worked side-by-side building vessels at the Hitchcocks'. They would spend the next twenty years together, doing what they did best. Against substantial odds, they would achieve notable success.

About the time David Deering watched the *Boxer-Enterprise* fight and began thinking about a career building ships, Thomas Donnell of Bath married a cousin and started raising a family. His oldest son Benjamin went to work in the Cox, Curtis, and Arnold yards in Bath's South

End, advancing over the years to the position of master joiner. He supposedly trained William Pattee, arguably the best of Bath's designer/modelers. The Donnells' home was on Russell Street, six blocks north of the Deering residence.

Benjamin's son William, born in 1837, attended school until the ripe old age of eighteen, rather a long education for a youngster who planned to follow in his father's footsteps. He went to work at Benjamin's side in the William Rogers shipyard. But then the Panic of '57 clamped down hard—so hard that Benjamin Donnell is said to have rowed someone from Bath downriver to Popham and back—twenty-four miles—for a dime. A decade later, that story would seem touchingly quaint in view of his son William's upward mobility.[7] For his part, William gave up shipbuilding during those hard times to go into the grocery business with his brother. There he learned proper business record keeping as well as, in the words of a descendant, "who to trust and who not to trust, signs of a good businessman."[8]

But, when the depression ended, William Donnell reverted to type. He resumed work as a joiner at the Hitchcock Brothers' yard, where he became friendly with fellow shipwright Gard Deering. He also became friendly with Clara Hitchcock, daughter of one of the yard owners. As the *Bath Daily Times* later put it, "the call of the shipyard was too strong and after marrying...Clara Hitchcock, he went into the shipbuilding business."[9] William was twenty-nine when he partnered with Gard Deering, thirty-three. Was it their relative youth that prompted them to stick their necks out? Was it perhaps the fact that Donnell's new wife was a Hitchcock? Both of the Hitchcock brothers had died and their yard was now idle. Who might get it up and running again? Who else? But to make a go of the place, Donnell would need some talented help. Gard Deering probably didn't need to be asked twice. Tom Hagan, another Hitchcock veteran, joined the team but left to start his own yard after the three completed their first vessel.[10]

It goes without saying that Gard and Bill were compatible. Both were Republicans, both Baptists, both fathers of infant daughters. Both were well liked, although Donnell's sociability eclipsed Deering's. Throughout their twenty-year partnership, Deering would be content to keep a low public profile, focusing his attention on his single great interest, shipbuilding. Donnell was a more prepossessing figure, more outwardly directed, more active in civic affairs

The Deerings and Donnells enjoy an outing at Popham Beach. They have driven right to the ocean's edge. In the foreground stands William Donnell. His wife Clara and their children shield themselves from the bright sunlight in the Donnell's shay. To the rear are Gardiner and Lydia Deering, who don't seem to mind the glare. Courtesy: Maine Maritime Museum.

and, as he grew older, a noted party giver and dresser upper. Donnell's bushy mustache gave him added presence; Deering's old-fashioned whiskers and beard were already going gray.

Perhaps coincidentally, a photograph of the Deerings and the Donnells at play, taken some years into their professional relationship, underscores the contrast between the two. In the picture's foreground, Donnell stands proudly beside a shiny one-horse shay in which his family is ensconced. Although the occasion is a seaside picnic, his natty dress includes a bowler hat and a conspicuous watch chain and fob. There is no mistaking the confidence in his gaze. In the background, Gard and Lydia Deering wait patiently in another shay, Gard's slouch hat shadowing his face. The Deerings appear ready for the photographer to finish so that life can resume.

At the outset of their partnership, then, Donnell was more of a known quantity around town than Deering. Having learned bookkeeping during his grocery venture, he brought that valuable skill to the business mix. Most important, he had secured the use of the Hitchcock yard on favorable terms.

War inflation had made wooden vessels more costly to make. Bath's shipyard production was in steep decline. Iron ships and steamers looked like the wave of the future. America's maritime trade had been emasculated by foreign competition. Bath people understood that the Good Old Days of their merchant fleets were over—or close to it. Open a shipyard? What could possibly go wrong?

CHAPTER TWO

Well and Substantially Built

Shipbuilding survived in Bath in the late nineteenth century because postwar builders were willing to kiss yesterday goodbye and embrace a changed world. It was understood that the City of Ships was no longer the City of Shipping. Accordingly, shipbuilding would no longer serve local merchant princes but would focus on a wider market. In other words, Bath's shipyards would supply vessels to clients far and wide. Some venturesome yards addressed Bath's technology gap by undertaking construction of engine-powered vessels and steel hulls—expensive, risky strategies requiring new know-how—with varying degrees of success. Then there was the Deering & Donnell yard, which operated on an entirely different business plan.

Beginning in 1866, Deering & Donnell thought small. Like larger yards, they intended to build only, not manage or own their products. The new partnership had no chance of competing with larger yards for bigtime contracts, or of employing new technology. There was, however, a chance to succeed in a niche market largely ignored by other yards: small wooden schooners. America's fishing industry still depended on that type of vessel, as did many coastwise traders. Moreover, the coastwise trade was restricted to U.S.-built vessels, so Deering & Donnell schooners would face no threat from cheaper, foreign-built vessels in that sector.

The yard's specialty, fishing schooners, could be built on the small side for a port such as Gloucester, Massachusetts, with a relatively shallow harbor, or a bit larger for, say, Boston. Fishing schooners led hard, often short, lives, thus ensuring a need for replacements and—importantly—periodic repairs. It was axiomatic that the best builders got their savvy through repair work because that was where a man learned what might go wrong with a vessel. Repair work also paid better, day for day, than new work. Whatever kind of work the partners undertook, they could not afford to stint. Judging from the results, Deering & Donnell's business ethic can be likened to the late twentieth century's Toyota strategy rather than to General Motors'. They built to last, assuming that quality would pay better in the long run.

Deering & Donnell's biggest challenge in this niche would be to keep costs low without sacrificing quality. That could be achieved by minimizing design changes, thus allowing the experience curve to take effect. Schooners were comparatively simple vessels to build, so rapid output would accelerate the learning cycles by which the yard could streamline production. Because many major structural components were delivered pre-sawn to size, ordering uniform multiples for future construction might also save time and money. Deering & Donnell's investment equity, which was probably heavily borrowed during the yard's startup period, could be rapidly recycled, avoiding the long waits endured by builders of large, long-term projects. Faster turnaround would permit lower prices. And of course, the two partners had access to a labor pool of seasoned, skilled, highly motivated shipwrights accustomed to a low wage rate.

The other trick, of course, was to generate a reliable, widening client base. They would build on speculation when necessary, trusting word of mouth and repeat customers to do the rest. In Deering & Donnell's startup period there was good reason for pessimism because in 1867 Uncle Sam revoked the federal subsidy by which small fishermen could make ends meet. All the more reason to cut costs but maintain quality.

The fact that Gard Deering and William Donnell were ready to risk their modest fortunes in an uncertain market testifies to their colossal optimism. In this case, colossal optimism was rewarded for, within a few years, the domestic market for schooners grew hot. Having been eclipsed by deepwater competition, American entrepreneurs turned more and more to the coastwise trade, where foreigners were forbidden to compete. The vessels best suited for such trade were schooners, which over time would grow to huge numbers and enormous size to keep pace with the nation's industrial expansion. There were hints of this trend in 1866 when Deering & Donnell started operations. Later, as coastwise shipping took off, our two young shipbuilders were perfectly positioned to exploit it.

Operations in the Deering & Donnell yard started in 1866 and, at least in the early years, were confined to warmer months when workdays were longer. A Donnell family tradition has it that each spring, the yard procured a pair of oxen for heavy hauling and stepping masts. When days got short in the fall, the oxen were slaughtered and their meat sold to the yard crew.[11]

Seasonal or not, during two decades of building, Deering & Donnell averaged three and a half vessels a year. Given their small size, there was space in the yard to work on three fishing schooners at a time if need be. The first was the *Hattie J. Hamlin*, 32 gross tons and 55 feet in length.[12] She was small even for a fisherman, smaller than David Deering's *Orville*. Her career provides us with a gauge of the yard's quality, for the *Hamlin* was still fishing, out of Mobile, in 1901. Then came the 44-ton *Lizzie D. Saunders*, sold to Rockport, Massachusetts, in 1867 and active until 1897. In 1867 Deering & Donnell established contact with the Gloucester, Massachusetts, fishing industry, a source of many sales over the next two decades. The 47-ton *Oceanus*, personally delivered to Gloucester by Gard Deering in 1870, was still fishing from that port in 1904.[13] A succession of these small, elegant vessels, sharp at the bow and with a graceful run aft, continued to slide into the Kennebec for twenty years.

Would you buy a schooner from this man? Many did, repeatedly. William T. Donnell, Gardiner Deering's partner from 1866 to 1886. Courtesy: Maine Maritime Museum.

In March 1869, William Donnell bought the old Hitchcock yard outright from his mother-in-law for $2,000, a financial stretch to be sure.[14] The stretch was pulled almost to the breaking point four months later when a fire broke out in the yard, gutting the blacksmith and joiner shops. Neither building was insured.[15] Damages were estimated at $1,500, a figure that seems high in view of the cost of the entire yard, but coming as it did at the height of the yard's busy season, the loss had to have been a severe setback. Severe, yes, but not fatal. Work continued, probably through the expedient of utilizing another yard's facilities. It is even possible that an entire project was shifted to another yard. The overall similarity of Deering & Donnell's 1869 vessels probably simplified construction somewhat. Whatever the case, the end result was that Deering & Donnell launched three schooners in that year of disaster.

Deering & Donnell's schooners were built with time-honored "vernacular" methods and two centuries' experience in refining reliable construction standards. Each hull's contours and proportions were based upon a wooden half-hull model built by a master to a fractional scale of the vessel's intended size. Many half models were built by fastening strips of wood together in layers and shaping the overall block into a hull form, the layers often indicating predetermined waterlines. A seasoned modeler's eye told him when his shaped wooden hull form, perhaps two feet long, was "right." A proper half-hull model might serve as the basis for many vessels.

A Deering & Donnell fishing schooner ready for launching, with interested parties on board and on the shipyard bank. Notice the vessel's slender, deep hull. Courtesy: Maine Maritime Museum.

Taking lines from the model, and tweaking them as necessary to fit the various size requirements of each job, builders scaled the lines up to full size, achieving precise dimensions of the proposed vessel's frame components. In the yard, those lines were drawn on the floor of a mold loft (a building with an uncluttered floor), and molds (patterns) derived from them determined the full-scale dimensions of the vessel's structural timbers.[16] Selecting the appropriate wood pieces and cutting them to fit the patterns came next, a labor-intensive process that filled the shipyard with noisy, hectic activity and generated the aromatic, boisterous scene you noticed during your inspection tour of Bath.

In a nutshell, and at the risk of oversimplifying: Assembly commenced with the laying of the keel, the vessel's so-called backbone, consisting of oak beams spliced together and layered for strength. Stem and stern posts were hoisted and joined to the keel, and the vessel's timbers (ribs), shaped from the mold loft's scaled-up patterns, were fixed to the keel at close intervals, gradually revealing the vessel's intended shape. Lateral beams became the foundations for decks. The scaffolded frame was planked outside and in (the inner planking called ceiling). To make them conform to the frame's contours, many planks were heated in a steam box until limber, then rushed to their intended position and pinned thereon while still hot. When they cooled, the planks would retain their intended shape. Oakum caulking would seal the gaps between planks.

Stepping a vessel's lower masts and bowsprit were toilsome, labor-intensive tasks for men and oxen alike. Vessels were customarily launched with only their lower masts in place. Rigging, which usually involved a crew of contract specialists, took place once the vessel was in the stream. Throughout this complicated process, Gard Deering and William Donnell were, of necessity, hands-on leaders every inch of the way.

Theoretically, any shipyard was a series of accidents waiting to happen. The countless steps involved in completing even a small schooner required thousands of custom wood and metal components and tools to make them that were potential instruments of destruction. Yet the rate of shipyard accidents in the age of sail was remarkably low. Occasional mishaps, however, were serious enough to attract public attention. Here are a few examples. Donnell himself suffered a broken in leg May 1872 while a crew was dismantling staging around the schooner *William H. Foye*. In September 1877, in Chapman & Flint's yard (just a short distance south of Deering & Donnell's), workers were taking down stairs from a vessel's staging when the pieces fell, "striking Mr. George Pushard with such force that he was taken up for dead. Dr. Bibber was called, and ascertained that probably no fracture nor internal injury was inflicted, although a large swelling was raised on his head, his right ankle sprained, and hip bruised."[17] In March of 1882, the *Bath Daily Times* reported that "in Deering & Donnell's yard, George Chick, while going to the grindstone to grind his scraper, slipped and fell and drove the scraper almost through his hand, making a fearful wound."[18] In 1883, Charles Matterson suffered a broken leg at Deering & Donnell when a large timber he was shaping slipped and struck him[19] In September 1882, Joseph Purrinton, a seventy-four-year-old carpenter at the yard, was murdered in his home when he apparently surprised a burglar—an unfortunate incident to say the least, but we shall not count it against the yard's safety record.

Nathan R. Lipfert, the Maine Maritime Museum's librarian, has conducted a statistical survey of work-related injuries among Bath's yard workers in the nineteenth century, derived from accounts in the local press. The survey shows that most shipyard accidents—56 percent—involved falls: tumbling from rigging, or from collapsed staging, or from a vessel's deck into her hold during construction, or simply tripping. Hits from flying or falling objects (often tools dropped from above by a co-worker) accounted for better than 19 percent of injuries; and cuts and blows from tools made up another 18.5 percent. Many accidents were caused by inexperience and bad weather conditions. Sickness and accident insurance were individual workers' responsibilities, not employers'. Probably less than half of Bath's yard workers had any kind of coverage, notwithstanding the fact that in hard times such as the 1870s, with wages at rock bottom, loss of a few days' work could spell disaster for an uninsured worker.[20]

The trim appearance of Deering & Donnell schooners was more than eyewash. Those vessels were fast. Take for example the case of the 70-ton *Dauntless*, built in 1870. She was returning from the Banks to Boston full of iced fish when a racing yacht fell in with her and challenged her to a contest. The *Dauntless's* skipper said yes and the race was on. Much to her challenger's surprise, the *Dauntless* showed a clean pair of heels to the yacht. Just after she had tied up in Boston, the yacht's captain came aboard the *Dauntless* and bought her and her catch outright. Unsolicited testimonials don't get much better than that.

Occasionally, Deering or Donnell would take a little time off for a busman's holiday and deliver a completed schooner to her new owner. This perk provided a welcome change from the daily grind in Bath while also saving the cost of a delivery captain. Where and how William Donnell acquired his sea legs remains a mystery; but in any event both "captains" racked up some interesting experiences during these getaways. Once, Donnell set sail in a new schooner for Gloucester, normally a two-day run at most. Nine days later, fogged in somewhere offshore and running low on provisions, he and his crew were probably growing nostalgic for the daily grind in Bath. Donnell was able to hail a passing schooner that assured him he was on course and near shore. Re-oriented at last, he took the vessel into Gloucester without further incident.[21]

Deering's favorite extracurricular adventure included a touch of piracy. It occurred during the depression year of 1875, after a Gloucester client had taken delivery of the newly completed,

72-ton *Lizzie*. The vessel had been built on the client's credit and had not been paid for, although the builders got wind of the fact that she was being provisioned for sea at Gloucester by the deadbeat owner. What happened next is best described in a later article that appeared in the *Bath Anvil*: "Mr. Donnell went to Gloucester and was unable to make any satisfactory adjustment but went aboard the Lizzie with a sheriff, got her papers and the schooner was towed across the harbor and laid up. But the situation was far from satisfactory and as she was liable to sale to satisfy other claims...the builders would have been left to whistle for their pay.

"So they decided on a coup. Capt. Deering engaged of Capt. B.W. Morse one of the Kennebec tugs to tow a vessel down[east] from Gloucester, and set out one afternoon. When they reached the fishing port at about two the next morning the tide was flood and the moon was just rising; and under these favorable conditions, and the guidance of Mr. Deering who was familiar with the port, they found the schooner, got her off the flats and brought her down to Bath. With her tied up at their own wharf and a keeper of their own on board, Deering and Donnell were in a much better position to negotiate with the Lizzie's owner, who came here, made a satisfactory settlement and had the Lizzie redelivered to him in Gloucester—and it is a tribute to the tact of Mr. Deering that she was not the last vessel his firm built for the same man. The incident remained for years a joke among the fishermen of Gloucester and when it was hard to settle a claim against a schooner in that port, the claimant would often threaten to invoke the 'Lizzie Law.'"[22]

The demand for Deering & Donnell's small schooners continued through the 1870s and into the 1880s, for the firm had indeed found a niche market. In 1872, the partners built their first fishing schooner for a Maine account: the 63-ton *Uncle Joe*, blithely named by Lydia Deering and commissioned by Joseph Maddocks of Southport, near Boothbay. Other Maine contracts followed. In subsequent years, new Deering & Donnell fishing schooners were home-ported in Portland, North Haven, and Eastport, Maine; Boston and Plymouth, Massachusetts; and Providence, Rhode Island. Others, having changed hands, eventually found their way back to Maine.[23] By 1886, the yard had completed fifty such vessels.

During the 1870s and 1880s the market for fish expanded and New England's fishing industry did likewise. Accordingly, the size of schooners began to creep up, allowing fishing crews to stay out longer and bring home larger catches. Speed to market was of course a vital factor, which is another reason Deering & Donnell vessels were in demand.

But, as before, the U.S. economy was subject to excessive gyrations whose trickle-down effect clobbered Bath's yards. The worst was the national financial panic of 1873, caused by the bankruptcy of the Northern Pacific Railroad and the collapse of Jay Cooke and Company, a bank that had backed it. The fallout from this disaster shut down Wall Street for ten days and precipitated an epidemic of bankruptcies. Uncle Sam's tight money policy made matters worse. America was plunged into another depression for the rest of the 1870s, and things grew quiet again on the banks of the Kennebec—so quiet that hundreds of shipyard workers left town to seek greener pastures. Those who stayed worked for a dollar a day, half or less of the going wage before the slump.[24] Production continued at Deering & Donnell, perhaps sustained by

The fishing schooner Uncle Joe, *built in 1872, seen here late in life. The* Uncle Joe *was Deering & Donnell's first schooner for a Maine buyer. She began life hailing from Southport. A caption on the reverse of this photograph reads, "... an old banker from Cundy's Harbor to Georges Banks 1906." Courtesy: Maine Maritime Museum.*

the decline in wages, perhaps also because the yard's smalltime niche was less impacted by big-time financial events. During the slump twenty-one schooners went down the ways. A few of these, however, were substantially bigger than the firm's usual output. For despite the grim economic picture, which did not brighten until 1879, a new opportunity loomed. Deering & Donnell began to think big.

As the United States urbanized and industrialized, the nation's needs grew and accelerated. Increased demand for the basics of everyday life such as coal, ice, and lumber offered bright prospects for the nation's protected coastwise trade. Despite rampant investment in roads and railways, shipping bulk products by land was expensive and often complicated. Coastwise shippers could compete effectively in this growing business if efficient, commodious vessels could be built to meet the challenge. The challenge was indeed met, and in the process wooden shipbuilding received another lease on life. Beginning shortly after the Civil War, America's coastwise shipping became the realm of the schooner.

Schooners possessed characteristics that suited them for coastwise trade. One was their fore-and-aft rig, by which they could sail closer to the wind than square-riggers and make headway in the lightest of breezes. Another was their simplicity, which made them cheaper to build than square-riggers and steamers and enabled them to operate with a much smaller crew. Another was their carrying capacity. None of their potential cargo space was crowded by an engine and its fuel supply. Traditional schooners, however, possessed a paralyzing drawback in an enlarging world: as they were built larger to achieve economy of scale, their spars and sail areas grew proportionately. These larger, heavier rigs required more manpower and, sometimes, caused structural damage to hulls. Such outsized configurations were exhausting to crews under normal circumstances and downright dangerous in bad weather. Adding manpower, however, could increase operating costs unacceptably.

Enter the tern schooner, which made the big schooner a reliable, cost-effective transport. As early as the 1830s, a few shipbuilders had overcome schooners' size limitations by adding a third (mizzen) mast. Doing so divided a vessel's sail area into threes (terns), thus reducing the sail area per mast, with a commensurate gain in ease of handling and size without an appreciable increase in crew. Shipbuilding was a tradition-bound business, so the tern configuration took decades to catch on. But in the late nineteenth century, when demand for efficient coastwise vessels shot up, Maine shipyards got the message. The tern schooner quickly became the industry standard for bulk hauling—somewhat akin to today's ubiquitous eighteen-wheel truck. Terns were able to load and unload cargoes at big and small saltwater ports and at upriver towns where shipping by rail was nonexistent or prohibitively expensive.

Profitability aside, terns also had an esthetic asset: by and large they were beautiful vessels, as many surviving paintings and photographs confirm. Although beamier and more straight-sided than, say, fishing schooners, they nonetheless sported sharp, slightly upswept bows and a graceful curving run toward the stern. Their lengthened hulls and proportionate sail plan looked "right" to landlubbers and sailors alike, and still do. Building of tern schooners began in earnest in Maine yards in the 1860s and expanded rapidly.

In 1872, Deering & Donnell built its first tern schooner, the *Walter B. Chester*, for Benjamin Brown of Wellfleet, Massachusetts. To the partners and their crew, building the *Chester* must have seemed a refreshing challenge after turning out fourteen generically similar projects in a row. At 421 tons and measuring more than 132 feet in length, the *Chester* dwarfed the yard's previous products, but she was the shape of things to come.

In 1873, with economic clouds darkening, the yard got an infusion of know-how and cash with the 319-ton tern *Ajax*. The prominent and respected Bath shipbuilder William Rogers, who had employed Donnell and Deering years before, had left town to get rich, got poorer instead, and so returned to pursue his first calling. Rogers started his comeback overseeing the *Ajax's* construction at Deering & Donnell. The *Ajax*, which featured a retractable keel extension (centerboard), was designed for a Rogers customer in Indianola, Texas. Then came the 585-ton *Georgie Shepard*, for a Boston shipper, and, in 1875, the 475-ton *Willis E. Shepard* for the same client. The partners had made a smooth transition into the tern schooner market.

Meanwhile, fishing schooners continued to splash their way into the Kennebec. These were years, remember, of severe economic depression, yet the yard stayed busy, although every buck counted. By way of illustration: To stay active, in 1875, Deering & Donnell low-balled a contract with a Gloucester client, offering to deliver a completed vessel, the *Martha C.*,

A pause in the workday at Deering & Donnell. At the wharf is one of the yard's early tern schooners, the 586-ton Georgie Shepard, *built for a Boston client in 1873. Here, ten years later, she has returned to have work done on her mizzenmast. In the stream, riggers are bending sail on the newly launched 704-ton* Josiah R. Smith. *Compare the* Smith's *freshly curved rail line with the* Shepard's, *which looks slightly hogged—sagging at bow and stern—from ten years' service. The rough-shaped timbers lying on their carpet of wood chips will probably be components of the next intended schooner. Courtesy: Capts. Douglas K. and Linda J. Lee.*

ready for sea, for $3265—under $41 a ton, a rock-bottom price. Because it never hurts to ask, the client requested a $15 price reduction. No deal! replied Donnell. For a while no one budged. After much correspondence, a compromise was reached: Deering & Donnell cut the price a whopping $10.[25] Apparently there was time even in the gloomy year of 1875 to stand on principle. A sawbuck was a sawbuck—and ten days' pay for a shipwright. True to her type, the *Martha C.* would give good service until, October 1894, when, transporting salmon and herring, she washed ashore on Bear Point, Newfoundland.[26]

Three more fishing schooners went down the ways in 1877; then things stopped short. More trouble: another fire swept Deering & Donnell, causing a reported $6,000 worth of damage (probably including construction materials). Understandably, the yard launched no vessels the next year. And in 1879, when the depression bottomed out, only two fishing schooners were completed. This was the nadir of Deering & Donnell's fortunes.

Once the nation had outlived the depression of the 1870s, Bath again became the City of Ships. In the first three years of the 1880s, Bath led the world in wooden ship construction, meanwhile breaking its own previous all-time record set in 1854. For the entire decade of the 1880s, Bath outdid itself, launching 346 vessels, 245 of which were schooners.[27] The city' shipyards accomplished this despite a labor shortage caused by many shipwrights' emigration during the recent depression. Not that business ran on an even keel, so to speak. In 1885, during a lull, a visitor to Bath commented in the press that the North End yards were momentarily empty, with but one vessel on the stocks, "contented and patient, only waiting for her owners to complete their job...." In the South End, all was silent, he said, except for Hagan's yard where a fishing schooner was under way.[28] Looks could be deceiving. Had our observer walked farther south, he would have heard the sounds of mallets banging away at Deering & Donnell. That yard had made a comeback, having completed twenty-nine schooners since the dark days of the depression. Eleven were terns; three, the *Alice Montgomery*, *Josiah R. Smith*, and *Gardiner G. Deering*, each measuring over 700 tons and 160 feet in length. The size increases were a response to the nation's growing demand for essential goods and a commensurate drive among maritime shippers for economies of scale. In the meantime, Deering & Donnell had responded in another significant way. The partners had made themselves owner-managers of a merchant schooner fleet.

It was probably just a matter of time before Gard Deering and William Donnell would decide to get a piece of the coastwise shipping action. Bath had a long tradition of builder-owners, albeit one that had been throttled by the Civil War. And other residents of the City of Ships were heeding that call. Furthermore, Deering & Donnell had lately supplied several tern schooners to out-of-town clients who were using them effectively as bulk transports. Furthermore, the partners could not have missed the growing numbers of terns being towed upriver to load Kennebec ice, a home-grown product that was in great demand in cities to the south and available just a few miles north of Bath.

Simple and elegant: The 92-ton Grover Cleveland, *with her topmasts rigged, is almost ready for launching at Deering & Donnell. Uphill at the extreme left is Donnell's home, soon to be remodeled into a South End showplace. Although a late and large example of Deering & Donnell's fishing schooners, the* Grover Cleveland *typifies their yacht-like grace. Launched in 1885 and originally registered to Boston, the* Cleveland *will still be sailing, out of St. Johns, Newfoundland, in 1928. Courtesy: Maine Maritime Museum.*

Beginning in 1879, Deering & Donnell pursued a two-pronged business strategy. The firm continued to produce fishing schooners, which by the 1880s were cash cows. And, over the next seven years, it built four new terns for outside clients. But at the same time, Deering & Donnell produced eight vessels for its own account, all tern schooners but one. These were the

Reuben S. Hunt (183 tons, 1879, a two-master), the beautifully named *Electric Light* (565 tons, 1880), the *Charles H. Haskell* (476 tons, 1882), the *Josiah R. Smith* (704 tons, 1883), the (at last!) *William T. Donnell* (511 tons, 1883), the (of course!) *Gardiner G. Deering* (718 tons, 1884), the *Oliver S. Barrett* (635 tons, 1884), and the *Samuel Dillaway* (811 tons, 1886).

Building in-house vessels was a much different financial proposition than contract work. To raise advance capital, the partners followed a practice that had been well established in Bath since early times: They sold shares in each of their schooners to venturesome investors. Most investors were probably local, acquainted with Deering and Donnell, and confident that the partners' management would earn attractive dividends. The estimated cost of a proposed vessel was customarily spread over sixty-four shares. Investors usually took a single share, finding

A step up in size. On a cold February day in 1882, Deering & Donnell's 732-ton tern schooner Alice Montgomery, *fully rigged and festooned with flags, awaits the moment of her launching, which presumably will occur shortly after her staging is removed. Is that Donnell and Deering standing at the bow? The* Alice Montgomery *will go to a Boston buyer. The project on the left is the* Charles H. Haskell, *intended for the partners' own account. Courtesy: Maine Maritime Museum.*

A visual masterpiece of balance, proportion and simplicity: The tern schooner Josiah R. Smith, *fourth in the line of vessels Deering & Donnell built for its own account, anchored in the Kennebec off the shipyard wharf. J. C. Higgins photograph, courtesy: Capts. Douglas K. and Linda J. Lee.*

it prudent to put their eggs in many baskets. If a potential investor was perhaps thinking of taking a bigger plunge, the new vessel might be named in his or her honor. Deering and Donnell may have held half a dozen shares between them per vessel; possibly less. Insuring one's investment was optional but recommended. Principal shareholders insured as a matter of course. Managing owners handled insurance transactions with underwriters.

Seldom did managing owners and their investors own the cargoes they shipped. Instead, vessels were chartered out, usually on a per-voyage basis. For example, a vessel's managing owners would contract for her to ship a cargo of ice, say, from Maine to Philadelphia; then proceed to Norfolk to load coal, and return with that to Boston. Dividends were paid to investors by the managing owners at the conclusion of each charter and after the vessel's total expenses had been deducted. Charters were usually procured by brokers in Boston and New York who, for a fee or a percentage, put waiting cargoes and available vessels together. Wire and cable permitted virtually instantaneous transactions.

Timing and speed were of course crucial. So was up-to-date knowledge of financial, political, and geographical factors that could affect business. Decisions, decisions! Freight rates were hypersensitive to economic fluctuation and gyrated accordingly. In hard times, it was tempting for managers to accept the security of long-term, fixed-rate contracts, even if the rates were low. But if and when rates edged upward, long-term security could come back to bite. Anticipating a forthcoming shortage or the imminent outbreak of hostilities somewhere, which usually drove freight rates up, could have a huge impact on earnings. It is in areas such as these that Deering & Donnell lacked savvy.

Indeed, the two partners had no prior experience in ship management, and were almost certainly babes in the woods when it came to financial markets and political issues. Not that that would have stopped them. Having taken a big risk back in '66, they were not daunted by uncertainty. Perhaps to an extent ignorance was bliss. And, thanks to telegraphy (and, soon, long-distance telephones), middlemen and short-term contracts reduced much of the risk. Always looming was the possibility of an unforeseen financial crisis—another panic—that could ruin the best-made plans.

Most important for managing owners was the need to keep vessels working, even if an occasional contract netted a loss. A vessel idling between charters was of course a vessel losing money for her investors. Worse, a vessel idling was a vessel deteriorating. Chiseled in stone was the principle that the best way to keep schooners in good shape was to exercise them constantly. When a vessel needed an overhaul, as most did every three or four years, those expenses were assessed proportionately to shareholders. With expense factors in mind, it is easy to see how Deering & Donnell's reputation for ruggedness, speed, and efficient repair were important business assets.

When a vessel was at sea her sailing qualities and her captain's skill became deciding factors. Wire and cable had increased managers' control over the masters of their vessels. Captains were authorized to draw upon an established account for ordinary expenses; but a major unexpected expense such as collision repair would now be telegraphed to the home office for approval.

Deering & Donnell's business records have scattered to the winds, but circumstantial evidence suggests that the partners did well by their investors—and themselves, of course.

As with other builders, the size and load capacities of their merchant schooners edged upward in the 1880s. Period photographs and reports confirm that they did not stint.

To Mainers, the most conspicuous employment for new schooners was hauling ice south from nearby Kennebec ice houses. The firm's new tern *Charles H. Haskell* was scarcely launched before she was thus laden, as reported in the *Bath Daily Times*, which made a practice of boosting local vessels with purple prose: Here is the *Times's* sendoff for the *Haskell*, built by Deering & Donnell for their own account, on 25 April 1882: "The schooner *Charles H. Hask[e]ll*,...now...fitting for sea...was built by Deering & Don[n]ell. This vessel, to all appearances, is not only substantially well built, but is well provided with all the necessary conveniences for a vessel of her class. Although not deeply laden, she has on board 742 tons of ice and bound for Charleston, S.C. May the best of success not only attend this fine and beautiful vessel, but also attend her gentlemanly master in all his future voyage of life."

After the *Haskell* came Deering & Donnell's namesake terns; then, in 1884, the *Oliver S. Barrett*. The 635-ton *Barrett*, launched on 24 March 1884, had cost $33,000, or just under $52

"One of the fastest schooners on the coast": The 634-ton Oliver S. Barrett, *built by Deering & Donnell for their own account and launched in March 1884. In this view it is probably April. The* Barrett *has received her suit of sails and is ready to sail. Notice the upswept bow, which will shed heavy seas. Behind her is the recently completed fisherman* Laura Bell. *Courtesy: Maine Maritime Museum.*

a ton, a testament to the yard's efficiency. She quickly earned a reputation as "one of the fastest schooners on the coast." In 1889, for example, she brought a cargo of salt to Bath from Turks Island (at the east end of the Bahamas chain) in fifteen days, under the command of Chester Wallace, who in later years would be a long-serving master of Gard Deering's vessels. That voyage also served as a honeymoon for Wallace and his bride Belle.[29]

The prime example of the yard's attention to quality and the press's doting notice, was the *Samuel Dillaway*, based on a model by William Pattee. Pattee, who reportedly designed 700 vessels during his lifetime, has been praised by schooner historians as "perhaps the greatest vernacular modeler of them all."[30] Some of his early training, remember, had come from William Donnell's father Benjamin. Pattee's model for Deering & Donnell, which may have also been used on the speedy *Oliver S. Barrett*, would be recycled effectively in the future. The results would speak for themselves.

The *Samuel Dillaway* was Deering & Donnell's last vessel. At 811 tons and measuring 170 feet in length, she was also the yard's largest. She went down the ways on 6 May 1886. Impressed by the *Dillaway's* details, a newsman reported that her captain would live in elegance. The vessel's after cabin was paneled in ash with black walnut borders and "stained cherry pilasters with [g]ilt trim." The captain's bed was canopied in black walnut.[31] Details like that might well attract the seasoned skippers needed by the partners. Incidentally, the schooner was

RIGHT: *Deering and Donnell's seventieth—and last—vessel. As yet unamed, she waits with dignitaries aboard and with her staging removed, ready to slide into the Kennebec on 1 May 1886. At 811 tons, she is also the largest vessel produced by the partners, who will put her into the ice and coal trades. Courtesy: Maine Maritime Museum.*

LEFT: *Anonymous no longer: At the Deering & Donnell wharf, the firm's last vessel prepares to depart. She will be towed upriver to load ice for Philadelphia. She has been dubbed* Samuel Dillaway *after a generous investor of that name. A new quarterboard displays her title. Courtesy: Maine Maritime Museum.*

launched without benefit of a name, but that gap was filled in when one Samuel Dillaway bought a large share in her.

The *Dillaway* made money for her owners, much of it through ice and coal cargoes. Though worked very hard, she lasted until 1916, and even then it took a South Carolina sand-bar to kill her off. We will come to know her better shortly.

You may have noticed that Gard Deering and William Donnell were talented and hard-working but not very lucky. Fortune did not smile upon their *William T. Donnell* (1883), which at times simply could not catch a break. The late Bath historian Mark Hennessy has outlined her early litany of misfortune: "In September [1886] the Donnell collided with the [tern schooner] Nellie W. Craig near Cove Point Maryland.

"In October, out of Bath with ice for Washington, she went ashore one day out near Hyannis, Mass., and for a time was thought a total loss.

"Hauled off and repaired, she went her way well enough until on December 3 she went on L'Hommedieu Shoals while out of Baltimore with coal for Boston. Freed, and leaking over 250 strokes an hour, she was towed into Vineyard Haven [Massachusetts] two days later by the tug Storm King."[32] If investors were expecting dividend checks they would be sorely disappointed. With passing years, although less accident-prone, the *Donnell* continued to be a poor earner.

But the *William T. Donnell's* headaches would momentarily be eclipsed by more important matters, for in 1886, Deering & Donnell decided to call it quits. They had just completed their seventieth vessel.[33]

When the national economy started upward in the early 1880s, Deering & Donnell came into its own, and a fourteen-year climb up the learning curve began to pay off dramatically. The shipyard was a beehive by 1881, completing four schooners (while all of Bath's yards built thirty-one), and managed to squeeze in some repair work on the side. These doings were closely followed in the *Times*. Every week, Bath residents could read about the latest develop-ments in the South End yard. Here are some examples from 1881: "Messrs. Deering & Donnell have three vessels in course of construction..." (18 April). "The schooner D. W. Hunt was launched from the yard of Deering & Donnell yesterday morning all rigged and ready for sea.

She was immediately towed up river and will load ice for a southern port" (31 May). "The schooner Ethel built by Donnell & Deering for Gloucester parties was towed to Boston by the [tug] Knickerbocker yesterday" (4 June). "Messrs. Deering & Don[n]el are getting out a keel at their shipyard for a vessel about 800 tons for Boston parties" (12 July). "The schooner David Hunt is unloading yellow pine at the yard of Deering & Donnell" (1 August). "Messrs. Deering & Donnell, as soon as the vessel on the stocks in their yard is completed, will build a schooner of about 800 tons. The frame has been cut in Canada" (13 August). "The schooner Eddie Huck has received a new quarter deck at Deering & Donnell's wharf" (19 October). And on top of this, the partners found time to manage the first two schooners of their growing private fleet. More progress: They could now keep in touch with local suppliers and shareholders by telephone. All in all, the shipyard was a picture of highly organized, carefully choreographed activity in 1881.

Reports from 1882 revealed even tighter organization and fancier choreography. "At Donnell and Deering's they have just got away two Gloucester fishermen, and are framing a 450 ton schooner.... They have behind this another schooner of about the same size. They have just finished enlargening their [yard's] reservoir which now holds 20,000 gallons. 'It is a regular quaker meeting all the time down here, at Deering & Donnell's; the men pay attention to business; nothing funny going on; the smartest and the most intelligent men in the city in our yard, you can say' said the teamster" (3 August 1882).

The enlarged reservoir was another sign of the yard's bigger schooners. Enough water could now be pumped into a hull on the ways to detect any leaks before the vessel was launched. The regular Quaker meeting now employed fifty shipwrights working year 'round, which was of course a factor in their short cycle times. Another factor as always was the practice of ordering precut components from disparate sources—timbers that arrived ready for assembly. The following tidbit, from 3 June 1882, is likewise revealing. In mid-1882 Deering & Donnell was simultaneously finishing up a 368-ton tern, at work on two Gloucester schooners and two more terns at the framing stage: "One frame is in the yard," noted the *Times*, and the other [upriver] in Pittston."[34] So busy were Deering & Donnell that they had subcontracted their latest hull to another yard. "This is an enterprising and a very reliable firm," chirped the

Three fishing schooners in various stages of construction at Deering & Donnell's expanded yard, 1885. The Grover Cleveland *(left) and the* Eliza A. Thomas *(right) will go to Boston owners; the* Mabel Kenniston *(center) is headed for Gloucester. An enlargement of the yard in 1882 has provided additional construction space. Where are all the shipwrights? Home. This photograph was taken on a Sunday. Courtesy: Maine Maritime Museum.*

Times on 8 July 1882. The *Times* was right on both counts.

Nothing succeeds like success. In 1883, Donnell purchased the adjoining Jewell shipyard, a small tract assessed at $800.[35] The additional space facilitated multiple projects. As a consequence, in that year Deering & Donnell launched seven schooners (two of them company terns), four in '84 (two of them company terns), and five in '85 (all contract fishing schooners). In the first months of 1886, three vessels went down the ways, including the large, handsome *Samuel Dillaway*. "Business is booming at the shipyard of Deering & Donnell," the *Times* reported on 27 January 1886. "At present there are 65 men employed." And this in the dead of winter. Then it all stopped. Gard Deering and William Donnell went their separate ways.

People have wondered ever since what it was that broke up such an effective team. Neither Deering nor Donnell gave any public explanation, so the community was at liberty to speculate. Even in a rumor mill like Bath, there was not much to go on; so, to this day, the breakup is puzzling. But when partners who have worked side-by-side for twenty years suddenly walk away from each other, clues about their decision lie all around. For reasons we will discuss later, subsequent generations of Deerings discarded their family history, obliterating any explanations from that side of the partnership. In contrast, Donnell's family nurtured its history, so there are clues to be found therein. But there is more to go on. In contrast to the gossipers of 1886, we can extrapolate the partners' intentions by reviewing what they did on their own after parting. Their separate paths suggest that they had come to a strategic disagreement by 1886. Neighborhood context also offers a few hints about the split. Bath had changed enormously over the last twenty years. So had Donnell and Deering, but in different ways.

Bath citizens liked parades and festivals, and almost any anniversary or holiday provided a pretext for public spectacle. In March 1881 the City celebrated the 200th anniversary of its first town meeting. Municipal life was not perfect, of course. Lately, because of ill-advised railroad speculation, Bath was on its way to accumulating the largest public debt per capita of any U.S. city. But such concerns went onto the back burner as the City of Ships saluted itself. On 19 March, in sunny, balmy weather, festivities commenced with bells ringing from every steeple, followed by a service at the Wesleyan church featuring music and a historical address. One of the key speakers was Mayor Thomas W. Hyde, an authentic Civil War hero and founder of Hyde Windlass Company, a manufacturer of deck machinery. (In 1888 Hyde would found Bath Iron Works, a yard that would specialize in high-tech naval warships.) To beautify the proceedings, the church's inside walls had been draped with banners emblazoned with "names of mark in Bath history." Donnell was one of those names.[36] Deering was not.

The fun continued that evening in the empty Patten Car Works building on North Street. The Car Works, a short-lived builder of luxury passenger rail coaches, had gone bust in the depression of the 1870s. Its idle barn was the only available building in Bath big enough for the expected crowd. Two thousand invitations had been issued; five thousand people showed up, crowding into the building to hear more music, more reminiscing about the Good Old Days, and more VIP speeches congratulating the community on its growth and success. Then came a grand march by costumed Masonic Knights Templar from all over Maine, after which there was a grand ball. All in all, a day to remember. It was generally agreed that the milestone celebration had been "worthy of the great shipbuilding city."[37]

In those untroubled days of the early 1880s, Bath had much to celebrate. The shipyards were humming and the Kennebec was full of schooners heading upriver to load ice and lumber. More schooners bunched together at the Maine Central Railroad's wharf in Bath, unloading another staple of the growing economy, Appalachian coal, most of which was trained inland. Other symbols of improving lifestyle were close at hand. In 1882, Alameda Hall opened in the downtown. This enormous pleasure dome featured periodic stage shows and concerts as well as a roller-skating rink (for those who weren't enjoying the other recent craze, bicycling). The Alameda also became the venue for future balls, public and private, in Bath. Some of these were lavish indeed, for the City of Ships was enjoying its good times. William T. Donnell was a principal owner of the Alameda.

In 1885, Bath established a municipal waterworks to pipe water from Nequasset Lake in Woolwich, east of the Kennebec. The taps turned on in 1887. Electric lights turned on in 1888, the year Thomas Hyde's new Bath Iron Works got its first contract and started on its way to make shipbuilding history.

What's for lunch? A day at the beach with the Deerings and Donnells. The adults, from left to right, are Lydia Deering, William Donnell, Gardiner Deering, and Clara Donnell. The younger folk are Donnell children. Courtesy: Maine Maritime Museum.

William Donnell reveled in all that growth and change, for his personal interests had widened. Now a middle-aged father of four (another child had died in infancy), he was a devoted family man. His son Harry, age twenty-two in 1886, was expected to follow in his father's footsteps. Over the years of his partnership with Gard Deering, William Donnell had become politically active. He was elected to the city's Common Council (part of its then bicameral government) and later served as an alderman in Bath's city government, 1869–1870, 1872, and 1880–1882, continuing intermittently thereafter. He hoped to go on to bigger things. He was a member, as was Deering, of Bath's Polar Star Masonic Lodge and of the Order of the Elks as well. In addition, he and his wife Clara had become mainstays of the city's enlivening social set and the events involved in it.

According to family tradition, Donnell had reached a point in his life by 1886 where he wanted to spend more time outside the shipyard pursuing his many other interests. But with the improving economy and the improving prospects in the yard, he probably found it harder than ever to squeeze a little private time away from the business. As the actual owner of the yard's real estate and its presumed bookkeeper, he would have had his hands quite full. It may have been the tug of war between shipyard duties and social aspirations that motivated him to remodel "the old Hitchcock mansion," a white clapboard Federal house that fronted on Washington Street and backed onto the shipyard, into a high-ceilinged, fashionably Victorian home.[38] Today we would call the result a trophy house. Then, however, it became known as the Donnell house. After its facelift, the rehabbed structure looked more suitable for the swankier North End, but it allowed Donnell to keep up with the Joneses and keep tabs on his business by looking out his window. The Donnell house became a magnet for the Donnells' partying friends, a circle that the attentive local press dubbed "the jolliest people in Bath."[39]

Deering's personal story during the same period is vaguer and briefer. Although well regarded, he was not, like his more sociable ex-partner, a colorful character around Bath. That would come later. In 1886, at age fifty-three, he was the father of four surviving children: Emma (born in 1862), Frank (1869), Harry (1872), and Carroll (1882). Deering's life was entirely absorbed with work. He was more of a hands-on master than his partner. Judging from his future innovations, most of the improvements in Deering & Donnell's efficiency were probably his. A confirmed teetotaler and, like his father David, a nonsmoker, he seems to have avoided the social spotlight. Politics? His entire career, if it can be called that, consisted of two one-year terms as an alderman from Bath's first ward. Organizations? His only documented extracurricular activity was membership in Bath's Polar Star Masonic Lodge. Gard's wife Lydia belonged to the Order of the Eastern Star, the female organization related to the Masons. Gard and Lydia attended the Corliss Street Baptist Church, built in 1868. Lydia was active in church affairs and Gard, like his wife a regular churchgoer, would in the future financially assist the congregation's building expansion. Fun? The only other surviving evidence of the Deerings' recreational social life during those years is a photograph of them picnicking with the Donnells, probably at Popham Beach at the mouth of the Kennebec. As he got older, Deering found just sitting on his porch after hours recreational. No gadabout, he got at least eight hours of sleep every night, which left little spare time after long days in the yard.

The partners had become two different animals from the pair of young shipwrights who

William T. Donnell's refurbished home at 259 Washington Street circa 1903. Immediately behind the house is his silent shipyard. The vessel looming overhead is not one of his—Donnell built no five-masters—but a product of the Percy & Small shipyard next door, probably the Elizabeth Palmer. *Courtesy: Maine Maritime Museum.*

stuck their necks out in 1866. Their endeavors had made them both well off financially if not wealthy. Deering had accumulated enough savings to acquire rental properties near his Pine Street home. But Donnell, of course, owned what to Deering was most important—the shipyard.

According to Donnell family tradition, there was disagreement between the partners about how to utilize that yard. Donnell, the story goes, was less money-oriented and perhaps more softhearted than Deering. Accordingly, he maintained that the yard should stay open year 'round to keep everyone fully employed, even if that meant financial sacrifice by the partners. Deering on the other hand saw nothing wrong with paying men off when work thinned out.[40] The story is perhaps consistent with the two partners' personalities but at variance with practical circumstances in 1886. With sixty-five men at work on multiple projects, and so busy that it had to subcontract a hull elsewhere, Deering & Donnell had long since outgrown its old practice of seasonal employment.

It seems more likely that the deciding factor in the split was disagreement about future strategy. Building and managing schooners was getting more lucrative every year. Tern schooners, which had become the tail that wagged the dog at Deering & Donnell, were nearing their size limitations by 1886. Coping with future growth and its technical challenge would necessitate redoubled effort—more time in the yard, not less. Such a prospect looked good to a workaholic like Deering. It may have looked like a trap to Donnell, who had other fish to fry.

So it was that Gard Deering and William Donnell came to a parting of the ways and a parting of the fleet. Donnell kept the yard—it was his, after all—and continued building there on his own. Deering was, well, on his own. Perhaps Deering received a cash settlement. As for their fleet of tern schooners, which now numbered seven, managing ownership was to be divided between the partners. Donnell's grandson, William R., who carefully studied his ancestor's career, later maintained that Donnell acquired control of the *Electric Light*, *Charles H. Haskell*, *Josiah R. Smith*, and the new *Samuel Dillaway*—a total tonnage of 2,556—while Deering became sole managing owner of the *Willliam T. Donnell*, *Gardiner G. Deering*, and *Oliver S. Barrett*—a total tonnage of 1,994.[41] (The little *Reuben S. Hunt* was apparently sold at the time of the split.) This division does not square with contemporaneous listings in *The Record of American and Foreign Shipping*, which published annual accounts of vessels and their managing owners. The *Record* doggedly continued to list all of the above tern schooners under the Deering & Donnell name for several years. Listings in the *Record* sometimes lagged behind the times, although it is difficult to see why Donnell and Deering would not take pains to publicize their breakup in that widely read trade source. The point is somewhat academic inasmuch as the two owned small percentages in all the vessels they had built and probably continued to do so, whoever was managing whatever. Common sense favors William R. Donnell's version of events; and, within a year, the *Record* would also commence listing new vessels under the sole names of G.G. Deering and William T. Donnell, for neither builder rested on his laurels.

Having taken leave of his everyday relationship with Deering, William T. Donnell departs our story at this point, so it is fitting to outline what lay ahead for him. Some interesting surprises awaited, not all of which were gratifying. He did however achieve his goals of political and social activism. In 1892–1893 he served as president of Bath's Board of Aldermen. In 1895 he was elected Sagadahoc County Commissioner. He served also in the Maine State Legislature. In 1903–1904 he was a member of the Bath's Park and Cemetery Board. Along with Deering he became a director of the First National Bank in Bath. He also invested in the Knickerbocker Ice Company of New York, which maintained several warehouses in towns up the Kennebec from Bath and chartered schooners to transport its ice south. When, in 1894, Parker Reed's *History of Bath and Environs* was published, like most for-profit town histories of the day, it included a "Biographies" section in which local bigwigs' careers were described. William T. Donnell was one of those bigwigs. Gardiner G. Deering was among the missing.

Wider aspirations notwithstanding, what Donnell knew and did best was shipbuilding. In his shipyard, starting in 1887, Donnell took the plunge into newfangled four-masted schooners and built eight, all for his own account, all of them of increasing size. His largest, the *Alice M. Colburn*, launched in 1895, measured 1,603 gross tons, with a length of more than 225 feet—a far cry from the 65-footers of the old days. But there he drew the line. When other yards' schooners grew into the five-master category, Donnell is supposed to have responded that any-

The 368-ton tern schooner William C. Greene *(right) was built on contract in 1882 to freight supplies from New Bedford to whaling ports of call in the Azores. Here she is tied up in her home port. To the left is the denuded hull of the Atlantic sperm whaler* Palmetto, *retired in 1890. Courtesy: Capts. Douglas K. and Linda J. Lee.*

thing that big would be "a floating birdbath." He apparently changed his mind by 1899 and ordered the frames for a proposed five master; but before proceeding he changed his mind again and sold the components. The *Alice M. Colburn* would be his last schooner.[42]

Donnell, as we know, believed that there was more to life than work. He and his wife became noted party-givers, occasionally throwing a shindig in the shipyard itself. They certainly enjoyed themselves. On one wintry Tuesday evening, for example, they and their friends traveled to nearby Brunswick in sleighs, danced at the Tontine Hotel, dined past midnight, and then sleighed back home in the wee hours. The jolliest people in Bath did indeed know how to have fun.[43]

In 1888 Donnell co-chartered the Sagadahoc Club, a members-only gathering place for the city's solidest citizens. Its clubrooms were, in the words of historian Parker Reed, "sumptuously fitted up and contained all the appointments of a high class gentlemen's club" including $4,500 worth of furniture—far more than the price of a fishing schooner.[44] A booster of Bath's bright future, Donnell wanted also to broaden the community's economic base beyond its maritime focus. To that end, in 1902 he and others founded the Columbia Shoe Dressing Company, an ambitious enterprise that proved a money pit and, in 1906, financially collapsed, taking Bath's Marine National Bank with it. In debt for $75,000 because of the Columbia failure, Donnell responsibly avoided bankruptcy and made good his debts, though he was almost ruined thereby and suffered remorse about the trouble the fiasco had caused others. Donnell's other investments included shares in western mining operations that likewise proved worthless.

He continued to manage his vessels but luck was not with him. In 1889, the *Charles H. Haskell* and *Electric Light* were both lost at sea, as was Deering's *Gardiner G. Deering*, in which Donnell held shares, in 1891. Insurance would have covered Donnell's investment but not the loss of future business. The depression of the mid-1890s and, later, his declining fortunes outside the yard, strapped him financially. His fleet was gradually sold off to others, including his former partner, who had prospered. The Donnell yard's last vessel, after a five-year hiatus, was the steam ferry *Hockamock* ("*Hinky-Dink*"), which began plying between Bath and Woolwich in 1901. Never much interested in steam power, Donnell left the ferry's construction to others.

His son Harry, who had learned shipbuilding and was expected to succeed William, did not do so. Once the *Hockamock* steamed upriver, Donnell's yard fell silent.

In 1910, William Donnell contracted heart trouble and, after several months' of ill health, died that year at age seventy-three.

It is also fitting, as the curtains close on Deering & Donnell, to salute the firm's fifty fishing schooners—vessels that gave the builders the upward mobility and efficiency to tackle other challenges. It was stated earlier that Deering & Donnell fishing vessels were designed for a rough and dangerous trade. Keeping that in mind, we can tie up a few loose ends while proving the point.

Fishing was and is one of the most dangerous occupations; so it may come as no surprise that many Deering & Donnell-built schooners met violent ends, albeit late in life for some. Witness these capsule summaries from the Gloucester fishing fleet: The 67-ton *Henry Friend* (1875) spent her life as a fisherman until she went onto Shovelful Shoal off Nantucket in 1894. The 96-ton *Gatherer* (1876), later registered to Boston, was abandoned at sea in 1923. The *Willie N. Stevens* (81 tons, 1877) went ashore and was lost at Blandford, Nova Scotia in 1896. The *James A. Garfield* (74 tons, 1881) drifted away from a wharf where she was loading fish at the Magdalene Islands, Quebec, and foundered in 1916. The *James Dyer* (81 tons, 1883) collided with a steamer and sank off Gay Head, Massachusetts, in 1896. The *John C. Whittier*, Deering & Donnell's penultimate vessel (104 tons, 1886), struck Flower Rock in Bonavista Bay, Newfoundland, and was lost in 1891.[45]

Maine vessels had similar epitaphs. Portland's *Eliza A. Thomas* (93 tons, 1885), was lost a year after her debut, at Malapeque, Prince Edward Island. Eastport's *Christina Ellsworth* (97 tons, 1885) went onto Green Island at the mouth of Burnt Coat Harbor, Maine, and was wrecked in 1891. Then there was the little *Frank C. Pettis* (30 tons, 1880), built for the oyster fishery in Providence. The *Pettis* moved to Virginia to ply the same trade but stranded off Cape Charles in 1890 while carrying oysters to New Haven.[46] Fishing, anyone?

Other vessels were luckier. The *Sarah M. Jacobs* of Gloucester (80 tons, 1879) was sold in

1899 and registered to Bolivar, Venezuela. She was still afloat in 1905. The *Emma* of Gloucester, later Portland (81 tons, 1883), was put under British registry and hailed from Port Natal, Cape Colony, after 1888. The *Henry Morganthau* (90 tons, 1885) ended up as the *Emilie T.*, sailing out of St. Pierre and Miquelon, a French enclave off the south coast of Newfoundland, in 1906. The *Mabel Kenniston* (83 tons), built alongside the *Morganthau* in 1885, ended her career the same way, renamed *Noel*. The *Grover Cleveland* (92 tons, 1885), was registered to St. Johns, Newfoundland, in the 1890s. She was still on the books in 1928.

The career of the *Carleton Belle* (139 tons, 1886), built for Samuel Nickerson of Boothbay, was perhaps the most curious. After years as a fisherman, she entered the Caribbean fruit trade. She was then converted into a New Bedford whaler and, from 1906 through 1915, hunted North Atlantic sperm whales in the waning years of that fishery. In 1916 she was converted into a "Brava packet" for the immigrant trade. Registered in Sao Vincente in the Cape Verde Islands, she sailed until 1927.[47] Let us doff our hats to the venerable *Carleton Belle* and the many nail-biting Cape Verdeans who crossed the Atlantic in her.

When Deering & Donnell ceased operations, Gard Deering, like his ambitious ex-partner, was faced with crucial decisions. At age fifty-three, and with some very good ideas in his head, he had the best part of his career ahead of him.

CHAPTER THREE

Proud of Their Production

Put yourself in Gard Deering's shoes. Breaking up with your partner has left you without a shipbuilding site or even an office in which to manage your charters. As a breadwinner your dependents include an unmarried daughter, twenty, and three growing boys, sixteen, fourteen, and four. As an entrepreneur, it's incumbent upon you to get back in business while the current boom lasts. And, at age fifty-three, you're not getting any younger. What would you do? Chances are buying a large house would be the last thing on your mind. Yet that is what Gard Deering did.

In 1886, the Deerings moved to a large, white-painted, four-chimney clapboard house at 606 Washington Street, within a few blocks of the business district. It was not by any means a new home. Its undeniably handsome Greek Revival flourishes, including a columned front porch, were now passé to Victorian taste. And anyone prone to headaches would have to keep the windows closed to escape the racket of the shipyards. Did Deering, despite his financial distractions, get this house at a price too good to resist? There must have been a method to his apparent madness, for, as will become evident, Gard Deering's sense of timing was impeccable.

The Deering family's newly acquired home on Washington Street, purchased just after the breakup of Deering & Donnell. From Illustrated Historical Souvenir of the City of Bath, Maine *(1899). Courtesy: Maine Maritime Museum.*

There was no time to lose. In February 1887, Deering leased the old Houghton Brothers yard at the foot of Federal Street, near his new home, and made plans to build more schooners. A yard for lease was usually a yard in neglect, devoid of labor-saving machinery.[48] Such was the case with the ramshackle Houghton yard. Period photographs show that Deering was content to leave things as they were. He wouldn't be there forever, and throughout his long shipbuilding career he preferred human sweat to machinery.

Rain or shine? The John C. Haynes *on her launching day, 18 July 1887, in Deering's leased yard at the foot of Federal Street. It is probably a sunny day because, although a few women wait under umbrellas, other rubberneckers sit calmly in the open. The add-on to the tumbledown structure at left is a steam box in which planks are heated so that they can be bent to fit a waiting vessel's contours. The* Haynes *is Gard Deering's first vessel as sole builder. He will keep her for his own account. Courtesy: Maine Maritime Museum.*

Over the next year he produced two 97-ton fishermen of the old Deering & Donnell persuasion, possibly contracts left over from the partnership's breakup. These were the *Ellen Lincoln* and *Reuben L. Richardson*. But after the *Richardson* splashed into the Kennebec in 1888 there would be no more fishing schooners. In the same startup period Deering also got out two big tern schooners based upon William Pattee's successful model for the *Samuel Dillaway*: the 720-ton *John C. Haynes* and the 828-ton *Horatio L. Baker*—both for his own account—acting as his own master builder and with his brother John as master carpenter. John S. Deering would continue to be Gard's regular master carpenter for years to come.

These vessels, like the *Samuel Dillaway*, featured a configuration that would later become important as schooner sizes increased: They were flush-decked, which increased rigidity and added cargo capacity. Flush-deckers were wet vessels in rough weather, although water spilled quickly overboard through their open rails. But with an increase in the deck's upward slope (sheer) and a raised stem forward, a flush-decker could keep her bowsprit above water in a plunge—very important when being driven before gale winds.

Investors in the *John C. Haynes* included names to conjure with around Bath: George P. Davenport, a wealthy eccentric who later became the city's greatest philanthropist; Capt. John Patten, one of Bath's savviest, public-spirited, and most venerated merchant princes; and Gen. Thomas Hyde of Hyde Windlass Company, the former mayor of Bath who had just created the Bath Iron Works. Shareholders like those were a strong endorsement of Deering's new enterprise. Another shareholder was the *Haynes's* first captain, William H. Hamilton of Portland. Hamilton had previously sailed in Deering & Donnell's *William T. Donnell*. He continued commanding Deering schooners until his death at sea aboard the *Lydia M. Deering* in 1899.

If Deering had been superstitious, an inauspicious event at the *Haynes* launching on 18 July 1887 might have given him pause. In the words of an attending reporter, "Philip Wildes who has been many years master workman at Houghton Brothers yard was among the large number of spectators who witnessed the launching of the Deering schooner Monday [18 July 1887]. As the schooner slid from the ways Mr. Wildes, all unconscious of danger, was standing about fifty feet from the end of the wharf. A rope which was in use to assist in getting the schooner off became entangled about his legs and threw him violently to the ground and before it could be cut he was dragged some twenty-five or thirty feet and nearly overboard. He received a flesh wound on the forehead and was considerably shaken up but no bones were broken. Mr. Wildes had a most narrow escape from being killed."[49]

Intended principally for the coal trade, the *Haynes* paid regular dividends until 1895.[50] In February of that year, outward bound from Hampton Roads with coal for Sagua La Grande, Cuba, she was rammed by a barge and lost. All hands escaped safely.[51]

The *Horatio L. Baker*, Deering's second tern, was finished to the same high standard as the *Haynes*. The *Baker* went down the ways on 5 September 1888 at a cost of $28,000, or $434.38

"Better than most gold mines": The Horatio L. Baker *(1888), seen here at Percy & Small's wharf about 1903. A fast flush-decker, the* Baker *served Deering and his shareholders until 1915. Stinson photograh, courtesy: Capts. Douglas K. and Linda J. Lee.*

per share. It should be noted that the *Baker's* cost to her shareholders included the shipyard's profit on her construction, as did the figures for all the subsequent vessels mentioned in this narrative. Construction profit was a major component of Deering's success.

Once in the water the *Horatio L. Baker* enjoyed an extraordinarily profitable career. It didn't hurt that, like other vessels of the Pattee model, she was fast. A year after her launching she sailed from Rockport, Maine, to Norfolk in three days, and in 1890 it took her only two days and four hours to sail from Portland to Baltimore.[52] (On an 1899 charter, however, she took thirteen days to get from Baltimore to the Maine Central coal wharf in Bath.) The *Baker* had her share of scrapes, including an expensive collision in 1893 with another Deering-built schooner, the *John S. Ames*, but she was almost constantly busy. And she lasted. In 1908, after twenty years' service, it was claimed that the *Baker* had "paid her owners 500 per cent, which is better than most gold mines."[53] In 1911, getting weary, she collided with a steamer in Delaware Bay and was badly damaged. In August of that year a storm blew out all of her sails, but she survived. In December, however, en route to Puerto Rico, she had to put into Jacksonville in distress. She lasted until March 1915 when, en route to Tampa to load phosphate rock, she was dismasted off Stirrup Light, Bahamas. That was the end. Her crew was rescued by a passing steamer, and the *Horatio L. Baker* was abandoned.[54]

Deering's last tern schooner for his own account was the 479-ton *John S. Deering*, which went overboard on 18 July 1891 at a cost of $29,000. It is not clear why, at a time when schooners were growing by leaps and bounds, Deering deemed it prudent to build so diminutive a vessel. Perhaps it was because she was intended for the hard-pine trade, which meant that she would be calling at southern ports where the water was shallow. But like her larger sisters, the *John S. Deering* would prove fast, making a passage from Savannah to Philadelphia in three days during her first year of service. In August 1895, she was driven ashore near

An expensive mishap: The Horatio L. Baker *being nudged to a Boston wharf after colliding with the four-master* John S. Ames *in October 1893. Her foremast appears severed and her main topmast is also gone, with damage to the main as well. She will be repaired in Deering's yard. N. S. Stebbins photograph, courtesy: Capts. Douglas K. and Linda J. Lee.*

Savannah. Deering assessed his shareholders, had her repaired, and she continued to serve until 1 March 1906 when, en route from Wilmington, North Carolina to New York, she was dismasted off Cape Hatteras and abandoned by her crew, all of whom were rescued. The *Deering's* waterlogged hulk was last seen adrift a thousand miles off the west coast of Ireland in July 1906.[55]

That year was also the death date for the tern *Oliver S. Barrett,* which Deering had successfully managed since his breakup with William Donnell. The *Barrett* got into serious trouble in 1901 when, under Capt. Gardiner Gould, she was en route from Jacksonville to Boston. Encountering heavy seas, Gould had to jettison the *Barrett's* deck load of lumber to save the vessel. He was knocked overboard and, before being rescued, was repeatedly bashed by boards tossing in the waves. When landed in Norfolk, he was treated for a dislocated shoulder and a broken leg. Upon recovery, Gould bought himself a small two-master and stayed local.

Worse came for the *Oliver S. Barrett* in September 1906, just two months after the *John S. Deering* disaster. Capt. Warren D. Campbell of Boothbay was freighting yellow pine from Port Royal, South Carolina, to Baltimore and encountered heavy seas. Struck by a huge wave, the schooner was thrown on her beam ends and overwhelmed by a second wave. One *Barrett* seaman clung to a floating board for more than four days before being rescued by a Danish steamer that landed him in Copenhagen. There were no other survivors.

Over his long solo career, Deering would lose a high number of vessels. Although the *John C. Haynes*, *Horatio L. Baker*, and *Oliver S. Barrett* did not die natural deaths, their careers were long and profitable, and each gave up the ghost at a time when their value had depreciated and charters were hard to come by. And of course Deering's own investment in these vessels was at most a few shares, covered by liability insurance. But losing a schooner denied him further income from the vessel, including repair work and management fees. By the time of the *Haynes's* demise, he was no stranger to such setbacks. In his early years on his own, Deering was further pinched by the losses of the *Charles H. Haskell*, and *Electric Light* in 1889 and the wreck of the *Gardiner G. Deering* in 1891, investments from his Deering & Donnell period. There would be many more such reverses because, in general, Deering vessels did not live charmed lives. A few were downright accident-prone. But as long as there was ice and coal to be hauled, Deering would keep at it. Shipbuilding was all he knew.

Today, a large schooner is so rare a sight on the Kennebec that it is hard to imagine the dozens that crowded that waterway in the Good Old Days, loading ice for New York, Baltimore, Philadelphia, Washington, and points south. The vessels, the shipyards, and the wharves have disappeared with few traces. Likewise, anyone cruising the Kennebec above Long Reach will have a hard time visualizing the region's onetime ice industry. The enormous warehouses that once lined the river in the west-bank towns of Bowdoinham, Richmond, Gardiner, and Farmingdale, and in the east-bank towns of Dresden, Pittston, Randolph, and Chelsea, have vanished so completely that it takes some imagination to comprehend their onetime size and national importance.

The tern schooner John S. Deering *at Daufuskie Beach, South Carolina, probably loading timber. Courtesy: Maine Maritime Museum.*

By the 1830s, winter ice cut on the frozen Kennebec was being stored until the river thawed, then shipped in local vessels to distant, warmer places. Strange as it may seem to today's readers, large blocks of ice, carefully cut for a close fit and packed in sawdust in a vessel's hold, could travel long distances through hot weather and still arrive at, say, New Orleans almost intact. Or how about Havana, or Rio, or even 'round the Horn to Valparaiso? It worked, and it was very profitable. But the ice trade was not big business until after the Civil War, when urban America's demand for fresh food, home storage, and household convenience skyrocketed. Demand was especially acute in population centers that relied on edibles shipped from the countryside. Such being the case, capital from the big cities flowed north to increase and systematize the ice supply.

The industry grew elsewhere in Maine and in other northern states, but Kennebec ice became

A tight squeeze. The Narrows, at the north end of Long Reach, looking from the eastern bank in Days Ferry across to woodsy northern Bath. Merrymeeting Bay lies beyond, and above that are the Kennebec icehouses. The tide is ebbing, creating a powerful current through the narrows—no time for a schooner under tow to attempt a passage. Courtesy: Private Collection.

a name to conjure with in the business. In addition to its purity, the stuff could be conveniently sawn out of the frozen river, stored a few yards up the riverbank and, a few months later, hauled away down the same river to a waiting market. By the 1880s, thanks to the infusion of outside investment capital, exposition-size warehouses had been erected on both sides of the Kennebec, each capable of storing many thousands of tons of ice. Local townspeople grew adept at cutting, hauling, sizing, and storing ice; local skippers grew adept at shipping ice; and local shipyards grew adept at building the right vessels for the job. For years the tern schooner was the optimal ice hauler.

Schooners with charters to load ice took a tow at the mouth of the Kennebec or at Parker Flats several miles below Bath. The tugs, belonging to the Knickerbocker Steam Towage Company of Bath, often towed multiple schooners lashed side-by-side to the icehouses. Above Bath, at Days Ferry, the river narrowed, creating tricky, often treacherous conditions between tide and current. Once through the Narrows, tows could proceed without difficulty into wide Merrymeeting Bay where the Androscoggin flows into the Kennebec, and then north a few more miles to a long straightaway that supplied ice in the wintertime and floated it out in the summertime. Thousands of tons, cached in gigantic wooden icehouses, were lifted block by block by steam-powered elevators. Then, assisted by gravity and steam, they slid on an inclined run, moving out of storage toward waiting schooners tied up at the house wharves. A machine placed on the loading schooners' main decks assisted in lowering the blocks into the vessels' holds. It may sound easy but it wasn't; and one of the most important precautions during loading was getting a tight fit between blocks.[56] Then it was downstream by tow and off to a distant port.

The surging demand for ice was a godsend for Maine schooners involved in the coal trade. Many such vessels, having discharged their coal in Boston, Portland, or even Bath, might have had to return to a coal port in ballast. Loading ice so close at hand made both legs of a coal run profitable, and on a grand scale. In 1887 it was reported that 4,000 vessels came up the Kennebec to load 930,000 tons of ice and, farther upriver, 47 million feet of lumber. One day in June 1890, forty-three schooners were tied up at Kennebec icehouses.[57] In 1894, when the industry reached its peak, a million tons of ice left the Kennebec.[58] It is easy to see why investors, William Donnell, for example, bought shares in the Knickerbocker Ice Company.

One of Deering's early four-masters, the David P. Davis, *loading at Weeks's icehouses in South Gardiner, Maine, where 35,000 tons of Kennebec ice could be stored for shipment. Towing a vessel this size through the Narrows north of Bath required favorable tide conditions, gentle weather, and precise timing. The* Davis *is decorated with flags; perhaps it is the Fourth of July. Courtesy: Capts. Douglas K. and Linda J. Lee.*

Maine's ice industry would inevitably have declined in the early twentieth century with the onset of electrical refrigeration. But things went haywire much earlier thanks to another of Bath's native sons, Charles W. Morse.

Remember the Deering & Donnell schooner *Lizzie*, whose builders had to tow her back from Gloucester to Bath in order to force payment for her construction? A key player in that 1875 escapade was Benjamin Morse, whose tugboat had the towing honors. By the late 1880s, Morse's Knickerbocker Steam Towage Company virtually monopolized towing on the lower Kennebec.

Benjamin's son Charles, born in Bath in 1856, graduated from nearby Bowdoin College in 1877. Learning a few tricks of the trade in business with his father, he went to New York City, prospered, and, very quickly, became prominent in the ice industry. Charles Morse soon set his sights on achieving total domination of that business. He began merging New York City's

Two Maine schooners wharfside at the Independent Ice Company, Washington, D.C., in 1894. William T. Donnell's Independent, *left, has discharged part of her cargo and, higher in the water, appears deceptively larger than Deering's* Edwin R. Hunt, *right, which is still full. Courtesy: Capts. Douglas K. and Linda J. Lee.*

ice companies, achieving a virtual monopoly of that city's business by 1895. He then moved to control ice companies in other major eastern U.S. cities. In 1895, he founded a Maine corporation, the Consolidated Ice Company, capitalized at $10 million, which secured control of all the icehouses on the Hudson River. He also manipulated his Knickerbocker Ice Company, buying up locally owned icehouses in Maine. In 1899, Morse merged Consolidated and Knickerbocker into a new entity, the American Ice Company, overcapitalized at $60 million, which used some of its assets to bribe officials and gain unfair advantages over remaining rivals. Such tactics purportedly cost Knickerbocker, in which William Donnell had invested, $2 million.[59] Now in virtual control of the U.S. ice industry—including freight rates—American Ice doubled its prices, making ice unaffordable to countless dependent Americans, many of whom suffered great hardship. It was alleged that because of Morse's forced price increase, New York City's death rate increased 5 percent.[60] In 1901, in keeping with his strategy, Morse also cut the supply of ice by halting all activity on the Kennebec, sending the local economy into a tailspin. Realizing that American Ice was over-leveraged, and now facing falling prices, Morse set up a holding company to safeguard his multimillion-dollar personal fortune, whereupon he resigned from the ice business.

Morse was a classic, home-grown example of the turn-of-the-century, public-be-damned robber barons who provoked federal antitrust legislation. Eventually, public investigation of his wide-ranging shady and criminal methods led to indictments and a fifteen-year sentence to federal prison. The "Ice King" would serve only two years before deceiving President William

Deering's Lewis H. Goward *unloading ice at the Independent Ice Company's 9th Street wharf in Washington, D.C. The tern schooner* Madalene Cooney *of New York (right) waits her turn. Courtesy: Capts. Douglas K. and Linda J. Lee.*

Howard Taft into pardoning him on faked evidence of ill health. He would then resume his career of making money and fending off further investigations. But that is another story.

The Maine ice trade never recovered from Morse's stoppage. Demand for Kennebec ice melted to a puddle that evaporated completely by 1910, leaving the industrialized riverbanks to go back to nature. But for decades, the business generated prosperity for river towns and charters for Bath schooners such as Deering's. And Deering's investors drew many of their fattest dividends from ice. An even bigger source of fat dividends was coal.

Coal was the lifeblood of industrializing America. It stoked the mills and furnaces of industry. It heated American buildings. It fueled the world's major navies. It even fueled the expanding rail system that moved it from its Appalachian sources to the waiting market. But getting coal from Appalachia to New England was still a complicated proposition in the 1880s. Shipping directly by rail was hindered by chokepoints in the rail systems, especially the Hudson and Connecticut rivers. The directors of the Norfolk & Western rail system found a more expedient method of getting vital coal to New England and beyond, and dedicated their resources to that enterprise. The answer was to move coal east to the coast by rail and ship it out by sea.

As demand increased, the Norfolk & Western persistently expanded its rail network into Appalachia's coalfields. Bituminous coal mined in Virginia, West Virginia, and Ohio was picked up at the source on an endless schedule by locomotives pulling endless lines of hopper cars, and moved on a gradual downhill course from the hinterlands to Norfolk, where it was discharged. The emptied trains then reversed course, climbing back to the coalfields for more. Freighting those coal cargos over long distances without the benefits of gravity, and ferrying it across rivers was simply too expensive. There was an easier way.

Chartered coastwise bulk haulers, mostly schooners, sailed through Hampton Roads to Norfolk and Newport News, loaded coal, and moved it out. By 1886, the Norfolk & Western tracks ran directly onto high piers at Norfolk's Lamberts Point, where gravity-powered apparatus could fill waiting schooners with hundreds of tons in a matter of hours. Coal made Norfolk one of America's leading ports, enriching mine owners and railroad stockholders in the bargain. Those profits, and the promise of more, might well be shared by Maine's shipbuilding communities, for there was a continuous need to refine the cheapest, most efficient way to move coal by sea. Obviously, economies of scale came into play. Bigger, faster vessels could move more tons more cheaply than the tern schooners in general use at the time. Steamers? No: In the 1880s, such vessels were too expensive to operate in the coal trade because their owners could not afford for them to idle in port, as so often occurred at crowded coal docks. That offered a chance for larger schooners to compete and profit. But how large? In a replay of the two-masted dilemma of twenty years earlier, tern schooners had reached their practical limits at about 900 tons. Four-masters would be the wave of the future, at least in the coal trade.

For the moment, however, big tern schooners could make money on coal charters.

We can get a close-up view of life in the ice and coal trade though the logbook of the large tern schooner *Samuel Dillaway*, 1893–1895.[61] The *Dillaway*, Deering & Donnell's last and largest schooner, was the model on which Deering based his big terns of the late 1880s, and he probably still owned in her during the mid-1890s. The *Dillaway's* experiences, typical of the trade, may also offer a few surprises about schooner charters of the period.

The so-called Gay Nineties were in fact beset by another financial panic and its aftermath. In 1893, economic jitters provoked a run on the nation's gold reserves and drained them to the legal minimum. A panic followed in which banks and railroads failed and countless businesses declared bankruptcy. By 1894, unemployment had risen to 20 percent or more, and the nation underwent the worst depression thus far in its history. The picture did not brighten until 1896. Deering shareholders came through the slump satisfactorily. They owed their dividends to the continuous need for ice and coal. Which brings us back to the case of the *Dillaway*.

Between November 1893 and October 1895, the *Samuel Dillaway*, kept in constant use, delivered ten cargoes of ice, seventeen of coal, and one of barrels, bridging the numerical gap between ice and coal cargoes by sailing empty.[62] "Constant use," may be a misleading term, however, because of the many interruptions and interludes she routinely sustained. The logbook, kept by a succession of at least seven different mates, opens on 8 November 1893 with the *Dillaway* at Boston, ready to sail light (empty) to Norfolk for a coal cargo. The usual route was a crowded coastal sea lane that ran from Boston southeast and around Cape Cod, then generally westward through Nantucket and Vineyard Sounds, passing Block Island and Montauk Point, then southwestward along the Atlantic coast of New Jersey, Delaware, Eastern-shore Maryland and Virginia to Cape Henry, at the mouth of Chesapeake Bay, then west into Hampton Roads for Norfolk or Newport News.

But in 1893, outward bound from Boston, the *Dillaway* almost immediately ran into trouble when she collided at night with another tern schooner off Cape Cod Light and had to return for repairs to her jib boom, all of which cost her five days' delay. After that, cautious Capt. Smith declined to sail her at night, anchoring in safe spots until daylight. Smith also preferred to anchor in heavy weather, riding out a storm before proceeding on his course. If time was money (it was), then such delays were expensive.

With a cargo of ice, the Samuel Dillaway *prepares to move downriver under tow past C. W. Morse's huge Consolidated Ice Company storehouse in Richmond, Maine. On the building's left end is the enclosed loading shoot that moves ice in blocks from storage to loading schooners. Courtesy: Maine Maritime Museum.*

The schooner arrived at the Lamberts Point coal docks, where she filled with coal in a day and was on her way back to Boston. On 7 December she "made fast at the Charlestown Bridge," but it took until Christmas Eve to discharge her cargo. Then it was back to Norfolk and thence with coal to New Bedford. For reasons that are unclear but suggest a lack of a charter, she lay at a New Bedford dock for an entire month. She then sailed for Philadelphia, but in Delaware Bay her windlass broke a cog. The crew had to haul the anchors by hand, a slow, exhausting chore. In Philadelphia she lost another four days while repairs were made.

The floes on the Kennebec must have gone out early in 1894, for the *Dillaway* was upriver loading 1,056 tons of commercial ice at the end of March. On 2 April she was heading downriver under tow by the tug *Adelia Chase*. As the mate put it in the logbook, the tug and schooner "came [to] the narrows and then towed through... at 10 am Ran us ashore on the Bay Sands and tried to Hall us off but could not. At 6:30 pm tug boats Seguin and Adelia Chase came out and Made Fast along side to wait for High Water. 10 Pm Floated and Backed off and started down the river." There were no further complications. The ice was unloaded between 11 and 14 April at the Great Falls Ice Company's wharf in Washington, D.C. From there it was to Norfolk, then to Boston, then back to Norfolk, and so on.

In May 1894, between charters, the *Dillaway* put in at William Donnell's wharf to have a long-overdue "donkey engine" installed which would assist in raising and lowering her anchors and sails and powering the pumps—a huge improvement in efficiency and, probably, crew morale. Towed to Richmond, she loaded another ice cargo that she delivered to Washington by the end of May; then she proceeded again to Norfolk where, over two days, she loaded 1,102 tons of coal for Boston. And so it continued for the rest of 1894: ice going south, coal coming north.

Between November 1893 and January 1895, the *Dillaway* lost three weeks of workdays to various delays, all part of the cost of doing business, apparently. Between January and October 1895, she lost almost two months more in various delays, including waiting her turn to load, waiting to discharge, waiting at Norfolk for coal (delayed by a miners' strike, which eventually diverted her to the secondary coal port of Baltimore), waiting at anchor for a tow, waiting at anchor for adverse winds to subside, and waiting for repairs after yet another collision. Another noteworthy factor in the cost of doing business was pervasive dependence on towage. Gone, apparently, were the days of intrepid skippers, bucko mates, and crack seamen.

In addition to the above 1895 delays, the *Dillaway* spent two more weeks in October at Donnell's yard undergoing general repairs. On 28 October 1895, just days after her refit and en route to load coal, the *Dillaway* "at 3:40 AM collided with barge Chemerig about five miles from Cape shore between Cape and Nauset Lights.

"We lay in colishan about 10 minutes before clearing barge

"After clearing second barge third barge struck us on the quarter

"Stood in shore after clearing barges about 2 miles and anchored at daylight got underway and proceeded to Boston for

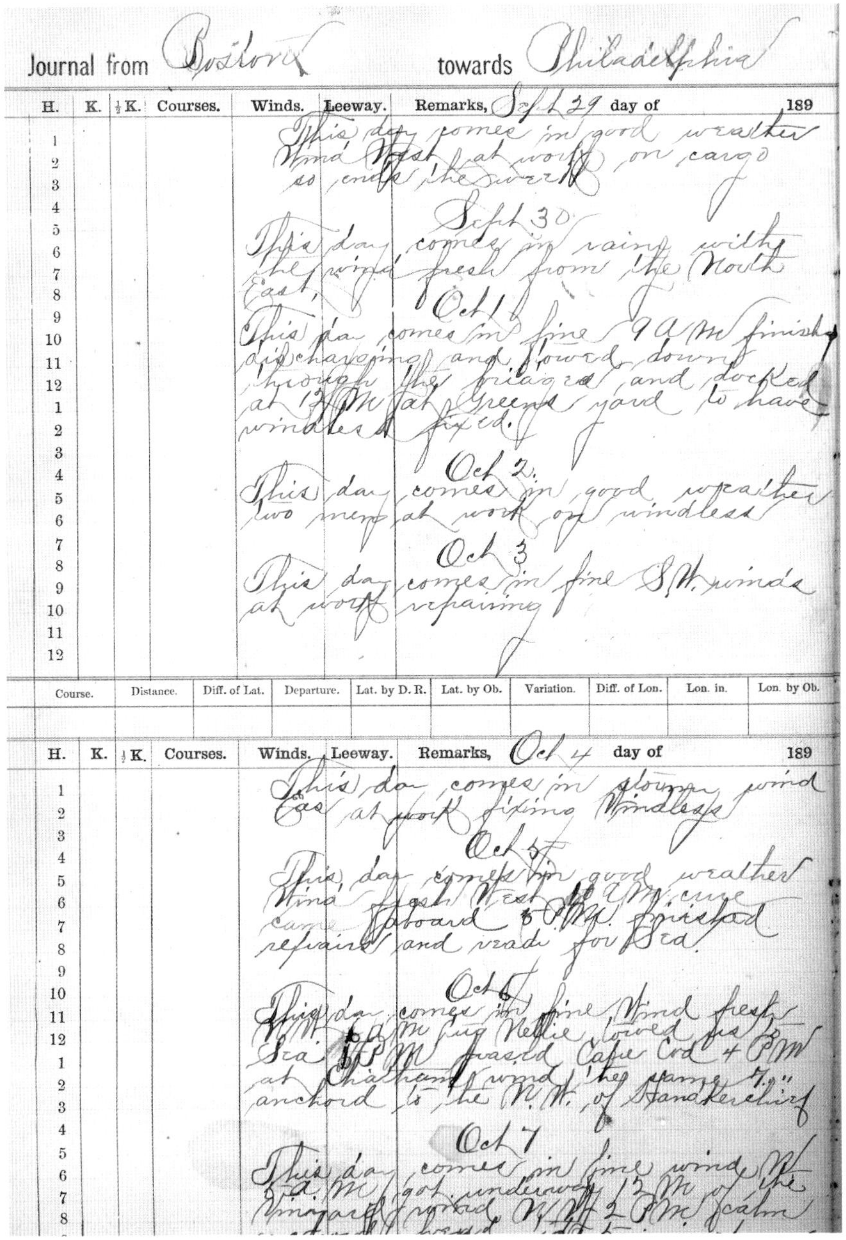
Journal from Boston towards Philadelphia

H.	K.	½K.	Courses.	Winds.	Leeway.	Remarks, Sept 29 day of 189
						This day comes in good weather Wind West at work on cargo so ends the watch
						Sept 30 This day comes in raining with the wind fresh from the North East.
						Oct 1 This day comes in fine 9 AM finish discharging and towed down through the bridges and docked at 12 PM at Greens yard to have windless fixed.
						Oct 2. This day comes in good weather two men at work on windless
						Oct 3 This day comes in fine S.W. winds at work repairing

Course.	Distance.	Diff. of Lat.	Departure.	Lat. by D. R.	Lat. by Ob.	Variation.	Diff. of Lon.	Lon. in.	Lon. by Ob.

H.	K.	½K.	Courses.	Winds.	Leeway.	Remarks, Oct 4 day of 189
						This day comes in strong wind East at work fixing windlass
						Oct 5 This day comes in good weather Wind [illegible] came aboard [illegible] finished repairs and ready for sea.
						Oct 6 This day comes in fine Wind [illegible] tug Nellie towed to sea [illegible] passed Cape Cod [illegible] at Chatham wind the same [illegible] anchored to the N.W. of Handkerchief
						Oct 7 This day comes in fine wind [illegible] got underway 12 M [illegible]

A page from the Samuel Dillaway's logbook, 1895. Courtesy: Maine Maritime Museum.

A doodle drawn in the Samuel Dillaway's *logbook by one of her many mates. Drawings and whimsies are common in personal journals but rare in logbooks, which were the official record of a vessel's voyages. Courtesy: Maine Maritime Museum.*

Repairs arrived in bost[on] at 5 PM in towe of Tug Juno," Another part of the cost of doing business.

Although the *Samuel Dillaway's* logbook ends in Boston, the schooner would be repaired again and stay active until going ashore on St. Helena Bar, South Carolina, in 1916. But her October 1895 collision, seen in hindsight, was another omen for Maine shipbuilders. The schooner had been hit repeatedly by a string of barges under a tugboat's tow. Here was another example of changing times and more efficient methods. It had occurred to many schooner crews and captains, to say nothing of builders, owners, and brokers, that if tugs were necessary to move schooners in and out of ports, might not tugs be better utilized as fulltime towboats, towing multiple, schooner-size barges the entire distance of a charter? Soon, strings of towed "clothes-line" barges (some of them ex-schooners) would be a common sight in the U.S. coastwise trade. They were also a dangerous sight, overly long and poorly lit—a moving menace to navigation before corrective regulations were enforced.

But of course there might also be ways to improve the efficiencies of schooners. For example, they could be made bigger—with a lengthened hull and an additional mast.

While the Deering & Donnell partnership was moving up the size ladder with tern schooners, other yards were moving to a new type. The first four-master, built in Bath by Goss, Sawyer & Packard, was the *William L. White*, in 1880. She had been conceived as a three-master but, at 995 tons, she would have been bigger than the largest tern, so adding a fourth mast made sense. A donkey engine was of course a must, and became standard equipment for the vessels that followed the *White's* example. The *White* ushered in another phase in wooden shipbuilding that gave the schooner a new lease on life. Unlike the slow growth of the tern schooner, however, this new phase went forward at a quickened pace. In 1882, Goss & Sawyer launched the first Bath schooner over 1,000 gross tons: the 1,138-ton, four-masted *Elliot B. Church*, which measured 192½ feet in length. Five years later came Bath's first 1,600-ton schooner: the four-masted, 227-foot *T. A. Lambert*, built at B. & F. Morse's yard.

Schooners grew in size to stay competitive with barges, and they kept growing. In 1897, with the launching of the *Frank A. Palmer*, at 2,014 tons and 274 feet the largest four-master

The Lydia M. Deering, *named for G. G. Deering's wife (aboard at the launching), and the first four-masted schooner built for his own account. Her shareholders include Gen. Thomas Hyde of Bath Iron Works, future shipbuilder Capt. Samuel Percy, and legendary designer Johnson Rideout. The* Lydia M. Deering *will continue to serve until 1915. Courtesy: Capts. Douglas K. and Linda J. Lee.*

A portrait of the 1,225-ton Lydia M. Deering, *painted in oil by Solon Francis Montecello Badger. Here she is passing Highland Lighthouse on the south shore of Cape Cod, probably bound to Norfolk for coal. Paintings such as this make an interesting, somewhat idealized contrast with workaday photographs. Courtesy: Parker Family Collection.*

Deering's 1,034-ton four-master William C. Tanner, *completed in 1890. In the foreground is a saw pit. With no power equipment in the yard, even basic jobs must be done manually. To the left is a massive tree trunk that may become a sternpost on Deering's next project. The* Tanner's *solid box rail will provide increased protection from seas. Possibly installed at the behest of the vessel's captain, Henry Johnson, it will apparently not achieve its purpose, for no future Deering schooners will have this feature. Courtesy: Capts. Douglas K. and Linda J. Lee.*

afloat, even that class had about topped out. From there it was just a short step to even larger, five-masted vessels—true superschooners. Building these giants became a virtual Bath exclusive; every Atlantic five-master but one was constructed on the banks of the Kennebec. Gardiner Deering would be a key contributor to this industry.

It cannot be said that Deering rushed into the breach. Down at the South End, William Donnell had launched the four-master *Katie J. Barrett* in 1887 and never looked back. It was two more years before Deering followed suit with the 916-ton *John S. Ames,* built on contract for Capt. Otis C. Chase of Boston and launched in 1889.

Immediately after the *Ames,* Deering got out a four-master for his own account, the 1,225-ton, 225-foot *Lydia M. Deering*. The investor roster for this long-lived vessel is noteworthy because Gard Deering's name (3 shares) is supplemented by those of his sons Frank (age twenty) and Harry (seventeen), with a half-share apiece. Deering planned to bring them into the business shortly. John Deering took another half-share. Besides his regulars, other owners included Capt. Sam Percy, thirty-three, a future force to be reckoned with in schooner building; and the legendary modeler Johnson Rideout (William Pattee's partner), who may have received a share for helping design the vessel. The *Lydia's* captain, William Hamilton, late of the *John C. Haynes*, was in for two shares.

Deering's venture into four-masters may have been delayed by the inadequacies of his leased surroundings, for in March of 1889 he purchased part of the Tom Hagan shipyard at the

The Edwin R. Hunt *(1892) at Galveston sometime during her twenty-five years of service in the Deering fleet. Note the sailor perched atop the mizzen crosstrees. Courtesy: Capts. Douglas K. and Linda J. Lee.*

foot of Federal Street, better quarters and handier to his home. The first Deering schooner was launched from that site in 1890. She was the *William C. Tanner*, a 1,034-ton four-master. Then came the little *John S. Deering*, mentioned earlier, his last tern schooner. Then, from 1891 to 1896, there followed a stream of four-masters. The first was the *Wesley M. Oler* (1891, 1,061 tons) built on contract. The rest were Deering's own: the *Edwin R. Hunt* (1892, 1,132 tons) at a cost of $52,060, the *David P. Davis* (1893, 1,231 tons) at a cost of $40,255, the *Lewis H. Goward* (1895, 1,199 tons) at a cost of $49,107, and the *Edward E. Briry* (1896, 1,613 tons) at a cost of $63,326. Deering launched nothing during 1894, a probable effect of the severe national depression. He likewise built nothing in 1897 and 1898.

In the Kennebec, ready for charter, the new David P. Davis *flies G. G. Deering's red-white-and-blue house flag with the device of a "D" within a diamond. One of her accomplishments during her eleven-year career will be a run from Boothbay, Maine, to Baltimore in thirty-four days, probably the all-time slowest passage between those points. Capt. Davis will rightly blame the weather. Courtesy: Maine Maritime Museum.*

Business was bottoming out in Bath in those years, although the *Times* tried to paint the rosiest possible picture. "PROSPECTS BRIGHT," ran a headline on 27 August 1898, "Business Along Our Water Front Looks Like Old Times." The question was, which old times? "The hum of industry along our waterfront increases as the days grow shorter," the report continued, "and to quote the words of one of our prominent shipbuilders 'prospects are very bright for fall work in the yards.'" But the hum of industry amounted only to one schooner lately completed, one in for repairs, and a crew sprucing up the pier at William Rogers's yard. Deering's yard, like most of the others, was quiet.

But Deering himself was busy, even after the *Haynes's* loss, as managing owner of a growing fleet: the vessels he had built on his own, and two others (the terns *Oliver S. Barrett* and *William T. Donnell*), that he'd inherited from his former partnership. Surviving records show that Deering came through the depression in stable condition. In 1893, the year of the panic, he had eight vessels with combined net earnings of $33,603. In 1894, when the depression was at

Gard Deering's shipwrights pose for a picture in the former Hagan yard, 1894. The science of cloning lies far in the future, so their mutual resemblance is difficult to explain. Behind them, the Lewis H. Goward *awaits their further attention. Courtesy Maine Maritime Museum.*

On 30 September 1895, the 1,119-ton four-master Lewis H. Goward *slides into the Kennebec. Just behind her to the north the Percy & Small yard is finishing up the* Charles P. Notman. *The floating logs in the foreground belong to M.G. Shaw's lumber mill. Courtesy: Capts. Douglas K. and Linda J. Lee.*

The Lewis H. Goward, *depicted in oil by an unknown artist. This work was probably intended to commemorate her maiden voyage, for the schooner retains the white paint scheme used in her launching. She flies the G. G. Deering house flag from her maintop. Courtesy: Parker Family Collection.*

its worst, nine vessels netted $29,368. Earnings rebounded in 1895, totaling $39,335 on nine vessels. Then, with ten vessels: $40,293 in 1896; $40,407 in 1897; $59,944 in 1898, and with an eleventh schooner added, $88,166 in 1899 and $109,568 in 1900.

That new eleventh vessel was another jump for Deering: an 1,800-ton, 225-foot five-master. Gard Deering had thought a great deal about shipbuilding as schooners morphed into superschooners. At age sixty-six he had an innovation or two of his own that he planned to

The Lydia M. Deering, *all sails furled and under tow, exemplifies an increasingly common sight in the coastwise schooner trade. The* Deering's *anchor looks ready to drop, so she is apparently approaching an anchorage. Courtesy: Capts. Douglas K. and Linda J. Lee.*

try. Bath shipbuilders were learning that building big schooners was a much different matter than terns. Schooner crews were learning that sailing them was, too.

The story of schooner evolution in the late nineteenth and early twentieth centuries is one of optimizing traditional technology and delaying obsolescence through successive innovations. In economic terms, the case of Bath's wooden schooners is particularly curious because, by the time of the Civil War, a vital component of the city's competitive edge in shipbuilding had disappeared. Maine's once readily available stock of critical timbers—oak for keels, hackmatack for securing beams to a vessel's sides, and mast pines, for example—had been exhausted. But wooden shipbuilding had become so entrenched that there was no question of

The fast, long-poop schooner Edward E. Briry *in the stream shortly after her completion in 1896. Launched completely bald, she has had her masts stepped upriver at the Bath Iron Works. She will soon test her mettle in a collision with the steamer* Fortuna *off Block Island. Courtesy: Capts. Douglas K. and Linda J. Lee.*

stopping, so builders bought the necessary timber elsewhere and had it shipped to Bath. By the late nineteenth century, schooners and trains delivered to Bath's yards oak and hard pine from southern states; knee-shaped hackmatack from Nova Scotia, Michigan, or wherever it could be found; and mast-size fir sticks from Oregon. As we have seen, one way to offset these additional costs was to send the patterns for a vessel's frame to the supplier, who precut components to size before delivery. In a way, building a big schooner was a bit like working from a kit. Increasing expenses were further offset by Bath shipwrights' accumulated know-how.

For as long as there was commercial demand for wooden vessels, it seemed that there were ways to cut construction costs and keep pace with changing times—power saws, for example, and, later, electrically driven machinery—although these expensive inventions did not interest Gard Deering. Another was rethinking the schooner form: exploiting its inherent virtues while overcoming such drawbacks as size limitation. Modelers and builders cleverly and courageously tweaked age-old technology, retaining the schooner's place in commerce by modernizing and enlarging it to achieve economy of scale. And for a while it worked.

But by the time four-stickers began splashing into the Kennebec, schooner builders were fighting a delaying action, postponing the day of reckoning when wooden vessels could no longer compete. How clear this reality was to people like Deering is difficult to estimate. By the 1890s there was ample evidence even in some Bath shipyards that rapidly evolving iron, steel, and steam technology was apt to win the ultimate race. But just as Bath builders kept on building wooden vessels after the wood ran out, so did they stick with schooners. If barges or steamers crowded schooners out of some markets, perhaps there were other niches in which

The Edward E. Briry *in service but between charters, her empty hull riding high above the water. Courtesy: Capts. Douglas K. and Linda J. Lee.*

The Wesley M. Oler *in 1891, ready for her Boston owner. Her design and durability will be sorely tested when she is caught at sea in the Blizzard of '98. Courtesy: Capts. Douglas K. and Linda J. Lee.*

they could operate or markets they could serve. In the meantime, bigger was better, because bigger and bigger vessels could haul cargo at lower and lower rates per ton. In the short run, this optimism would be vindicated. But not of course in the long run. With the possible exception of Noah's Ark, building large vessels out of wood can be stretched only so far. Bath's glandular schooners would soon reach that limit. And, as we shall see, relentless economizing produced unwholesome shipboard conditions that compromised competitiveness. Cost cutting can be taken only so far.

So it was that by the 1890s, schooner hulls were being lengthened and widened to a point where they were very sensitive to a variety of stresses. Lacking rigidity, they tended to twist or sag under pressure. Viewed as cargo receptacles, big schooners' hulls can be likened more to baskets than boxes. With passing years, these baskets had enlarged but the construction components had not kept pace. One schooner authority puts it another way: "Vessels kept getting bigger but trees stayed the same size."[63] Made up of countless pieces spliced and cobbled together, a large schooner's shape could change when she was filled. Even when empty, the overall structure's uneven weight distribution provoked drooping or rising in spots. The bow and stern sections, heavier than the rest of the hull, tended to hog (sag) over time. Wave action could cause longitudinal or lateral flexing that might cause seams to open. Wind pressure on sails caused masts to exert strenuous force on the hull. All sailing vessels were subject to such stresses, but with the enlarged wooden hulls of the four- five-, and, later, six-masted giants, these effects were magnified, sometimes with serious consequences for manageability, safety, and of course longevity. To combat these weaknesses, the big schooners were reinforced by countless metal straps and braces, some of which reinforced the reinforcements ("the wood was there to hold the steel in place!")[64]

To illustrate the mixed blessings of progress, let us consider the case of the Deering-built four-master *Wesley M. Oler* of Boston, which was tested to the limit in the notorious Blizzard of 1898. Her tribulations ran the gamut of problems awaiting big new schooners when conditions turned ugly. For the *Oler*, and for our purposes, what happened in November of '98 was The Perfect Storm. At 1,061 tons and 191 feet in length, the *Wesley M. Oler* was not much bigger than the largest tern schooners. She was however, built to exacting standards, equipped with the latest gear, and part of a line of Deering schooners that would grow from to big to bigger to huge.

The *Oler*, having loaded a cargo of molasses in barrels at New Orleans, encountered a series of gales as she made her way across the Gulf of Mexico, around the southern tip of Florida, and north along the Atlantic coast in November 1898. On the morning of 28 November, well off the Capes of Delaware, she was struck by a powerful west-northwest wind—the beginning of the blizzard. Like every big schooner, the *Oler's* options were few because of her massive fore-and-aft rig. She was already running under shortened sail, so she did the best thing under the circumstances: she ran before the wind, hoping it would weaken before her canvas blew out. The wind shifted to the northeast and strengthened. In such circumstances, a square-rigger, with an elaborate repertoire of manageable sails, could have reduced sail to a minimum, just enough to maintain headway in the heavy gale. But that was not an option in a four-master, with her limited array of gigantic sails whose booms slatted dangerously in violent weather. Her crew's best bet at that point was to keep her off the wind as much as possible to relieve pressure on masts and sails, and try to hold her there. The *Oler* fought back, plowing through heavy seas and howling wind, and laboring badly. The relatively low upward curve (sheer) of her bow did not repel water well and her jib boom went under every time a head sea struck her. If those impacts should damage the bowsprit, the foretopmast (whose stays connected to it) could fall. In such a calamity, an old-fashioned vessel could have minimized damage by cutting the hemp rigging, freeing dangerous debris and relieving strain. But the *Oler* was not an old-fashioned vessel. Her standing rigging was made of wire, which remained taut under all conditions and could not be cut away in an emergency.

The Wesley M. Oler *(second from left) at Bangor sometime before her ordeal. Courtesy: Capts. Douglas K. and Linda J. Lee.*

When the wind blew out the mizzen, thus subtracting a huge, unmanageable sail and easing strain, Capt. William Harriman knew that the best course was now to run before the wind.[65] As the *Oler* was wearing around, a heavy sea struck on her starboard quarter, carrying the second mate overboard. The *Oler* had not yet gathered headway, so the crew had time to act, but the best they could do under the chaotic circumstances was to throw lines to the injured mate, to no avail. Then the schooner went before the wind and the mate was lost. The boarding wave that claimed the *Oler's* mate had stripped her of every movable object big and small on her port side. Part of her starboard rail, "six by six hard pine edge bolted through and through," was gone.[66] A 1,500-pound anchor lashed to the forward house had been torn loose and hurled into the fore rigging. But now there was a breather as the *Oler* gained headway, and the crew used the time for emergency repairs. It took a day to clear away the wreckage.

The gale continued. Then, with the blizzard abating, hurricane-force winds came on. In the course of the next two days, keeping before the wind, the *Oler* was blown helplessly on a 360-degree course, plunging into heavy seas that swept her entire length. At the worst moment, a sea destroyed the wheelhouse and swept the schooner's yawl boat from its stern davits. And throughout the blizzard and hurricane, her enormous booms slatted violently and unpredictably, making them potentially lethal to anyone in their crazy path.

Relative calm returned on 3 December. The exhausted crew bent some spare sails and headed for Bermuda, 200 miles to the southwest. Despite the mayhem and damage, the molasses cargo was undamaged and the *Oler* had developed no serious leaks. Her cargo was transshipped to Boston and, for the next two months, she underwent repairs.

The *Wesley M. Oler's* ruggedness had served her well but her low stem and schooner rig had not. It was one thing to sail *Samuel Dillaway*-style, hugging the coast and anchoring at night. It was quite another to sail offshore for long distances in dicey weather. The *Oler's* size did not save her; just the opposite. A longer, less rigid, schooner might not have made it in such circumstances.

The *Wesley M. Oler* went back to her trade and continued therein until November 1902, when, en route to New York with guano, she put into Nassau in distress. Apparently her repairs were too complicated or expensive to be attended to there, so she was taken under tow for the States. Off Cape Hatteras, in a gale, she parted her tow hawser and pounded to pieces at Hatteras Inlet. All hands were lost.[67]

Less than four months after the Blizzard of '98, the Deering four-master *David P. Davis* delivered her cargo of Boothbay ice to Washington, D.C., completing what was undoubtedly the longest passage in history between those points: thirty-eight days. Not that the *David P. Davis* (1893, 1,231 tons) wasn't fast; she was, after all, a Deering schooner. It was the schooner-hostile weather again. The *Davis's* captain, Albert P. Davis (another ex-Donnell master) explained things as best he could in a report to Gard Deering. It had taken thirty-four days, Davis wrote, to reach Sandy Hook, New Jersey. He was unable to wire Deering there about his vessels' situation because "we had no boats to get ashore in. We lost a small boat and stove a big one…." According to the skipper, after leaving Boothbay in a snowstorm, the *David P. Davis* had almost reached Montauk when a northwesterly wind hit, bringing with it five days of snow. The *Davis* behaved much like the *Wesley M. Oler* had four months back: "We laid vessel to and she got used up so I ran for the Gulf stream. We had nothing but gales and wind for 3 weeks steady. They came from all directions and it made such a cross sea we could not lay to. She would put her [jib] boom right under. So we had to run her any way the wind was fair.

"I think we went all over the Western Ocean 2 or 3 times. We spoke a steamer and told her to report us. Also spoke another steamer and obtained some stores. The Capt. was very kind. We had no boats seaworthy so he loaned me one of his boats and sent us stores."[68] That got the *Davis* to her destination at last.

The *Davis* kept busy and paid Deering shareholders regular dividends until 1904. On 26 February of that year, freighting phosphate rock from Punta Gorda to Baltimore, she collided in dense fog with an unidentified schooner off Hatteras and was totally dismasted. The crew manned the pumps until exhausted, then abandoned ship. The passing steamer *Toledo* rescued four of her crew, and a boat from the Diamond Shoals Light Vessel rescued the other six.[69] But what of the mysterious schooner that tore a hole in the *Davis* and departed without identifying herself? In an explanation that was without a doubt supplied by Gard Deering, the *Bath Anvil* later reported that the culprit was the Bath-built four-master *Benjamin F. Poole* of Providence. "The Poole went her way without

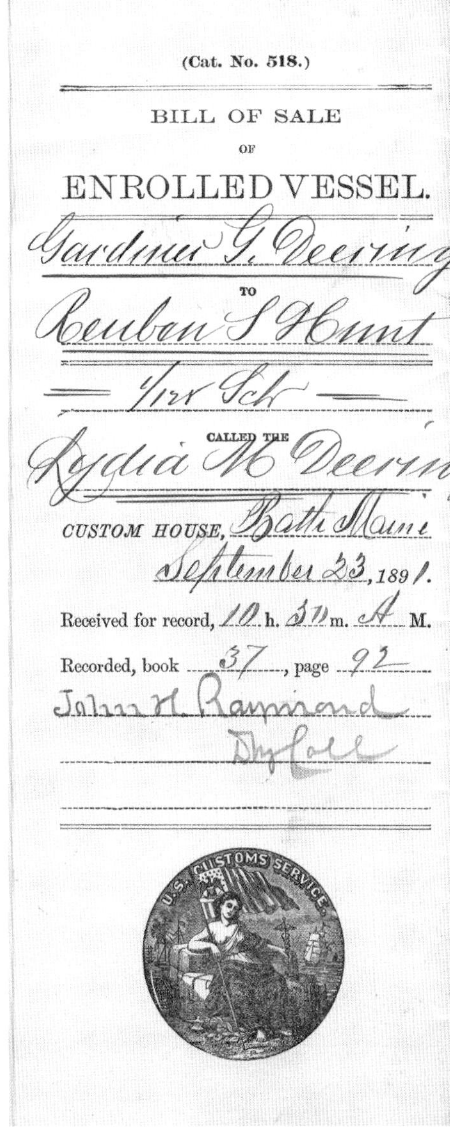

(Cat. No. 518.)

BILL OF SALE

OF

ENROLLED VESSEL.

Gardiner G. Deering

TO

Reuben S. Hunt

CALLED THE

Lydia M. Deering

CUSTOM HOUSE, Bath Maine

September 23, 1891.

Received for record, 10 h. 30 m. A M.

Recorded, book 37, page 92

John H. Raymond

Dy Coll

A folded bill of sale for a half-share in the Lydia M. Deering, *September 1891. Courtesy: Maine Maritime Museum.*

Sections 4170, 4171, 4192, 4193, 4194, 4196, and 4312, Revised Statutes. Cat. No. 518.

THE UNITED STATES OF AMERICA.

BILL OF SALE OF ENROLLED VESSEL.

To all to whom these Presents shall come, Greeting:

Know ye, That* I Gardiner G. Deering, of Bath, State of Maine Owner of Three Sixty-fourths (3/64) of the Schooner or vessel called the Lydia M. Deering of Bath of the burden of Eleven hundred seventy three 57/100 tons, or thereabout, for and in consideration of the sum of One dollars, lawful money of the United States of America, to me in hand paid, before the sealing and delivery of these presents, by† Reuben S. Hunt, of Bath, State of Maine the receipt whereof I do hereby acknowledge and am therewith fully satisfied, contented, and paid, have bargained and sold, and by these presents do bargain and sell, unto the said‡ Reuben S Hunt, his

A bill of sale for Reuben S. Hunt's 1/64 share in the schooner Lydia M. Deering. *The* Deering *was two years old at the time. Courtesy: Maine Maritime Museum.*

making her identity known and did not report the collision but a little clever detective work proved her connection with it and a satisfactory adjustment was effected."[70] At the time of her loss, she was valued at $40,000 (about what she had cost to build) and had paid her shareholders 175 percent.[71]

In February 1902, Deering's four-master *Edwin R. Hunt* (1892, 1,132 tons) was caught in a nasty gale off Delaware's Atlantic Coast. As reported in the press, the *Hunt* "arrived in Vineyard Haven considerably damaged. The vessel's spanker was badly torn and he spanker boom and gaff broken. The mate had his hands badly frostbitten and one sailor was so badly frozen that he was taken to the Marine hospital. She was coal loaded from Newport News for Portland, to which place she will probably tow."[72]

Gard Deering and his investors had more than their share of disasters and close calls, although mishaps and occasional losses were accepted as occupational risks by builders, investors, and mariners. And small wonder. Schooners were getting bigger and more numerous, and their coastwise sea lanes, narrow and riven with dangerous shoals, were increasingly crowded. In 1897, the year after her launching, the four-master *Edward E. Briry* (1,613 tons) was damaged to the tune of $2,600 when she collided at night off Montauk with the steamer *Fortuna* of Boston. After impact, three of the *Fortuna's* crew jumped aboard the *Briry* but the steamer drifted away. The rest of her crew gave her up for lost and were taken off by the schooner *Laura L.Sprague* of Lynn, Massachusetts. The *Fortuna*, however, did not sink. Came daylight, and she was found to be in reasonably good shape, whereupon she was taken into Vineyard Haven and later Boston for repair.

The *Edwin R. Hunt* had a near miss in March 1902 when sailing out of Chesapeake Bay in close company with the schooner *Marguerite* of Taunton, Massachusetts, "with fair wind and a big spread of canvas when [the] Hunt's wheel rope suddenly jammed and she veered toward the *Marguerite.* The Hunt's crew yelled and the Marguerite was kept off just in time to save her from full impact by the onrushing Hunt. The quarters came together solidly, just lacking force necessary to stave planking."[73] The *Hunt* was another steady earner for Deering, and we shall follow her later career more closely. Her own violent end lay far in the future.

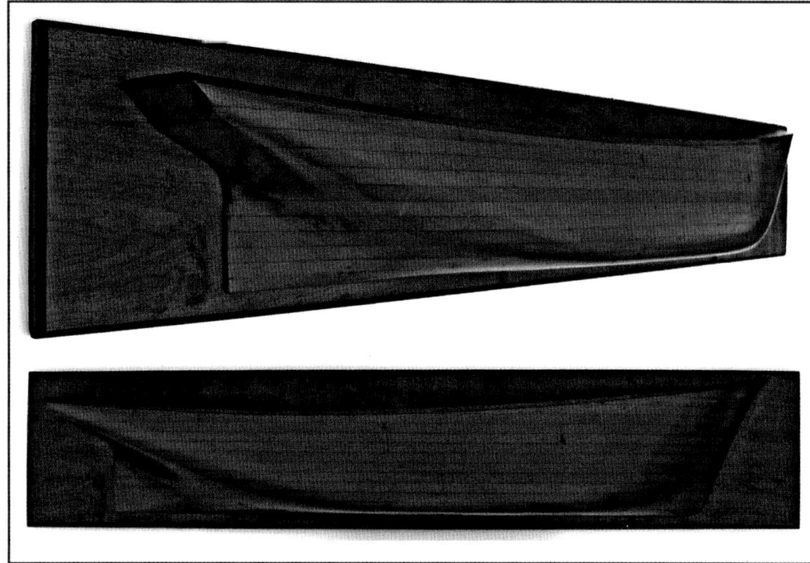

Two views of the layered half-model believed to be Fred Rideout's design for Deering's big schooners. The proportions here befit a smallish foremaster, but such models could be scaled up for larger projects. The model's length is 43 inches. Courtesy: Capts. Douglas K. and Linda J. Lee.

Deering's tern schooners, as we have seen, were fast vessels, and his larger schooners were especially so. His four-masters were based on a model by Fred Rideout whose father Johnson was William Pattee's partner. (Pattee, remember, was responsible for modeling Deering & Donnell's and, later, Deering's best terns.) Upon Johnson Rideout's death, Pattee made Johnson's son Fred a partner in that well respected design firm. Fred Rideout's model inspired the unusually swift four-master *Edward E. Briry*, and was probably the model also for the *Lewis H. Goward* and *David P. Davis*. That same design would be the basis for Deering's forthcoming five-masters as well.

One function of longer hulls is that they sail faster than shorter ones, so Deering often received good news about his four-masters' performance, which did not hurt business. The *Edward E. Briry* was known as one of the fastest. In 1905, when she was nine years old, she earned a degree of fame under John Ross's command when she raced with four other big schooners freighting coal from Baltimore to Boston. One of her four contestants was the *Alice M. Colburn*, William Donnell's last vessel. The *Colburn* took an early lead. By day three,

G. G. DEERING,
SHIP BUILDER.
VESSELS REPAIRED.
Washington, St.

Bath, Me., April 12th 1894

G. W. Gaurly,

Dear Sir.

I have not got any use for knees just at present but if you wish to send in a Car load I will sell them for you. I have a call for Knees quite often, a few at a time, will pay you for them when they are sold. Prices as follows. 5 in 75¢ 6-in $1,05 7 in, $1.70 - 8 in $2,70 - 9 in $3,70. 10-in $5,20 this is for Knees Planed.

Yours Respect,
G. G. Deering, Pr -

An 1894 business letter from Gard Deering to a supplier discussing a supply of knees, important components in wooden shipbuilding. Deering devised a way reduce the industry's dependence on hanging knees and strengthen schooner hulls in the bargain. Courtesy: Maine Maritime Museum.

when the racers reached the south shore of Cape Cod, the *Briry*, though she had lost her foretopmast, closed in on the leading *Colburn*, which was fifteen minutes ahead. By the time they approached Boston on day five, the *Briry* led, and it was she who took the first tug, a half-hour ahead of the *Colburn*. How sweet it must have been for Deering to hear that one of his schooners had bested the pride of William T. Donnell's fleet. The *Edward E. Briry*, named for a prominent Bath physician who also served as that port's boarding officer, stayed in Deering's fleet for years, making at lest one transatlantic voyage to Lisbon with coal.

Deering's four-master *Lewis H. Goward* (1895, 1,119 tons), which in the early twentieth century followed the trend of chartering schooners for transatlantic voyages, loaded kerosene, rum, flour, tobacco, sewing machines, and watches in 1906 and took them to Freetown, Sierra Leone, in thirty-four days, which was considered crack sailing. She returned in ballast to Tampa in thirty-one, covering 280 miles a day for five consecutive days.

And then there was the *William C. Tanner* (1890, 1,034 tons) the smallest of Deering's four-masters. On 20 December 1909, bound from Rockport, Massachusetts, to Key West, she sailed instead to Oblivion. Nothing was ever heard of her again.

In 1899, Deering took another step upward with his fourteenth schooner, the *Henry O. Barrett*. With five masts, more than 1,800 gross tons, and measuring almost 245 feet between her hull's perpendiculars, the *Barrett* was an adaptation of the Rideout model already used with such success for the *Edward E. Briry* and others. She cost more than $71,000 ($1,111 per share) to build and could load 3,300 tons of coal, so she can aptly be designated Deering's first superschooner. That term was not used at the time,

With every sail set in the lightest of breezes, the Edward E. Briry *ghosts along in Vineyard Sound. Courtesy: Capts. Douglas K. and Linda J. Lee.*

but it fits the same way as do such accepted designations as superfrigate (for the U.S. Navy's oversized, overgunned frigates that fought effectively in the War of 1812) and supertanker (for the colossal oil freighters that transport Mid-east crude worldwide). In each case, "super" designates more than giant size; it implies the extention of existing technology beyond its tradtional intentions, come what may. The *Henry O. Barrett* was just that, a creative extension of existing technology in the service of greater size.

Like all builders of big schooners, Deering had been dogged by the growing scarcity of wood components and troubled further by the stress factors that were magnified as schooners grew in size. With the *Barrett,* he devised an important shipbuilding innovation that spoke to both issues. Wooden vessels were strengthened by right-angled brackets called hanging knees, fastened at the juncture of a vessel's frame and her deck beams. For purposes of strength, it was necessary for each knee to be fashioned from a single piece of timber. Accordingly, knees were made from the naturally occurring "L" formed by the base of a hackmatack (tamarack) tree trunk and its adjoining root. Schooner-size hackmatacks were getting hard to come by and by the late nineteenth century were being hunted down in the boggy woods of such diverse places as the Maritime Provinces, Virginia, and Michigan—all part of the cost of doing business.

Or was it? Beginning with the *Henry O. Barrett,* Deering devised a substitute for hanging knees that eliminated the hackmatack problem and actually strengthened a schooner's longitudinal strength. Instead of knees, he bolted large, hard-pine longitudinal timbers (shelves) to the frame and to the adjoining deck beams above. The shelves were braced by other timbers, resulting in a stiffer and therefore stronger hull than was possible using knees. This idea was a substantial departure from conventional methods, and it is a tribute to Deering's powers of persuasion (and of course his reputation) that he was able to convince the American Shipmasters' Association to authorize the procedure. It was a success and quickly became widespread among schooner builders.

Unlike his four-masters, built with very long poops on their main decks, Deering's *Henry O. Barrett* was flush-decked. The *Edward E. Briry* and her predecessors may have encountered stress problems associated with long-poop vessels that Deering wished to avoid. Conventional vessels usually had a raised section aft, called a poop, which ran forward from the stern to within a few feet of the main. The after house was recessed into the poop deck. Other vessels adopted a long-poop configuration, extending the poop forward past amidships, thus providing protected space above the main deck in which to store cargo. This arrangement had become popular on square-riggers during the cotton and emigrant trades because it provided additional, nontaxable space where light cargo (including passengers) could be stored, thus making a voyage more profitable. Later the long poop was also known as a Brazil deck, taking its name from the lucrative South American trade in which tern schooners freighted Maine lumber to Rio de la Plata ports. Such voyages, which usually took a year round trip, were considered an extension of coastwise trade, so there was no hesitation about employing fore-and-afters in it. With a Brazil deck, a schooner could deliver an extra load of dry lumber, stored above decks in the poop.

This oil rendition of the Edward E. Briry, *appears to have been based on the photograph taken in Vineyard Sound. It is attributed to Antonio Jacobsen, and so would probably have been painted during a* Briry *visit to New York City. Courtesy: Capts. Douglas K. and Linda J. Lee.*

As schooners grew in size the long poop became a regular feature in general coastwise shipping. A look at the accompanying photographs of the *Edward E. Briry*, for example, reveals that her poop, indicated by an open rail, extended forward of her main (second) mast. An open, unsheltered space existed between the break in the poop and the forward house. The vessel's essential donkey engine, boilers, and hoisting machinery resided in the forward house, an advantageous arrangement that optimized performance and kept the equipment's heat above decks. However, in heavy weather, water from boarding seas often piled up in the recessed area between the poop and the forward house, sometimes flooding the latter and, more important, adding dangerous weight at a weak point in the schooner's hull. Deering, who was always concerned with durability, overcame that problem by flush-decking the *Henry O. Barrett* and her big successors. Flush-deckers had their disadvantages: They could be very wet in heavy weather, and their boilers, which extended below the main deck in the recessed forward house, created uncomfortably hot working conditions below, but Deering deemed the tradeoff worthwhile. He had seen the advantages of flush decks in his terns such as the *John C. Haynes* and *Horatio L. Baker*. With an upswept stem, there was less chance in a flush-decker of boarding seas straining the hull forward, and the unitized deck provided a greater degree of overall rigidly, something badly needed in any superschooner.

Deering's abandonment of hanging knees had aroused considerable interest in the City of Ships by the time the *Henry O. Barrett* went overboard on 8 May 1899. The *Times* reported her unusual construction and scrupulously enumerated her other details: "In her construction the very finest material was used and the corps of efficient mechanics who assisted in the work of building are proud of their production." The corps of efficient mechanics included master carpenter John Deering and joiner William McNeal, who had joined Deering in 1896 and would rack up twenty-three years' service in the yard.

But to continue: "The Barrett has three decks. The poop runs the whole length making a flush deck. The keel is white oak, 211 feet long. There are only ten pieces in it....

"The planking is five inch hard pine fastened with locust treenails [pins] and composition butt bolted. The decks are white pine. There are four hatches. The cabin is arranged with every convenience for the comfort of the officers and contains six state rooms furnished in hard wood. Amidships is the house for the galley, carpenter shop and store room.

The Henry O. Barrett *(1899), the first schooner to be built without the support of hanging knees. Besides eliminating an expensive component, Deering's alternative method actually improved the longitudinal strength of the* Barrett *and her successors. The innovation was quickly adopted by other shipyards. Courtesy: Maine Maritime Museum.*

"In the foreword house is the engine room and forecastle [crew quarters]. The vessel is heated with steam. The masts are 111 feet long, 28 inches in diameter, of hard pine. They are thoroughly caulked to keep the water out. The rigging is wire set up with turn buckles. She will spread about 8000 square yards of canvas. The vessel has the latest improved steam gear: engine, windlass, steam capstan and three pumps of Hyde Windlass Co. make. She will carry two 6000 pound anchors and 210 fathoms of 2 ⅛ chain."[74]

The *Henry O. Barrett* was named for a Boston executive of Braman, Dow & Company, an industrial supply firm founded by Henry's father Oliver, namesake of Deering & Donnell's 1884 tern. Her first captain was A. P. Davis, late of the *David P. Davis*. True to expectations, in November 1900, the *Barrett*, under Capt. R. B. Swain of Fairhaven, Massachusetts, "made the run from Cape Henry to Boston in sixty hours, which is very quick time...."[75] By the end of

The Henry O. Barrett *under tow in Portland Harbor. Beyond the tug is the first Atlantic five-master, the* Gov. Ames *of Fall River, built in Waldoboro, Maine, in 1888. Courtesy: Capts. Douglas K. and Linda J. Lee.*

that year she had paid her shareholders $408.23 per share—about 37 percent of their investment.

The *Henry O. Barrett's* kneeless construction was fully vindicated. But the flush-deck configuration, undeniably a sound decision, was not enough to spare "Captain Joshua B. Norton. 55, of Rockland, Maine, and James Conley, a New Brunswick man, [who] were swept overboard when the Henry O. Barrett...was pooped by a tremendous sea in Vineyard Sound" in December 1905.[76]

Building the *Henry O. Barrett* was possible because of an upturn in the economy that continued until 1902. During this period of prosperity, Deering moved his operations to a more commodious location in the South End.

In his ten years at the former Hagan shipyard, Deering had gotten out eight schooners: one tern, six four-masters, and one five-master. The old Hagan yard was convenient to downtown Bath and Deering's home but at very close quarters with other operations and short of working space. Despite its drawbacks, it had the three assets crucial to any piece of real estate: location, location, and location.

In 1899, the Hyde Windlass Company to the north, which supplied the patented engines and deck machinery to all of Bath's shipbuilders, needed to expand. Might Gard Deering sell Hyde Windlass his adjoining shipyard? There was a very spacious yard in the South End, not far from Donnell's, that might be just right for Deering. It is safe to say that Gen. Thomas Hyde made Deering an offer he couldn't refuse. In the end, everyone was surely happy. After launching the *Henry O. Barrett*, Deering pulled up stakes, moving his business almost a mile downriver, and Hyde successfully expanded into the old Hagan-Deering shipyard.

"Gardiner G. Deering has traded for the John McDonald shipyard at the South End," reported the *Times* in October 1899. "The property was owned by Chapman & Flint of New York. It is one of the largest and best located yards in town.... It is stated on good authority that Mr. Deering is to build a large five-masted schooner, commencing operations next year."[77] Deering probably gave that tidbit to the *Times* to promote interest among potential investors. But his construction plans were put on hold until 1901.

Deering's newly purchased shipyard had a long history before his possession, and had reached a degree of glory under Chapman & Flint's ownership, when operations there were run by John McDonald. A native of Nova Scotia, McDonald had impeccable shipbuilding credentials, including foremanship of Donald McKay's East Boston shipyard, where the legendary clipper *Great Republic* had been built. Before coming to Bath in 1869 he had managed Chapman & Flint's yard in Thomaston, Maine. At Bath he built thirteen ships, four barks, four tern schooners, and a yacht, all of which enjoyed matchless reputations for quality. McDonald's last vessel went into the Kennebec in 1891. Deering bought the idle shipyard from Chapman & Flint heirs.[78] The property included no power equipment as McDonald had been a believer in hand work. Deering was of the same mind, so he did not see that as a drawback.

Percy & Small's William C. Carnegie *(1900), built in Deering's newly acquired yard in Bath's South End. In a pinch, Deering has obligingly leased his yard to his hard-pressed neighbors and his kindness will be well remembered. The* Carnegie *is larger than any past or future Deering project. In the foreground is Deering's blacksmith shop. Notice the suitably gentle slope of the open terrain—perfect for shipbuilding. Courtesy: Maine Maritime Museum.*

Just north of Deering's newly acquired location was the shipyard of Capt. Sam Percy and Frank Small. They had lately moved operations to a spot between Donnell's yard to the north and Deering's to the south, and intended to construct superschooners of the very latest design. To accomplish this task they, unlike Gard Deering, were prepared to install the last word in construction equipment, and they set about to do so.

In 1900, Percy & Small made plans for a new departure: a six-master, the *Eleanor A. Percy*. The first six-sticker was sure to make headlines and win prestige for its builders, and of course Percy & Small considered it vital that the *Eleanor A. Percy* achieve that prestigious goal, so the firm was in a race to completion with Holly Bean's shipyard in Camden, which was also building a six-master, the *George W. Wells*.

Before setting up the *Eleanor A. Percy*, however, Percy & Small needed to finish a scheduled five-master, the *William C. Carnegie*. There was not enough space at Percy & Small to work on both vessels at once. But what about the idle yard next door? Gard Deering had just bought it

At last! On 13 August 1900, following a two-day delay that disappointed a large assembled crowd and mortified Sam Percy, the William C. Carnegie *agrees to budge. The big splash is not a moment too soon for Gard Deering, who has plans of his own for a new superschooner. The dilapitated structure to the right will shortly be refurbished. Courtesy: Maine Maritime Museum.*

but hadn't started anything of his own there. If Deering would agree to put his own plans on hold and lease his property just long enough for Percy & Small to build the *Carnegie* at that site, work could begin immediately on the six-master at Percy & Small. Sam Percy, the senior partner of Percy & Small, put the proposition to Deering.

Percy, who was twenty-three years younger than Deering, had of course known the old man for years. Professionally speaking, the two were a study in contrasts. Deering liked to keep things to himself and his wallet in his pocket. Percy eagerly exploited publicity and ran an expensively mechanized operation. As he later explained, "Our yard and Kelly & Spear's had as good machinery and were as well equipped as any wooden shipyards in the country. We had a Daniels planer, run by electricity, that could do a pile of slabbing. If a plank was a quarter or a half an inch too thick, it was planed down; this was called slabbing. In the old days such work took a lot of the dubbers' time. Slabbing by the old method of hand-hewing made for a big labor bill.... All timbers that in the old days called for adze-work—dubbing—was now planed. But, when it came to the fitting, then the old shipwrights could not be displaced by machinery."[79] No doubt Percy had said much the same thing to Deering. The two were undoubtedly cordial; and Percy, like Tom Hyde the year before, was in a tight spot. But Percy's lease proposition was asking a great deal of a man who lived to build schooners and who at age sixty-six had just made a major investment in doing so. Gard Deering agreed. The *William C. Carnegie* was built at Deering's while workmen got busy on the *Eleanor A. Percy* next door. Accordingly, the *Carnegie* went into the Kennebec on 13 August 1900; the *Percy* did likewise on 10 October.

Because Sam Percy had agreed to relinquish the leased yard in time for Deering to initiate his own planned project, Percy & Small workers had to divide their time between the two projects, sometimes concentrating on the *Carnegie* to meet Deering's deadline. Alas for Sam Percy, Holly Bean's six-master won the race to launch, although the *Eleanor A. Percy* could claim to be the largest schooner (and at the time the third largest wooden vessel) afloat.[80]

The *William C. Carnegie's* launching proved a further disappointment for Percy. On the hot summer day of 11 August 1900, thousands of spectators in a festive mood assembled to watch her go down the ways. Some—including Deering, perhaps—may have chuckled when a bottle of genuine French champagne (strictly for medicinal purposes) was broken on the *Carnegie's* bow to christen her. But when the big moment came for the vessel to slide into the Kennebec, she declined to budge. What an anticlimax! It took two days to fix the problem, and Monday's launching could not match Saturday's festive though thwarted anticipation.

But meanwhile, thanks to his favor to Percy, Gard Deering had made a friend for life.

Six days a week, early in the morning, Bath's South End suffered a momentary brownout when Percy & Small powered up its complicated, noisy equipment. Sometimes that juice was being used for Deering's projects next door, for whenever Gard needed the assistance of a power saw or a planer, he had only to ask Sam Percy, who was ready to help. It was a bit like having milk without buying a cow. All in all, putting his plans on hold for a few months turned out to be a very good investment for Deering. Between Tom Hyde and Sam Percy, Deering had done quite well with the new yard before lifting a timber.

But now, with the *William C. Carnegie* gone and a dedicated crew of veteran shipwrights on hand, it was time for Deering to get busy again. At age sixty-seven, he had no thought whatever of retirement, which is why he had invested in a new shipyard. His father David, who had died in 1889, had worked until the age of eighty-five. Gard Deering was only sixty-seven. He still had plenty of time.

Gardiner G. Deering in his late sixties, presumably looking forward to his next series of superschooners. Courtesy: Maine Maritime Museum.

CHAPTER FOUR

The Very Best Business Judgment

It couldn't last forever, of course. Gard Deering had been through enough national financial panics to understand the principle of making hay while the sun shone. While shipping basked in good fortune, he built a rapid succession of schooners: the four-masters *Malcolm B. Seavey* (1901) and *Elisha Atkins* (1906), and the five-masters *Mary F. Barrett* (1901), *Gardiner G. Deering* (1903), and *Dorothy B. Barrett* (1905). In between, and on contract, he turned out the tern schooner *Fairfield* (1902). The 564-ton *Fairfield*, built for Weston & Company of Jacksonville, Florida, for $36,527.43, was the last vessel Deering produced for an outside client. She entered the lumber trade.

This expanding schooner fleet raises a few interesting points about Deering's business sense. As managing owner of about a dozen vessels (the precise number depending on attrition and new launchings) he was certainly a busy man. He also found time to manage his rental properties in the old neighborhood. In the years after the turn of the century, he achieved community recognition for his longstanding financial sense, becoming a board member of the First National Bank of Bath and a co-founder of the Bath Trust Company.[81] In a smaller way, his fourteen serving captains had recognized him by chipping in and presenting him with a five-piece silver service on his seventieth birthday.[82] Although he never sought the limelight, his venerablility and achievements had made him one of Bath's Grand Old Men. And one need not take the word of local potentates on that issue. We have the word of no less a potentate than Charles M. Schwab. In June 1903, having come to Bath in his private railroad car to attend the foreclosure of financially troubled

The 564-ton lumber schooner Fairfield *(1902), built for a Jacksonville client, interrupted a long line of four- and five-masters. She was Deering's last tern schooner and his last vessel built to contract. Here she is in 1914, home-ported in New York. Courtesy: Maine Maritime Museum.*

Bath Iron Works and Hyde Windlass, Schwab, then president of U.S. Steel, met Gard Deering. As the *Bath Daily Times* later reported, the two had a "most delightful chat on the steps of the Iron Works just before that plant was knocked down under the hammer wielded by United States Senator James Smith, Jr., of New Jersey."[83] When it came to maritime investment, Schwab could have used some advice from a man like Deering, but that is another story.

As the *Times* also stipulated in October 1910, Deering was "a man of the very best business judgment and 'Gard' Deering's word is just as good as his bond and as quickly accepted. He has served in both branches of [city] government, might have been mayor numberless times had he been willing to accept but his love for his business, his family and his home has been too great to tempt him to enter politics...."[84]

But how much business was enough? Shouldn't a prudent fleet manager, sensitive to economic instability, take care not to overbuild lest those expensive vessels sit idle in bad years? Deering's belief that the United States would recover its former greatness in maritime commerce was a matter of record. Perhaps it was that conviction that overcame fears of future slumps and kept him building through thick and thin. Another contributing factor was his obvious zest for the trade, which sharpened as he got older. A third was his reputation as a builder who always had something going on in his yard, even in the leanest times when shipwrights' jobs were scarce and production dwindling elsewhere—a source of personal pride but personal obligation as well. Now white-haired, bearded, and serene of expression, he remained as hale as a man half his age. Like all senior teetotalers, he attributed his good health to "temperate living."[85] Within a few years he would delegate some of his responsibilities, but meanwhile, there were schooners to build for his fleet.

The flush-decked *Malcolm B. Seavey* (1901) was built at a cost of $63,325. She measured 1,247 tons, was 203 feet long, and could carry a 2,000-ton cargo. For an extra measure of speed she had been fitted with disproportionately tall masts. Deering believed that her robust construction and wire rigging could handle the extra strain. The *Seavey* was named for Henry O. Barrett's grandson. Barrett owned two shares of the new schooner, Gard Deering owned a whopping fifteen (at least at first), his wife Lydia and his sons Frank and Harry owned one share apiece. So did Capt. Charles E. Patten, former mayor of Bath (and, as a Democrat, a rare

The 1,247-ton, 203-foot Malcolm B. Seavey, *launched in 1901, Deering's first vessel built in his new South End yard. Courtesy: Capts. Douglas K. and Linda J. Lee.*

political bird). Because Deering vessels were getting expensive, many investors, like master builder John S. Deering, took half a share. In addition to Maine investors, the roster of shareholders was quite diverse, including parties from Boston, Fall River, Syracuse, Philadelphia, Baltimore, and the Washington, D.C., area. Obviously, Deering had a broker working on his behalf. The *Seavey's* first captain, Elisha D. Atkins of Allston, Massachusetts, owned a share and a half of his new command, as was usual with Deering skippers.[86] Atkins had for ten years been master of the *Horatio L. Baker* after serving on that vessel as mate. Before the *Baker* he had been on the Deering & Donnell-built *Alice Montgomery*. His intrepid career would cover thirty-six

A post-launching photograph of the Mary F. Barrett *(1901, 1,833 tons) an enlarged version of the* Henry O. Barrett *and named for the original Henry's wife. She is posed just off Deering's shipyard, her bow pointing north. Courtesy: Maine Maritime Museum*

years commanding Deering schooners, including 119 round trips for coal without losing a vessel or a man. Much later in life, a widower, he would marry Gard Deering's widowed daughter-in-law.

The 1,833-ton, 241-foot five-master *Mary F. Barrett,* a larger clone of the *Henry O. Barrett,* was built at a cost of $77,605 (rounded up to $80,000 in the press).[87] At the time of her completion Gard Deering surprisingly owned 35/64 of her; evidently fewer investors than expected had come forward. Those who did included several who owned in the *Seavey,* such as Henry O. Barrett, who took three shares. The co-owners of the Crowell & Thurlow shipping fleet of Boston (which would someday own a few old Deering schooners) took two. Oddly, the schooner's first master, R. B. Sargent, former skipper of the *Oliver S. Barrett,* had no stake in her. Deering's huge personal ownership meant that he had built most of this vessel on speculation. She was named for Henry O. Barrett's wife.

The 241-foot flush-decker was launched on 26 November 1901, fully rigged and ready for

In this unusual photograph the Mary F. Barrett, *loaded, sails wing-and-wing (with her sails alternately to port and starboard before the wind) in Nantucket Sound. The sails to starboard are somewhat overexposed, but they're there. Courtesy: Capts. Douglas K. and Linda J. Lee.*

An oil portrait of the Gardiner G. Deering *by S. F. M. Badger. She is as fast as she looks. During her long life she will be much battered by accidents. Courtesy: Parker Family Collection.*

sea, with Capt. Sargent already moved into his elegant quarters. According to the *Bath Enterprise*, she was "designed for the general carrying trade," which meant mostly coal—3,500 tons worth. "There was no christening," the *Enterprise* added, "as Mr. Deering never christens his vessels but considers himself lucky if he gets them overboard without their sticking on the ways as has been the case several times when launchings have been attended by these ceremonies."[88] Mr. Deering had probably not forgotten the near disaster at the *John C. Haynes* launching. And, as a teetotaler in a nominally prohibitionist state, he may have wondered just what libation was proper in a new vessel's christening.

Working next door to Percy & Small may have had other effects on Gard Deering besides his sweetheart arrangement with that yard. He could not have overlooked the hoopla of Percy & Small's launchings, which, besides being fun, served a promotional purpose. Judging from the short investor lists for Deering's last two vessels, some similar public relations couldn't hurt. He certainly did not miss the fact that Percy & Small built enormous superschooners, vessels in a size category beyond his own products. In future years, his output would be four- and five-masters that never achieved the scale of the *Eleanor A. Percy*, much less Percy & Small's future colossus, the *Wyoming*. Instead, Deering continued building vessels of assorted sizes, schooners that stopped short of the ultimate economies of scale but retained enough versatility to service many ports with many cargoes, not just coal. And of course he kept on building as long as the economic picture remained bright. He had another motivation to build: As we have seen, he had lost three vessels, the *David P. Davis* in 1904; the *John S. Deering* and *Oliver S. Barrett* by 1906. With those losses and the 1905 sale of the underachieving *William T. Donnell*, he was left with but one tern, the *Horatio L. Baker*. There would be no more. Deering's departed terns were replaced with larger vessels.

His next, and largest yet, was the five-masted *Gardiner G. Deering*, the second schooner to bear that name. The new vessel was close to 2,000 tons and more than 250 feet in length. One share in her cost $1,326.48, which meant that building her cost $84,894.78 ($90,000 in press reports). Before going down the ways on 14 March 1903, she was anointed with a bottle of good old Maine Poland Spring water. Deering's daughter Emma, now Mrs. Calvin Rogers of Bath, did the honors. As usual, John S. Deering had been master carpenter.

Her first captain was John E. Ross of Sackville, New Brunswick, and, lately, Arlington, Massachusetts, who was between commands of the *Edward E. Briry*. Ross took the *Deering* to Baltimore to load coal. She would later also carry ice. She was of course too big a vessel to load upriver on the Kennebec but suitable for loading pond ice at the Herrick Ice Works on Deer Isle, which she freighted to the Caribbean.[89] Like so many Deering vessels, this one was

The Deering fleet in service: Left, the super-schooner Mary F. Barrett *at a Maine coal dock. Below, the* Mary F. Barrett, *docked in the La Have River at Bridgewater, Nova Scotia, probably to load a gypsum cargo. Courtesy: Capts. Douglas K. and Linda J. Lee.*

collision-prone and proved it within a year of her launching. On the foggy night of 7 March 1904, off Point Lookout, Virginia, she came into smart contact with the steamer *Essex*. Capt. Ross's telegram to Deering, printed in the *Bath Daily Times*, tells the story: "'Run into by Merchants and Miners Steamer Essex at twenty minutes past one. Cut into main hatch on port-side, filled with water, and lay on her beam end, in seven fathoms of water...in wide channel. No one on board. The crew landed here, the vessel can be saved.'" The *Times* continues with a dispatch from Newport News: "'The prow of the steamer caught the schooner above her second mast and almost cut her in two. The Essex had two holes stove in her starboard side ten feet above the waterline. Captain Ross and his crew of eleven men including five Japanese were saved by the boats of the Essex, and were taken aboard by that vessel.'"[90] As soon as he received Ross's wire, Gard Deering rushed to Newport News to have a personal look at the damage. He concluded that the virtually sunken schooner was worth saving. Accordingly, a Baltimore salvage company raised her and towed her to that port for extensive repairs. This near disaster would not be the *Gardiner G. Deering's* last, but she did prove to be a long-lived vessel. And she was fast, of course. In 1916 she made a run from New York to Newport News to Portland in nine days including time at the loading dock. Her best days still lay ahead.

On a wintry day in 1905, the new Dorothy B. Barrett, *festively decorated with signal flags, is anchored in the Kennebec off the G. G. Deering wharf. Notice the small chunks of ice in the river and Bath's snowy South End beyond. Courtesy: Capts. Douglas K. and Linda J. Lee.*

The five-sticker *Dorothy B. Barrett's* tonnage was close to 2,100 and her length was 259 feet between stem and sternpost. She reportedly cost $89,000. She was named for Henry and Mary's ten-year-old daughter, who on 8 December 1904 christened her namesake, à la Percy & Small, with a bottle of French bubbly. Her first master was Walter M. Ervin, forty-two, a Nova Scotian who had been seafaring for twenty-seven years, including captaincies of the

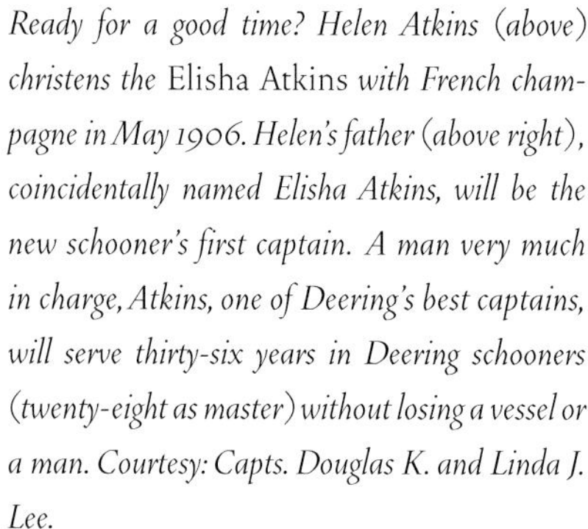

Ready for a good time? Helen Atkins (above) christens the Elisha Atkins *with French champagne in May 1906. Helen's father (above right), coincidentally named Elisha Atkins, will be the new schooner's first captain. A man very much in charge, Atkins, one of Deering's best captains, will serve thirty-six years in Deering schooners (twenty-eight as master) without losing a vessel or a man. Courtesy: Capts. Douglas K. and Linda J. Lee.*

David P. Davis and *Henry O. Barrett*. The *Dorothy B. Barrett* quickly built a reputation for speed and ease of handling, which made her a moneymaker, except for an interlude after being struck in August 1911 by the U.S. Navy destroyer *Mayrant*. She escaped this mishap with only light damage.

Sometime after her collision her captain was William (Hungry Bill) Merritt of Portland. Why Hungry Bill? Alas, the reason for the moniker has been lost over time, although Merritt's descendants recall that the Captain had a large appetite and could balance several peas on his knife, which is surely enough of an explanation. Merritt had previously been master of the Portland four-master *Stella B. Kaplan*. As we shall see, an interesting career lay ahead for him in Deering schooners.

By the time he launched the *Elisha Atkins*, completed at a cost of $71,533, Deering had overcome his former reluctance to celebrate such events on a grand scale. The Bath press, which bathed every launching in superlatives, duly covered the birth of the *Atkins* and her successors, leaving us with some vivid details.

For local people who had just survived another Maine winter, watching a new vessel slide into the Kennebec was a perfect spring outing. So, on the first Saturday in May 1906, just before noon, "the handsome four-masted schooner Elisha Atkins was launched from the yard of G.G. Deering Co. in the presence of a vast throng. She was christened with champagne by Miss Helen G. Atkins of Wollaston, daughter of Capt. E.D. Atkins who is to command the new craft. The Atkins is one of the largest four-masted schooners afloat, measuring 200 feet in length, 40.9 feet beam, 21.1 feet depth of hold while her gross tonnage is 1259 tons. She is almost ready for sea and is designed for the general trade which she will enter in a week or so." Deering would surely forgive the overzealous reporter's exaggerated claim about her size; she was no bigger, for example, than the *Lydia M. Deering*, launched seventeen years earlier. But there is more: "The launching banquet at New Meadows Saturday afternoon, by the G.G. Deering Co., was a fitting celebration of one of the most successful launchings ever held in this city, and was enjoyed by a large company, including all the launching guests from out of town, the master workmen and their wives and numerous local guests. The party were conveyed to the [New Meadows] Inn, when they had landed from the schooner immediately after the launching...and Landlord Cahill was in readiness for them with one of his famous shore dinners over which the guests from abroad were delighted.... One of the guests who has been a frequent visitor to the Shipping City for launchings says 'It is worth a trip to Bath to sit down to one of Cahill's dinners.'" Dozens of celebrants partook, including several Deering captains and their wives, Deering's wife Lydia, the Deerings' daughter Emma Rogers and sons Harry and Frank with their spouses, and a long roster of out-of-town investors. When dinner was over the group adjourned to the inn's lawn overlooking the New Meadows River, listened to congratulatory speeches, and concluded with "a vote of thanks to the G.G. Deering Co. for the delightful entertainment and wishing all kinds of success for Captain Atkins and his new command."[91] Quite a change from the days when Gard Deering declined even to christen his vessels at launchings.

Two views of the Elisha Atkins *in service. Completed in 1906, this vessel will remain active until 1924. Courtesy: Capts. Douglas K. and Linda J. Lee.*

The *Elisha Atkins,* incidentally, was not named for her first master as has sometimes been claimed, but for an out-of-town investor of the same name. The vessel proved to be another hard worker in the fleet. With her addition, and subtracting the *John S. Deering* and *William T. Donnell* (lost and sold, respectively, in 1905), and the *Oliver S. Barrett* (lost in 1906), the fleet numbered twelve vessels. Actually, it was now more than ever a company fleet. In 1905, still intent upon growing his business, Deering, his wife, and his sons formed a family corporation.

Now past seventy, Gard Deering had decided to formalize his business and take his sons into it. The decision was hardly premature. His oldest son Frank was thirty-five, his middle son

ARTICLES OF AGREEMENT.

We, the undersigned, Gardiner G. Deering, Frank. M. Deering, Harry G. Deering, Carroll A. Deering, and Lydia M. Deering, all of Bath, in the County of Sagadahoc, and State of Maine, hereby associate ourselfs together by written artifles of agreement for the purpose of forming a corporation under the laws of the State of Maine for carrying on the business of owning, controlling, managing, building, repairing, buying and selling vessels and vessel property, owning and operating a Marine Railway, or Dry Dock, dealing in real estate, shipbuilding materials and general merchandise, and conducting a Ship brokers, and commission, ~~and insurance~~ business.

Gardiner G. Deering
Frank. M. Deering
Harry G. Deering
Carroll A. Deering
Lydia M. Deering

Bath, Maine April 20th. 1905

The G. G. Deering Company incorporates: Articles of Agreement signed by Gardiner and Lydia Deering and their three sons, April 1906. Courtesy: Maine Maritime Museum.

Harry was thirty-two, and his youngest, Carroll, was twenty-two. On 20 April 1905 these four and Lydia Deering produced a typewritten "Articles of Agreement," in which they associated themselves into a Maine corporation "for carrying on the business of owning, controlling, managing, building, repairing, buying, and selling vessels and vessel property, dealing in real estate, shipbuilding materials, and general merchandise, and conducting a ship brokers and commission business." The statement of intent covered everything Gard Deering had been doing for decades plus a few future possibilities. Originally included in the business roster was insurance, but that had been wisely struck out by the time the four Deerings put their signatures to the paper. The new entity, G.G. Deering Company Incorporated, itemized its assets. The shipyard was valued at $25,000, the entire company's assets totaled $50,000. Capitalized at that figure, 1,000 shares of stock were issued at a par value of $50. Frank, Harry, Carroll, and their sister Emma Rogers each were given eight shares. Gard Deering kept the remainder, an estimated 960 shares, leaving no question about who wore the pants in the family. Lydia apparently received eight shares. She had lately shown signs of mental deterioration and had withdrawn from her usual church and social activities. She would shortly become a patient in a Massachusetts sanitorium without lasting results. Gard had assumed full responsibility for Lydia's uncertain future; perhaps including her in the corporate charter was part of his plan. At the time of incorporation, the partners' shares in the existing thirteen vessels came to $170,000.[92]

With this milestone, Deering's grown sons became more visible players in the shipyard, although the details of their contributions remain hazy. All had probably assumed roles in the operation some years before its incorporation. Frank had a nodding acquaintance with the sea—as a passenger aboard vessels, not a seaman—which was apparently the sum total of the sons' nautical experience. Frank, who had learned the workings of the yard under his father and uncle, became the yard foreman. In 1908, master carpenter John Deering retired at the ripe old age of eighty. It is very likely that Gard, an energetic whippersnapper of seventy-three, assumed many of John's duties, for Gard remained conspicuous in the daily shipbuilding activities. Harry handled much of the office work and Carroll was bookkeeper. According to Coe's *Maine: Resources, Attractions, and Its People*, Harry quickly became "an expert manager of the enterprise" and assumed the corporate presidency because of his "excellent business ability and sound judgment of ships and their possibilities."[93]

Bath, Maine,

We are building a four-masted schooner, which will probably be ready to come off some time in July. She will cost about $1200 per 1-64th, possibly less. She will carry about 2200 tons of coal, will be sailed at $40 per month and 5% of the gross stock. We have a first class man to go master of her, and would be pleased to have you take an interest in her, and do not think you would be making any mistake by doing so.

Yours truly,

Sound interesting? A general solicitation letter to local investors. The proposed schooner is probably the Elisha Atkins *(1906). Courtesy: Maine Maritime Museum.*

The business continued to function as it had before incorporation. Changing economic times would soon create a shakeout in the yards, but G. G.Deering's would outlast almost all of them, earning Gard the title Dean of Bath Shipbuilders. People around Bath began to see the Deering yard as a living reminder of the Good Old Days, and Deering himself admitted that his was a dying art: He was, he said, operating an "old man's home" in the yard—a sort of refuge for the kind of shipwrights who, as Sam Percy admitted, could not be replaced by machinery.[94] Years later, people would recall Deering's confidence that, despite all the evidence to the contrary, America's merchant marine would regain its former worldwide stature—with a place of course for wooden vessels.

Gard Deering's structural innovation for schooner hulls had found favor and earned him respect, but there was another innovation he enjoyed discussing. On all of his vessels, captains' and mates' quarters were finely detailed and comfortable. The same could not be said for crew quarters—a condition that pervaded the schooner trade, although such accommodations were a cut above the standard in square-riggers. Sometime in the early 1900s—exactly when is un-

Out of service: With the crew posing by the company fence, The drydocked Mary F. Barrett *awaits attention in Hoboken, New Jersey. Courtesy: Capts. Douglas K. and Linda J. Lee.*

certain—Deering decided to make shipboard life more enjoyable for common seamen. In a business obsessed with hardnosed cost cutting, this was indeed something of an innovation. Deering decided to adapt the conventional midship house on his vessels to provide dedicated dining and recreation space for the enjoyment of off-duty sailors. His expressed rationale was that better conditions would attract better, more satisfied, crew. The competitive edge he would gain would more than offset the added expense.

After a later interview with Deering, The *Bath Independent* reported the first results of this experiment: "When the crew arrived on board they took a look at the usual fo'c'sle and began to kick. They said that there was no chance for them to eat. Mr. Deering took them to the house amidship, with its table and chairs, its floor neatly covered with oil cloth and asked how they liked that for a dining room. 'Oh,' said one of the men, 'this is only a bluff to keep us here until we get underway, then we'll have to get out.' 'No you won't' said the captain of the craft, 'as long as you use the place right it will be yours.' The men appreciated it and when they went to their meals they took their hats off and behaved themselves as they might if in a lodging house on shore. When they got to the end of the voyage and were paid off their spokesman went to the captain and said 'Cap'n if you don't mind and you want us again we'll kind o' hang around and when you're ready we'd like to ship.'"[95] The story came right from the lips of Gard Deering but the amusedly condescending depiction of sailors may have been the reporter's contribution. In any case it squared with conventional wisdom about schooner sailors at the time. According to Deering, the midship house was a good investment also because it kept seamen from tossing their uneaten food overboard, thus allowing the cook to recycle the tidbits into hash "'or some other dish which is pleasing to the crew.'"[96] The dedicated midship house became a regular feature of Deering schooners thereafter.

That such an innovation as a crew dining room could be considered a bold departure hints at the deteriorating conditions aboard schooners at the turn of the century and later. Like virtually all schooner managers of the period, Deering was pinched by never-ending pressure to keep schooners economically competitive. As a rule, these pressures alienated sailors from owners and often created tense relations on board. One factor that sustained schooners' competitiveness was their minimal crew costs. A middling four-master like the *Wesley M. Oler* could get by on a fraction of the manpower necessary to operate a square-rigger of similar size—six men—and a less skilled crew at that. A superschooner such as the *Gardiner G. Deering* needed a complement of only ten or eleven although, as we have seen, there were tight spots in which more manpower might make the difference between life and death. The usual complement was a captain, two mates, an engineer, a cook, and four or five seamen.

A tough day on the Malcolm B. Seavey. *The vessel may have sustained storm damage. Courtesy: Capts. Douglas K. and Linda J. Lee.*

Under normal conditions, crack seamanship was not called for, although at the turn of the century coastwise sailors were paid better than their deep-water counterparts.[97] In 1910, looking back on his management career, Deering recalled that his seamen's wages, once eighteen to twenty dollars a month, had advanced to twenty or twenty-five. The increase had kept pace with inflation but was not on a par with wages of land-based skilled laborers, who were now working a nine-hour day. In particular, G. G. Deering sailors made substantially less than the $33.66 average for the coastwise trade at the time.[98] Because of the ongoing need to minimize costs, schooner sailors were customarily paid off at the end of each charter, which created a ready labor pool in the large coastal ports of the United States. If, as was often the case, a schooner idled in port waiting her turn to load, or undergoing repairs, or awaiting a new charter, sailors were routinely discharged to save the owners money and recruited again as needed at sailing time.

In response to what they perceived as intolerable wage conditions, sailors formed the Atlantic Coast Seamen's Union, which because of recurrent economic jitters and fluctuating freight rates was unable to win wage concessions. To combat unionism and fight costly, discriminatory piloting and loading practices in the coal ports, schooner operators formed the Atlantic Carriers' Association, whose primary goal was to break the Seamen's Union. Gard Deering, Sam Percy, Frank Small, and William T. Donnell were among the association's members. The Association's union busting strategy was to recruit Afro-Americans and foreign sailors who were accustomed to low wages, thereby undercutting union wage demands. So it was that West Indians, Cape Verdeans, Canadians, and Scandinavians become fixtures in the schooner trade. The association even set up a sweetheart union, The American Seamen's Federation, for this purpose. An unusual example of this recruiting practice was the *Gardiner G. Deering's* five seamen mentioned above, all of them Japanese and, perhaps, hard-put to understand commands at the time of that schooner's disastrous collision.

Why people go to sea: The Elisha Atkins, *deeply loaded and making brisk time. The daring Capt. Atkins has ventured out onto the bowsprit with his camera to capture this exciting image. Courtesy: Capts. Douglas K. and Linda J. Lee.*

For decades these circumstances undermined morale at sea and created tensions in port. For example, the logbook of the *Samuel Dillaway* reveals that while tied up in Boston in August 1894, the vessel's crew "had [a police] officer on board all day to protect them from Union men."[99] Some altercations between "union men" and Deering sailors probably had a racial component. Twenty-seven years after the above incident, in Portland, a gang of hoods forced their way aboard the aging *Mary F. Barrett*, beat up her black crew, and threw James Walker of New Bedford overboard to his death.[100]

The *Samuel Dillaway* logbook also confirms that mates were as expendable as common sailors, being changed in port after port, hardly a practice designed to cement a solid chain of command or an effective team in an emergency. On 30 May 1895, one W. Sunderland, mate and log keeper of the *Dillaway*, recorded that "at 10 PM anchored off Nobska Leting go port anchor Capt. Interfering with my Business, told him if he thought i didn't know enough to let an anchor go he had better do it himself, ordered to my room and off duty." And off the *Dillaway*, to be replaced by another revolving-door mate.[101] What emerges is a picture of relative strangers working at close quarters (with or without a dining room) and, sometimes, strenuous conditions.

As a rule, masters had achieved their captaincies by starting young and working their way up through mates' berths to command, a system that favored those who accepted traditional shipboard practices and, for better or worse, were apt to perpetuate them. Many skippers believed, with some reason, that the labor situation had caused a decline in sailor quality and character. Captains and mates often went armed and, as we shall see, sometimes believed themselves to be in danger from crew. All in all, shipboard life was not designed to bring out the best in men. Nor was the time-honored sailor practice of riotous behavior when ashore.

Before itemizing a few shipboard occupational disasters of Deering schooners, it is proper to bear in mind that for the most part, day after day, month after month, these huge windjammers earned their keep without melodramatic interruption. Yet, understandably, their rare melodramas dominate the record, because they exemplify the persistent uncertainty of the trade.

In June 1903, while Deering's *Edward E. Briry* was en route with coal from Philadelphia to

Ongoing maintenance. Sometime before her voyage to Nowhere, the William C. Tanner *rests on the Quigley Shipyard's marine railway at Camden, New Jersey. Her box rail, unique in the Deering fleet, makes her less graceful in appearance than her sisters. Courtesy: Capts. Douglas K. and Linda J. Lee.*

Boston, mate Carl Johnson got into an altercation with James Finch, a West Indian "colored seaman," who allegedly refused orders, scuffled with Johnson, and bit him on the arm. Johnson shot and killed Finch. Murder? After nine months the case went before the United States Circuit Court in Boston. Four members of the crew, all men of color, had been held as material witnesses. As was common, they were put behind bars to keep them from shipping out, and thus spent nine months in the Charles Street jail.

Johnson was charged with murder. When at last the trial went forward he, on the advice of his pro-bono lawyers, pleaded guilty to manslaughter, for which he received a three-year sentence and was fined one dollar. The four seamen who had been incarcerated for the period before the trial were "released" and awarded $240 each for their inconvenience.[102]

Given the realities of the shipping lanes, the weather, and the structural limitations of vessels, there was always a nagging possibility that, regardless of skilled seamanship, collision or storm or worse could cause havoc, as when Capt. Joshua B. Norton and his Canadian mate, James Conley, were swept off the *Henry O. Barrett* to their deaths in December 1905.

Norton had been the *Barrett's* third captain since her 1899 debut. Hinting at a jinx on the *Barrett*, the Rockland, Maine, *Courier-Gazette* pointed out that "in the five years since she was built, at Bath, three captains have died. The first one was that all-around favorite and good fellow, A[lbert P.] Davis, of Somerset. The vessel was built for him, and he was the owner of quite a good deal of the stock. In less than a year he died of typhoid fever. Then [Robert] Swaine of Fairhaven took the vessel, and after a short time his health, never good, failed, and he went home to die at the age of 42. Capt. Norton, apparently in his prime, and enjoying his full strength at the age of 57, followed Davis and Swaine."[103]

Norton was freighting 3,500 tons of coal from Newport News to Boston. Near Block Island the *Barrett* was overtaken by gale winds from the west. She proceeded before the wind toward Martha's Vineyard in a confused sea caused by opposing wind and tide. "The Barrett was abreast of Quick's Hole when the big wave came rolling up the stern. The helmsman stated that he heard Captain Norton shout as the sea rolled up, 'We are among the breakers,' to which the mate replied, 'No, sir.' Then the sea tumbled aboard, completely flooding the entire poop deck of this vessel and carry[ing] the two officers overboard." With her yawl boat and after house gone, the *Barrett* limped into Woods Hole. Capt. Henry Haines of the *Lewis H. Goward*, anchored nearby, sent his mate aboard the *Barrett* to see her to Boston. Capt. Norton, who had the distinction of being the only Rockland-area skipper of a five-master, was eulogized as a man "of very jovial disposition and he invariably brightened up the atmosphere of any office he happened to drop into by his never failing fun and jollity."[104]

In 1918, off Monhegan, the *Mary F. Barrett* collided with the schooner *Lottie G. Merchant*, killing thirty-five-year-old crewmember, Newfoundlander Ronald McDonald.

Or take the case of Capt. Henry Haines, one of Deering's most stalwart and expert skippers, who in March 1910 was swept off the deck of the *Lewis H. Goward* and drowned during a gale. Gard Deering, who received the news via a cable sent by the *Goward's* mate, made a public statement. "The news was pretty hard to receive," he told the *Times*. "Capt. Haines was one of the best men that ever sailed the ocean, an honest man, an expert mariner and one who was loved and respected by everybody who knew him. He had been in command of the Goward since she was built in 1895, and previously was in command of the schooner John C. Haynes."[105]

In between charters: The long-lived Lewis H. Goward, *in for repairs. Courtesy: Capts. Douglas K. and Linda J. Lee.*

Cape Hatteras was a particularly hazardous point in the coastwise trade, especially for Deering vessels. In April 1911, the *Lydia M. Deering* sailed from Jacksonville for Boston with railroad ties. She ran into a northwester off Hatteras. It was the same old story: run before the wind and hope for the best. Capt. Gamage, manning the wheel, summoned the mate, James Horner. According to the *Bath Daily Times*, "the latter had taken scarcely a dozen steps when a big sea broke over the stern and took the unfortunate man over the side. Three hundred railroad ties were also washed into the sea. Looking at the mate, the others saw him grasp one of the ties in his effort to keep afloat. He was soon compelled to release his hold, being weighted down with heavy rubber boots and oilskin clothes. Because of the fury of the storm, it was impossible to attempt a rescue. Horner was 48 years old. He joined the Deering last December."[106]

Aside from shipboard violence, the above disasters engulfed men who were seasoned veterans, not novices, so it is difficult to see how they might have cheated their fates. Such misfortunes were accepted as occupational hazards—and of course part of the cost of doing business.

Business was good until 1907. Then the nation was gripped by another financial panic, which originated in New York when banks, having overextended their credit, began to fail, taking businesses down with them. The crisis began when the Knickerbocker Trust Company, one of New York's largest banks, was compromised financially, first because of its link to Bath's own Charles W. Morse, second because it used Morse's tactics to overspeculate, dangerously diluting its resources. Loss of confidence led to a run on Knickerbocker that spread to other banks, creating a credit shortage, massive business failure, and a 50 percent drop in the stock market. Total economic collapse was averted when Uncle Sam and J.P. Morgan stepped in with stopgap federal funds and major banking repair, respectively. The crisis passed by 1908; but once again, the repercussions of relentless financial speculation had spread far and wide, touching the City of Ships.

The Panic of '07 caused freight rates to fall, which was particularly damaging to wooden shipyards because it coincided with declining investor confidence in schooners. Labor strife was one reason for this decline. So were costly delays that schooners often experienced at coal ports, idling while new steamers got faster service. So too were the increasing numbers of tow-boat-barge combinations whose expenses were low enough to undercut those of their sailing competitors. By 1908 there were only three Bath shipyards devoted to wooden vessels: the Kelley-Spear Company in the North End, Percy & Small, and G. G. Deering.[107]

Deering completed no schooner during 1907, but one was under way. In January 1908 the yard launched the four-master *William R. Wilson* (1.385 tons, 214 feet), a slightly larger version of the *Elisha Atkins*, built at a cost of about $75,000. The *Wilson* was master carpenter John S. Deering's swan song. Festivities at her launching were somewhat restrained: a fairly large crowd of stalwarts, bundled up against the cold, stood among the shipyard timbers waiting. Since the *Dorothy B. Barrett* launching, someone had decided that it was unseemly for a little girl

Above: Well-wishers and dignitaries gather at the bow of the William R. Wilson *on a brisk January day in 1908, just before her launching. The Deering yard's blacksmith shop is in the foreground. Stinson photograph, courtesy: Capts. Douglas K. and Linda J. Lee.*

Right: The William R. Wilson *goes overboard, January 1908. The motorcar in the foreground may be Gard Deering's. Dr. Bruce Nelson Collection, courtesy: Capts. Douglas K. and Linda J. Lee.*

Floating ice gathers around the hull of the new William R. Wilson *as she receives her finishing touches at the Deering wharf. Stinson photograph, courtesy: Capts. Douglas K. and Linda J. Lee*

to manhandle a champagne bottle, so ten-year-old Doris Stetson of Bath strewed roses and carnations instead and waved Old Glory as the *Wilson*, painted virginal white, slid down the ways. After the launching, attending dignitaries took lunch aboard in the stream. The *William R. Wilson's* first captain was George Mohr of Baltimore, late of the *Horatio L. Baker*. Work would soon begin on another four-master, for G. G. Deering Company was still able to keep its Old Man's Home busy and show a profit in the schooner trade.

As he came into his own, Gard Deering had also become something of a curiosity, a relic of the past who could ride out the nation's economic gyrations and keep at his trade when all

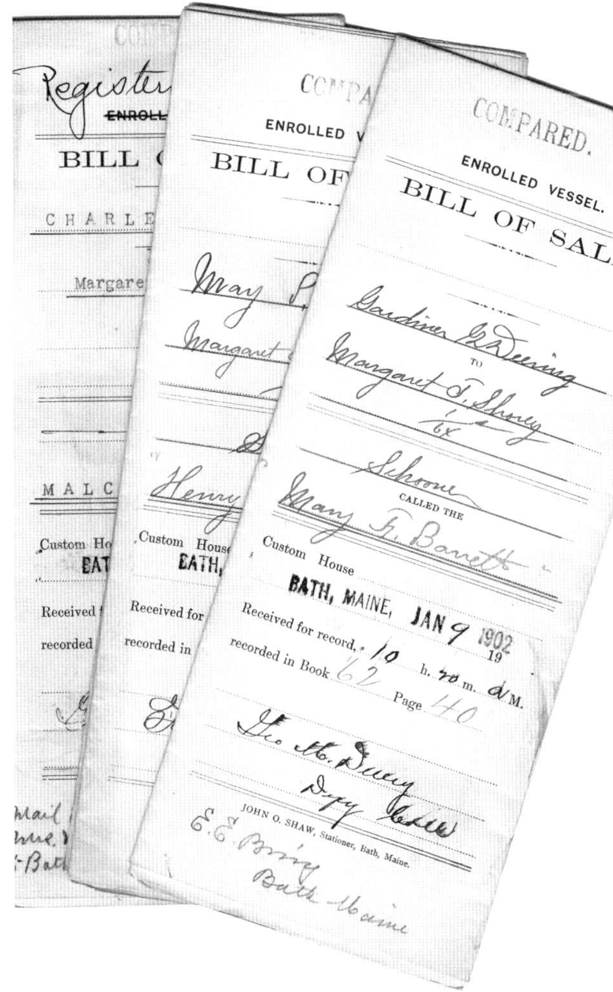

Loyal support: Bills of sale for Margaret Shorey's shares in three Deering schooners, the Malcolm B. Seavey, Henry O. Barrett, *and* Mary F. Barrett. *Courtesy: Maine Maritime Museum.*

but a few had given up in Bath. Better still, he kept other people working at it, too, as noted in the *Bath Independent* in 1910. The whys and wherefores of this phenomenon were deemed front-page news: "With three big schooners tied at the wharf undergoing repairs, and a big one on the stocks almost ready for launching, the Deering yard at the south end presents a scene of old time activity which is pleasing to the people of Bath and interesting to the visitor. It reminds one of the days when our whole water front presented a similar picture and brings to mind how much credit is due Gardiner G. Deering for the activity he has displayed in keeping his workmen busy and in turning out craft which have always been a credit to the city and the builder." Aside from his curiosity value, Deering was news in 1910 because not a single schooner was launched in the City of Ships. And the two launched the next year would be his. "In Gardiner Deering," said the *Independent*, "the city of Bath has a citizen in whom it has every right to be proud."

How did G. G. Deering Company continue to flourish? Deering was only too happy to reveal a few details. One was his ability to find uses for his fleet outside the coal business—phosphate, for instance. Phosphate rock, usually shipped out of Punta Gorda or Port Tampa, was used in the making of fertilizer. It was a lucrative but dangerous cargo, requiring very careful handling. The chief problem was its weight. Phosphate carriers, which were never loaded to their capacity, had a floor installed above the keelson upon which the rock was carefully piled in a pyramidal mound. Tapering the mound concentrated the cargo's weight along the keel to promote stability and maintain a high center of gravity. God help a phosphate schooner whose cargo shifted in rough weather. Rough weather was a distinct possibility, however, because phosphate vessels operated in the Gulf of Mexico during hurricane season. Another requirement was a dry hold to prevent the porous cargo from sopping up water, thereby taking on weight. God help a phosphate schooner that sprung leaks in a seaway.

The phosphate trade was hard on schooners, but Deering thought his fleet was up to the challenge. "I have four of my vessels carrying phosphate rock from Port Tampa to New York,

Baltimore, Norfolk, and Philadelphia," he explained. "They do a good business but of course they have to be strong built craft to carry that cargo."[108] Aging or poorly maintained vessels need not apply. Even Deering, however, may have underestimated the perils of the trade. Within the next three years, two of his vessels would be lost carrying phosphate rock. In 1915, a third such carrier would be abandoned in a hurricane but luckily salvaged afterward.

Another aspect of Deering's competitive edge was his vessels' speed. Within a few years, new opportunities for long-range freights would emerge that were tailor made for Deering's fast, sturdy schooners. He was pleased, he said, that his fleet had suffered few mishaps or losses at sea, which would indeed have been an advantage had it been true. In fact, Deering vessels were unusually prone to accidents and disasters. Since going into business for himself, and including the vessels he had brought with him from Deering & Donnell, his loss rate was 30 percent. By the end of his career, the loss rate would be 50 percent.

Deering considered his dedicating midship houses for crew use an authentic innovation, a step toward improving shipboard morale and therefore his vessels' competitive performance.

He enjoyed another advantage: His business had reached a point of predictability, which allowed him to exercise his acute sense of timing. He could afford to start a new vessel on his own schedule (or at his own convenience) and proceed on speculation without first filling her roster of investors: "I usually begin a schooner without a timber head being sold," he said, "but that doesn't worry me much for I find that by the time she is ready for business she is usually well taken."

Which brings up the point about the old man's timing. In the past and in the future, he would sometimes take a business step that looked out of phase with the realities of the day but that would soon produce a payoff. Perhaps other personality traits contributed to this prescience—he seemed to be a man comfortable with himself and aware of his limitations, but unafraid to follow his instincts. The building went on.

If you had decided to visit Bath in the early 1900s, you would have noticed many changes from your previous visit—if you could remember back that far. Bath had maintained its objective of keeping up with the times. The city's population was a little less than 10,000. The downtown, with a number of land-based factories, had a solid, surprisingly urban look to it. The effect was enhanced by the Bath Street Railway's trolleys ferrying people north and south along Washington Street, passing the city park anchored by the Patten Free Library, an elegant monument to community pride. There was no chance of staying at the once grand Sagadahoc House; that landmark had burned down years ago, taking part of the downtown with it. Adequate places of lodging were available, but you would want to steer clear of the American House on Water Street unless you were looking for what sailors liked to call a good time.

On your way to a South End launching? Take the trolley. In this winter view, a car makes its way down Washington Street near the G. G. Deering yard. Long Reach and the Woolwich shore are in the background. In warm weather, the Bath Street Railway cars are fully open at the sides. Courtesy: Maine Maritime Museum.

Depending on the season and the weather, you would find interesting diversions: roller skating, bicycle riding, motoring, shows at the Alameida, band concerts, steamboat rides to Popham Beach. But this was the City of Ships, so you would surely want to take in the action on the waterfront.

Alas, in a few decades the action had slowed dramatically. The innovative Bath Iron Works was going through a difficult period. To the south along the waterfront things looked grim. Gone were the sounds and smells of the wooden shipyards that had characterized Bath until lately. Well, not entirely gone. If you hopped a trolley and rode a mile south of the business district, things started looking and sounding like the Good Old Days. Just south of William T. Donnell's silent yard stood Percy & Small, whose workers and machines were probably getting out another superschooner. Noisy wasn't it? Just beyond was the G. G. Deering Company yard, where you would surely find something else interesting. Did you come to town for a Deering launching? Then you were in for a really good time.

If you were in Bath on Labor Day Weekend, 1909, you could watch the white-painted four-master *Mary L. Baxter* go overboard. At 1,036 tons and 188 feet in length, she was about the right size to replace the Deering fleet's *William C. Tanner*, although that similarity might have been a coincidence. Eight months before, the *Tanner* had departed Rockport, Massachusetts,

Not again! Another minor cliffhanger occurs as the Mary L. Baxter *stays put instead of sliding down her ways into the Kennebec as planned, on 31 August 1909. But stick around. Courtesy: Maine Maritime Museum.*

Don't blink! After monumental efforts to dislodge her, the Mary L. Baxter *suddenly makes a run for the Kennebec. To the extreme right is the tug* Seguin, *which has lent a hand to get the new schooner moving. Courtesy: Maine Maritime Museum.*

for Key West and had simply vanished, utterly and forever. With the *Tanner's* subtraction and the *Baxter's* addition, the Deering roster now stood at thirteen. The new schooner cost $64,000 to build (one share in her was $1,000), and her master carpenter was William P. Dodge.

On your way to the *Mary L .Baxter* launching, your southbound trolley would have taken you past the Deering house, where on off days dark-suited, white-bearded Gard could be seen sitting on his porch. But not today, obviously. A startling sight would have grabbed your attention just north of Deering's yard. At Percy & Small, the largest wooden vessel in the world was under construction, the six-master *Wyoming*, designed to carry 6,000 tons of coal. In the stocks, her 329-foot length stretched her from Washington Street to the edge of the Kennebec. She would go overboard in December, the last of the six-masters.

But 31 August 1909 belonged to the four-masted *Mary L. Baxter*, a less prepossessing but arguably more graceful creature. And speaking of graceful creatures, eight-year-old Mary L. Baxter, daughter of banker and political bigwig Rupert H. Baxter, was on hand to do the honors. With the words, "I christen thee *Mary L. Baxter*," which was surely a thrill for her, she scattered roses and carnations to the winds, then waited with the other on-board VIPs for her namesake to slide into the Kennebec. Nothing happened. This was exactly the sort of thing that had prompted Gard Deering to dispense with christenings some years back. The *Mary L. Baxter* remained motionless before the restless crowd. Or, as an attending reporter put it, "The vessel appeared loath to depart from her comfortable berth o[n] the shore to make her initial dip into the waters of the Kennebec, and for nearly three-quarters of an hour the mountain of wood and iron balked the efforts of the sturdy crew of carpenters who were trying to make her slide. Big bumpers of timber, two hydraulic pumps and the tug Seguin were called into the service, and almost everybody was ready to leave the yard except the veteran shipbuilder G.G. Deering, and some of his men. At last their efforts were crowned with success, for at 12:15, almost without warning, the craft settled and made a run down the ways at a racehorse clip. It was a silent and swift journey, and some of the spectators who did not happen to be looking at the moment nearly missed seeing her go overboard."[109] While people in rowboats gathered the strewn posies, lunch was served aboard: hot rolls, chicken salad, and coffee.

Or was your Deering date for the July 1911 launching of the four-master *Montrose W. Houck*? This vessel's birth was another example of Gard Deering's out-of-phase sense of timing. In 1909, the schooner had been started uptown in the old New England Company yard by Capt. James Hawley. She was based upon a model of Bant Hanson, a prodigiously talented Rideout protégé who designed Percy & Small's colossal *Wyoming* and had inherited the Pattee-Rideout mantle. But the lights were going out in most Bath shipyards, so work stopped on the vessel, not be resumed until January 1911 when Deering bought her on the stocks. She was completed where she stood at a cost of $65,000 and, though modeled by Hanson, she approximated Deering's other four-masters in size: 1,104 tons and 191 feet. Hanson, who acted as master builder, incorporated Deering's kneeless construction into the vessel's lower hold but she had hanging knees between decks.

Schooners were not famous for catchy names. But *Montrose W. Houck* was an awkward name to give any vessel, to say nothing of a helpless child. The original Montrose had overcome this handicap and, in adulthood, managed a New York grocery wholesale firm with his brother

Honk if you love schooners: Spectators blend their car horns in a loud salute as the Montrose W. Houck *goes down the ways in Bath's North End. The startled horse and driver in the foreground do not look pleased. The* Houck*, designed by Bant Hanson, was bought by Deering in a partial state of construction and completed in the New England Company yard. The automotive effect is something new in launching festivities. Courtesy: Maine Maritime Museum.*

Courtney (!). The Houcks, a referral to Deering from their Maine business associates the Baxters, would find more New York investors for Deering. So *Montrose W. Houck* it was.

Her launching was attended by almost 2,000 spectators, including "summer people" who arrived by excursion boat and natives who had taken Maine's interconnecting trolley lines to reach Bath. The *Houck's* deck was crowded with people, and if you were not a VIP you would have had to jostle to get close to the ways. But it would have been worth it because of a new wrinkle in such festivities. Those spectators with automobiles had driven into the yard and parked in a line. When the magic moment arrived, and Frank Deering's daughter Alice had scattered flowers from the bow, the *Houck* slid into the Kennebec to the raucous salute of car horns. While lunch was served to the people aboard, the steamer *Wiwurna* took the *Houck* under tow downriver to the Deering yard for her finishing touches. Under Capt. Ira Colberth of Bucks Harbor, Maine, late of the *Horatio L. Baker*, she entered the coal and phosphate trade.[110]

Acquiring and completing the *Houck* when shipbuilding was almost at a standstill exemplified Deering's unique take on the business. He apparently believed in the old blueprint for success: Buy when everyone else is selling—which everyone was during the current slump. In the *Houck* transaction, Deering also won the services of Bant Hanson, whose know-how would be applied to the company's next vessels. Later in 1911, Deering purchased the late William T. Donnell's leftover four-master *Alice M. Colburn*, surely at a nice price. The *Colburn* would prove to be a good investment. In coming years Deering would prosper using the other half of the blueprint for success: He sold when everyone else was buying.

Or was your Deering date for the 1911 launching of the *Lydia McLellan Baxter*? If so, on your way to the South End you would have noticed that there was nothing on the stocks at Percy & Small. That yard was making ends meet solely through repair work. So, being the only new schooner in Bath, the *Baxter* was sure to attract a crowd when she went down the ways.

While this $74,000, 1,352-ton four-master was under construction, Gard Deering had boasted that "he did not believe that the craft he is now building would leak 24 hours after she was launched even if she was not caulked at all. He takes particular care in the planking and says that in his long experience he never saw a finer lot of hard pine than he is putting on the

Left: The Lydia McLellan Baxter *goes down the ways seconds after her christening. She is only partially rigged; Gard Deering rushed the launching to avoid a predicted December storm. Courtesy: Capts. Douglas K. and Linda J. Lee.*

Below: Now completely rigged, the Lydia McLellan Baxter *rides at anchor in the current just off the Deering shipyard. The sun on her white side effectively conveys the austere grandeur of a large schooner. Courtesy: Capts. Douglas K. and Linda J. Lee.*

craft now building at the yard. He said that when he commenced building the crew expected to put on two, three or four strakes of plank in a day and now they get on about one but that one is put on right."[111]

Obviously, Gard Deering had learned a thing or two about publicity, which proves that you can teach an old dog new tricks. Further proof was that the new schooner was named for Mary L. Baxter's younger sister, "Baby Lydia," who, at age four, was the youngest sponsor ever to christen an American vessel, especially one built in her name. Lydia's tender age attracted wider than usual press coverage. It didn't hurt that she was angelic, photogenic, and a good interview, telling a rapt reporter before the launching that she enjoyed dancing classes and expected Santa Claus to bring her another doll for her large collection. Lydia would need no excuse from school to attend the upcoming launching; she was too young to attend school.

Little Lydia and Her Roses Made Bright the Launching

The Little Four Year Old Beauty Who Christened Her Namesake of the Deering Fleet, at Bath.

BABY LYDIA McLELLAN BAXTER
Who Christened Her Name sake at the Bath Launching.

Four-year-old Lydia McLellan Baxter, the youngest and cutest sponsor ever to launch a schooner. And why not? The new vessel was named for her. Courtesy: Maine Maritime Museum.

Lydia Baxter on deck moments before her namesake's launching, dressed in a white fur ensemble and armed with a cluster of roses and carnations. Courtesy: Capts. Douglas K. and Linda J. Lee.

Fearing an approaching storm, Deering decided to launch the *Lydia McLellan Baxter* early, on 5 December, when she had only her lower masts in place. So, if you stood among the Deering yard's snow-swept wood chips or, better still, were aboard the white-painted vessel at its moment of birth, you would watch history being made. "Lydia is a decided blonde and the picture, which she presented today as she stood holding a big bouquet of roses and pinks, around which she could hardly clasp her chubby hands, will never be forgotten by those, who were fortunate enough to see her.

"Lydia's eyes are the bluest of the blue, her cheeks as pink as the roses she held and she was dressed in a white fur coat and white hat, trimmed with rose buds. Wholly unconscious of the admiration of the hundreds of spectators, she played her part to perfection and a sweeter sponsor could not have been found.

"As the four master left the ways, just at the appropriate moment, she delightedly scattered the flowers, and utter[ed] the christening words." Enough superlatives? Never! "The schooner Lydia McL. Baxter is one of the handsomest and best constructed vessels in the well known Deering fleet."[112] Long lives lay ahead for both Lydias.

Unless you were a hopeless grouch or sensitive to cold, that christening was well worth your trip to Bath. So, perhaps, was your view of the big vessel as it loomed above you on the ways. Even though she was not quite in the superschooner class, she was a bit overwhelming up close. Although admittedly the last word in quality, she, like the rest of her class, had little of the symmetry and proportion that had graced Deering's erstwhile tern schooners. Her stretched profile, slab sides, and flattened bottom achieved an ark-like effect. Apparently, designers of big schooners had abandoned the principle that if a vessel looked right it was right. Noticing the many seams of hard-pine planks that Deering had praised, your instincts might suggest that it was risky to expect big wooden vessels like this one—and her even larger brethren—to bear up safely when loaded to capacity and driven hard. And your instincts would be correct.

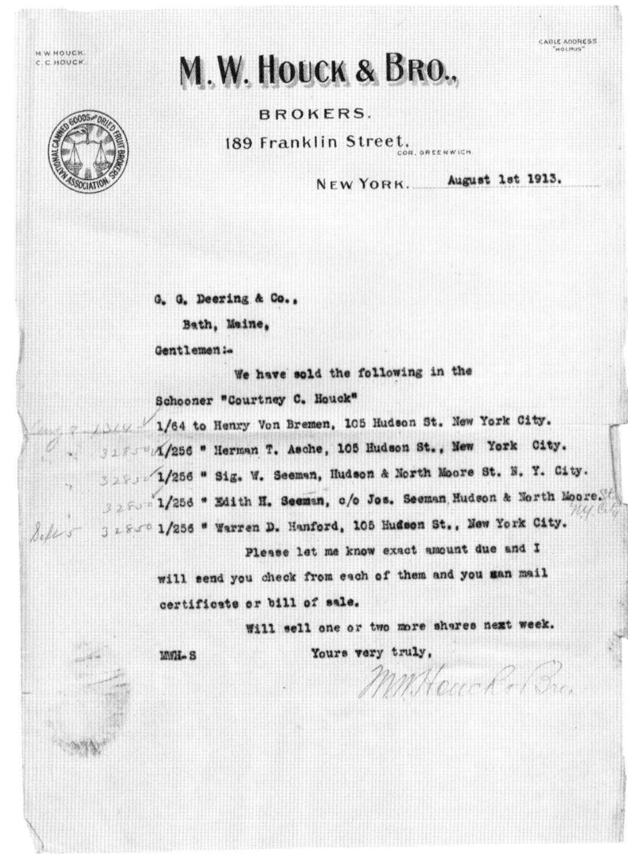

M. W. HOUCK.
C. C. HOUCK.

CABLE ADDRESS "HOLMOS"

M. W. HOUCK & BRO.,

BROKERS.

189 Franklin Street.
COR. GREENWICH

NATIONAL CANNED GOODS AND DRIED FRUIT BROKERS ASSOCIATION

NEW YORK. August 1st 1913.

G. G. Deering & Co.,
Bath, Maine,

Gentlemen:-

We have sold the following in the Schooner "Courtney C. Houck"

1/64 to Henry Von Bremen, 105 Hudson St. New York City.
1/256 " Herman T. Asche, 105 Hudson St., New York City.
1/256 " Sig. W. Seeman, Hudson & North Moore St. N. Y. City.
1/256 " Edith H. Seeman, c/o Jos. Seeman Hudson & North Moore.
1/256 " Warren D. Hanford, 105 Hudson St., New York City.

Please let me know exact amount due and I will send you check from each of them and you can mail certificate or bill of sale.

Will sell one or two more shares next week.

MWH-S

Yours very truly,
M.W. Houck & Bro.

Networking: In 1913 the Houck brothers find shareholders in New York for the new five-master Courtney C. Houck. *Courtesy: Maine Maritime Museum.*

Deering's building in 1911 was soon offset by unforeseen disasters. In August of that year, the *Malcolm B. Seavey* was proceeding north to Baltimore from Port Tampa with phosphate rock. It was hurricane season. Off Cape Romain, South Carolina, she encountered heavy seas and anchored. For two days she was pounded by hurricane-force winds and seas, including a comber that swept away her forward houses. The strain started her leaking. Because the galley had been flooded, destroying many provisions, the crew was put on short rations. Another huge sea swept the *Seavey*, washing Comus and Momus, the resident cats, overboard. Soon there was eight feet of water in the hold. On the storm's third day the port anchor chain parted, causing the *Seavey* to drag inshore. She struck and quickly broke up, only her fore section remaining above water. The crew took refuge in the masts' crosstrees. One sailor did not make it. Capt. Henry Dodge was also swept overboard but was rescued in weak condition and lashed to a mast. On the fourth day, with the storm abating somewhat, the *Seavey's* distress signal was spotted. With heroic determination, her crew was rescued by a boat from the steamer *Mohawk* of Charleston that approached near enough for the survivors to jump into the sea and be snatched aboard. Capt. Dodge reportedly was incoherent for days afterward.[113]

Five months later the four-year-old *William R. Wilson* was freighting 2,200 tons of Baltimore coal to Port Tampa when, off Key West, fog and heavy seas did her in. She drove hard onto Alligator Reef and quickly broke in two—a total loss. The crew was rescued.[114]

In 1913, less than two years after her launching, the *Montrose W. Houck's* time was up. Loaded with phosphate rock for Baltimore and encountering heavy seas midway between Capes Hatteras and Henry, Capt. Colberth attempted to tack her. When she failed to come about (missed stays) and lost headway, Colberth tried unsuccessfully to anchor. The vessel dragged ashore near the Paul Gamiel Hill lifesaving station.

A distress signal set from the foremast—the only mast still standing—was spotted at daylight at the station, from which a surf boat was launched. The *Virginian Pilot* later provided this vivid account: "Time after time the hardy surfmen tried to launch their life boat, and as often as they pushed it off the beach the heavy sea upset it; throwing them into the raging water that eddied around their armpits. Finding that they could not get through the roaring surf the lifesavers resorted to the Lyle gun, trying to throw a life line across the foundering schooner. This method...also failed for the schooner was so far out the shot with the line attached fell short....

"All though the morning hours Captain Colbe[r]th and the nine men on the Houck, clinging to first one part of the vessel and then another as it began to go to pieces, watched

YOU ARE INVITED WITH YOUR FRIENDS TO ATTEND
THE LAUNCHING OF THE
SCHOONER "MONTROSE W. HOUCK"
FROM NEW ENGLAND CO'S SHIPYARD AT BATH, MAINE
AT 11.30 O'CLOCK
TUESDAY, JULY TWENTY-FIFTH
NINETEEN HUNDRED AND ELEVEN
G. G. DEERING CO., - - BUILDERS AND AGENTS
LUNCH WILL BE SERVED AFTER
THE LAUNCHING

YOU ARE INVITED TO ATTEND THE LAUNCHING OF THE
SCHOONER "COURTNEY C. HOUCK"
FROM OUR SHIPYARD AT BATH, MAINE,
AT THREE O'CLOCK
TUESDAY, JULY THE EIGHTH
NINETEEN HUNDRED AND THIRTEEN
E. D. ATKINS
MASTER
G. G. DEERING CO.
BUILDERS AND AGENTS
LUNCH WILL BE SERVED ON BOARD

"You are invited . . .": Special invitations for the launchings of the Montrose W. Houck *(1911) and* Courtney C. Houck *(1913). Courtesy: Maine Maritime Museum.*

Above: A cast metal commemorative plate originally affixed to one of the Courtney C. Houck*'s quarter bitts (perpendicular timbers aft protruding above deck, to which lines could be attached). Courtesy: Capts. Douglas K. and Linda J. Lee.*

Right: Beating the smoke? At sea aboard the fast five-master Courtney C. Houck*. Elliot family photograph, courtesy: Capts. Douglas K. and Linda J. Lee and Maine Maritime Museum.*

the efforts made to rescue them. With despair in their hearts they saw the life line fall hissing into the water a hundred yards short of them…they had about given up hope of being saved when the life boat came bobbing over the white capped waves and took them off….

"The rescuers were just in time for the schooner was fast going to pieces on the outer shoals under the heavy pounding of the waves, whipped into fury by the 30-mile north wind. The nine men, exhausted from a twelve hours' battle with wind and water, nearly frozen to the marrow from the incessant lashing of the waves, had been without a mouthful to eat or a drop to drink since the vessel struck early yesterday morning. All of the masts had fallen, and the timbers of the schooner were breaking away one by one. The surf boat safely landed the schooner's crew and late yesterday the Houck was reported a total loss."[115]

These losses were partly offset by another Deering superschooner launched on 13 July 1913. Named for Montrose Houck's partner and brother, and christened by his wife, the five-masted *Courtney C. Houck* was modeled on the *Dorothy B. Barrett* but was slightly smaller, with a tonnage of 1,627 and length of 213 feet. She cost $84,096. Elisha Atkins took her. She was characteristically fast, freighting phosphate rock from Tampa around the southern tip of Florida and north to Baltimore in twenty-six to thirty days. Atkins and his longtime mate Bill Struck were determined to outsail steamers and bent every sail. As later reported in the New York *World*, "Capt. Atkins sent some cases of oranges on a steamer to Baltimore to get them in a hurry, and then he beat the "smoke" in with the Houck. Since then he has never had much use for coal, except in a galley stove."[116] It wouldn't be the last time Atkins beat the smoke into port.

The Edwin R. Hunt's *skipper, shaded by an awning rigged over the spanker boom, watches as a sailor checks the powered yawl boat's rudder. The* Hunt *is probably in a hot southern port, for even the yawl boat has sun protection. Courtesy: Capts. Douglas K. and Linda J. Lee.*

The long-serving *Edwin R. Hunt* has left us a logbook, now at the Maine Maritime Museum, that provides details of coastwise schooner life in 1913 and 1914. It makes an interesting comparison with the earlier *Samuel Dillaway* logbook because it shows that, after twenty years, some of the same problems dogged the coastwise trade. It also shows that, in the slack year of 1913, vessels like the *Hunt* made themselves useful with a variety of cargoes. From February 1913 through August 1914 the *Hunt* made sixteen trips: four with coal, two with lumber, three with railroad ties, one with an unidentified cargo, and six light.

The *Edwin R. Hunt* was twenty-one when the events described in her logbook commenced. She was under the command of Charles Gilbert, about whom little is known. Gilbert had apparently been in square-riggers and ran a very, very tight ship. He observed the sabbath aboard the *Hunt*, which suggests a kind of enforced piety, but not necessarily goodwill, nor good relations. Mates fell like dominoes before him. The first of these, who attentively set down daily details, may have tried to make a point in doing so, for being on the old *Hunt* was risky business in bad weather.

Sunday, 2 February 1913, found the *Hunt* en route light from Philadelphia to Norfolk for coal. On her second day out she ran into southeast gales and reduced sail. Seas washed over her deck, stove in her forward house, and flooded the galley and cabin. With her first three lower sails shortened (reefed), and with only two topsails set, the schooner went before the wind. Water continued to come aboard. The *Hunt* was a long-poop vessel, apt to gather water on deck forward, which could produce strain. Sure enough: "...found 6 ft water in vessel and started all pumps.... Bad weather.... Vessel laboring heavily."[117] The pumps were kept going the next day (one failed), as the vessel continuously shipped water. When the storm blew itself out, the water in the hold was reduced to three feet, which made the schooner manageable.

At Norfolk, the *Hunt* underwent repairs. Caulkers came aboard to close seams, a new pump was rigged, and a new fore gaff replaced one broken in the storm. On 12 February, still at Norfolk, the port anchor chain parted and the anchor was lost. The captain went ashore and found a replacement. On 13 February, loaded with coal, the vessel set sail for San Juan. She encountered gales en route: "deck constantly flooded" on 18 February, "everything flooded" on 20 February, but the cargo was delivered and unloaded whereupon the *Hunt* sailed light to Port St. Joseph, Florida, for a lumber cargo.

No lumber awaited her at Port St. Joe, so she idled for six days ("Sabbath observed"). More time was lost because only four stevedores could be found to load the wood once it started dribbling in on trucks. The *Hunt* filled and added a deck load. Ready to depart for Boston, she was stopped by adverse winds. On 15 April, the mate noted that the "pilot dare not take us out." Another mate continued the logbook on 16 April: "Captn advised pilot not to take any chanses but he said everything was allright. 1.45 pm Passed out over the Bar vessel pounding heavy several times Captain ordered pumps sounded before letting Pilot go Vessel not making any water let Pilot go 2.30 pm."

Anchored in Vineyard Sound on 10 May, another new logkeeper recorded that the *Hunt* lost another day when the tide turned, preventing her from getting under way. She reached Boston on 14 May, unloaded, and, according to still another new logkeeper, proceeded to Green's shipyard where she was hauled out, caulked, and rerigged. When the work was done she sailed light for Norfolk. Sound familiar? Then it was coal for San Juan where, after unloading, the crew performed maintenance while stevedores slowly loaded the *Hunt* with an unspecified cargo, probably sugar. The mate continued the logbook although the vessel was not at sea: "[20 July 1913.] ...Sabeth day observed. Second officer drunk and disorderly. Sailor Oscar also drunk and disorderly. Sailer Oleph on shore in police station.... Pumps attended." Oscar and the delinquent second mate were paid off on Monday. Each day at San Juan the *Hunt* lost time waiting for trucks to arrive haphazardly and tardily with cargo. Then it was off to Moss Point, Mississippi, for 8,658 railroad ties which, after a day's delay by adverse winds, she took to Boston on a month-long voyage. At Moss Point and at Boston, she changed mates yet again. Under tow away from Boston's Commercial Wharf on 8 October, the *Hunt* lost another day to minor damage. While this was attended to, a fire was discovered below the galley stove. "Fire did not blaze out," recorded the new mate on 10 October, "but must have been smouldering there for two or thee days between the deck iron and sheet metal under deck." Shipshape again, but light, the *Hunt* headed for Savannah. She continued this way, taking coal south and bringing lumber and ties north, through July 1914, at which point the logbook ends.

Exclusive of her downtime for repairs, over seventeen months the *Edwin R. Hunt* lost twenty-two days doing nothing because of adverse winds or delays in port. She sailed light 37.5 percent of her time at sea. And, judging from the changes in her logbook handwriting, she had sailed under six different mates who came and went anonymously—except for the last, one J. M. Borden. Before he left the *Hunt* at Boston on 22 July 1914, Borden, infuriated by his

Distance.	Diff. of Lat.	Departure.	Lat. by D R.	Lat. by Ob.	Variation.	Diff. of Lon.	Lon. in.	Lon. by Ob.

¼ K. Courses. Winds. Leeway. Remarks, Tuesday 21 day of July 1904

Comes in Hazy and wind West. 7 30 am passed Cape Cod Lighthouse
6 pm Docked at Mystic wharf. took a heavy squall at Boston L house got all sails wet Captain will not let us quit to night, have to stay and dry sail, to morrow.
Good God I wish I was clear of the d— old tub. The Engineer says she makes 7 foot of water every twenty four hours lying still. Good God what a cuss. Still I know damned well the old man would take her around Cape Horn if the owners said so. no wonder they call him the Cowboy Captain

"The most miserable days of my life": Mate J. M. Borden kisses off the Edwin R. Hunt, *leaving behind a written tirade against Charles Gilbert, "the Cowboy Captain," in the schooner's official logbook. Let the next* Hunt *mate beware. Courtesy: Maine Maritime Museum.*

days on the old schooner, broke logbook-keeping rules and vented his spleen against the *Hunt* and her skipper, Charles Gilbert. It was, to say the least, an extraordinary departure from protocol. But because it became part of the *Hunt's* offical record, it has survived to this day: "6 pm docked at Mystic Wharf. Took a heavy squall at Boston L[ight]house got all sails wet. Captain will not let us quit tonight, have to stay and dry sail to morrow."

There had obviously been a disagreement between crew and captain about wages. Thus, "Fine weather dried all sails and furled them.... 3 pm Capt came on board to pay off crew. Crew wanted money before commissioner. Capt told them to take their money or go to hell Crew went down to get their money. Capt put each mans money in an envelope made them sign clear. Then knocked the hell out of them gave them their money and let them go. Called me aft. Called me a son of a bitch gave me two black eyes and I think he has broke some of my ribs. Docked me five dollars for [in]subordination gave me balance. Made me sign clear. Kicked my ass and made me get out of his cabin. I would take him to court but good God he would find me and kill me.

"Now whom so ever goes mate in this vessel next if you see this before you go to sea get out don't go with him. But if too late and you have started on the voyage let me advice you, you cant treat this man as the general run of Coasters. He is an old deepwater man. He is engineer, mate, 2nd cook and sailor and takes no bluff from any man. He works from daylight to dark and if you don't keep busy god help you, so beware, if he ever hits you his fist is like the hoof of a mule. Thank god I am clear of him.

"A little more advice before I close. Keep your sailors working and let no man loaf. If you do it is hell to pay you get plenty to eat but whats the good. He takes it all out of you in work. I must take my duds and get before he catches me at this. I would not want to be within 100 miles of Boston when he sees this. Still give the devil his due, if you know your business and work like hell you will never go with a better man than Chas Gilbert the Texas Cowboy Captain.

J. M. Borden, Mate for 36 the most miserable days of my life."

The day after Borden made his escape, if he had gotten a safe distance from the Cowboy Captain, he might have read in a newspaper the disturbing news from Europe. Austria-Hungary had delivered an unacceptable ultimatum to Serbia. Five days later war was declared. Europe's two power blocs, hopelessly enmeshed in mutual military commitments, were unable to prevent a widening of the conflict. By August 1914, all the major European powers were at war. The nightmarishly destructive conflict, expected to be brief, lasted for years and spread around the world. By 1917, isolationist America had been sucked into its vortex.

Viewed against such a backdrop, the affairs of wooden ships and shipyards would seem trivial. But like every other nook and cranny of Western civilization, Maine people would be profoundly changed by the conflict. Rather ironically, the high-tech monster of European war would give the low-tech, dying schooner trade an unexpected reprieve.

A big ship in a small river: The Courtney C. Houck *discharges coal at the border town of Calais, Maine. Notice the coal derricks on the wharf. This view is from the east shore of the St. Croix River in St. Stephen, New Brunswick. Courtesy: Capts. Douglas K. and Linda J. Lee.*

At the beginning of 1914, G. G. Deering's fleet, because of additions and losses, numbered fourteen vessels. There were no immediate plans for more. Wasn't it just a matter of time before Deering's vessels, like almost everyone else's in the business, became uneconomical to operate? Although he was now the preeminent builder of wooden vessels in Maine, did Gard Deering worry that schooners were being forever squeezed out of their niche markets?

Apparently not. He had, for example, bought the *Alice M. Colburn* at the bottom of the schooner market. Suddenly she and her kind (including, as we will see, the tired *Edwin R. Hunt*) were hot properties. Another example of optimisim: In June 1914, when Percy & Small investors were hard up for dividends, Mrs. Osceola Cahill, widow of Percy & Small's promoter, grew discouraged about the future. To cut her losses, she sold all of her shares in Percy & Small vessels to Gard Deering, reportedly for less than the original cost of a single share.[118] A few weeks later the guns were booming and the entire picture had changed. Inasmuch as Deering was not clairvoyant, he must have been propelled by positive thinking, which flew in the face of conventional wisdom. In any event, once again he had bought when everyone was selling. And now the European War was changing everything—for the better, if you were a schooner owner.

Still at it: Freed by his sons of some management chores, Gard Deering personally supervises schooner construction well into his eighties. Here he inspects some precut and numbered timbers for the yard's next vessel. Courtesy: Maine Maritime Museum.

CHAPTER FIVE

The Oldest Active Shipbuilder

One economic effect of the Great War was that belligerent nations consumed more resources at home. As a neutral power, the United States stood to benefit by providing raw materials and finished goods to both sides. In addition, Latin America's coal supply, which had been imported from Europe in European vessels, was choked off. South America thus turned to the United States for coal. American shippers, who for generations had regarded South America as an extension of their coastwise trade, were only too ready to oblige. Prices started up, doubling the cost of living over the next four years. But freight rates far outstripped inflation. They began rising slowly, then accelerated, eventually reaching more than twenty times their prewar figure in such markets as coal. Europe's unspeakable disaster was manna from heaven for America's dying schooner trade.

The G. G. Deering Company, which had always done well even in hard times, now stood on the threshold of a bonanza. Schooners would earn big money taking coal, lumber, and other essentials to South America and returning with cargoes such as coffee, linseed, salt, and hides to the States. The European meat grinder continued at full speed, its insatiable demand driving transatlantic freight rates through the roof. With charters often prepaid regardless of risk, American schooners took up transatlantic runs to neutral European nations such as Portugal and Spain. The vessels were not designed for Atlantic commerce, but coastwise steamers and barges were edging them out of domestic charters, and soaring long-distance freight rates were simply too much to resist. Aging schooners, which before the war had gone begging, now began to look valuable. And the need for more shipping revitalized Bath's wooden shipyards.

With a fleet numbering fourteen, Deering was well positioned to exploit these opportunities.

Would you refuse an order from this man? Capt. Alden M. Chaney, longtime skipper of the Lewis M. Goward, *about 1915. Courtesy: Capts. Douglas K. and Linda J. Lee.*

But the company was no luckier than before and in 1915 lost two vessels. As mentioned earlier, the *Horatio L. Baker* was dismasted and abandoned in March while on her way to Port Tampa for phosphate rock. And in August the old *Lydia M. Deering* went down. She had left Sabine, Texas with lumber for Boston, under the command of George Murphy who, the year before, had lost the tern schooner *S. G. Haskell* of Deer Isle on a lumber run from Brunswick, Georgia. The *Deering* ran into an August hurricane, her last, in the Gulf of Mexico. She was lost along with Murphy and one other man. The rest of the crew were rescued by a passing vessel and eventually landed in New Orleans.[119] The elderly *Baker* and *Deering* (especially the *Baker*, as has been seen), had more than earned their keep.

By 1916, investing in schooners had become respectable again. In March of that year, Deering launched another superschooner. The five-masted *Jerome Jones* (1,891 tons, 250 feet) could carry 3,000 tons of coal. Inflation was gaining momentum, so the vessel's cost was a cool $96,000: $1,500 a share. She was named for one of the founding members of Jones, McDuffee & Stratton of Boston, advertised as "The Largest Wholesale and Retail Crockery, China and Glassware Establishment in the Country." The *Jones* launching had been scheduled for 18 March but was postponed because a late-winter storm had filled the yard with snowdrifts. Two weeks later, on 31 March 1916, the South End schools declared a holiday for the rescheduled event, and the yard was reportedly filled by "several hundred people, including many visitors from out of town." Captain E. L. Nash, late of the *Gardiner G. Deering*, and with a quarter of a century of command behind him, was captain of the new vessel. Jerome Jones's granddaughter Rosalie was the christening sponsor (roses and pinks again, eagerly gathered up by souvenir-seeking boys).

It should come as no surprise that the ceremony "was a pretty one." The huge new vessel was adorned with a set of flags given by her namesake. "She was built under the personal supervision of G. G. Deering, the oldest active shipbuilder in the United States. Mr. Deering is in his eighty-third year and has been building for half a century and in the construction of the Jones nothing has been spared to make her as near perfect as possible.... Every man employed on the craft is proud of her.

"The Jones has an unusually heavy Virginia oak frame cut by the J. S. Hoskins Co. of

Baltimore. She is a novelty from the fact that every tree-nail used in the construction is locust....

"The after house is 30 x 33, containing the cabin, captains' room, spare state rooms and dining room, finished in mahogany, ash and North Carolina pine, and Master Joiner M. A. McNeil, who has been with G. G. Deering for twenty years, brought out a combination of unusual beauty and pleasing effect. The captain's cabin is heated with steam and the floors are polished hard wood. The amidship house...contains the galley and mess room.... The forward house has the forecastle, engine room and engineer's room." Her master builder was Charles Robinson and her plumber was C. W. Rogers, Deering's son-in-law.[120] Perfectly positioned to cash in on rising freight rates, the costly *Jerome Jones* more than paid for herself within a year of her launching.[121] The brightest optimist in Maine could not have foreseen such a shipping boom. And it would get boomier very shortly. With the *Jerome Jones,* and adjusting for losses, Deering's fleet now numbered thirteen. Within two years, the *Jones* was renamed *Frank M. Deering* after Gard's son and partner. There must have been a story behind the change but, alas, it has been lost to us.

Meanwhile, Gard had radically redistributed his controlling interest in the company. Early in 1916, having bought his daughter Emma's 8 shares, he gave his sons Harry and Frank 300 each. Carroll received 200 shares. Lydia had 16, which left Gard with 160 of his own, making him a minority owner. This change was probably in recognition of Gard's advanced age (he was now eighty-two), his sons' maturity (Frank was forty-five, Harry forty-four, and Carroll thirty-four), and the increasing complexity of the business. The shares, originally valued at $50 each, were now appraised at $175.[122] For his part, Gard could focus on day-to-day supervision of the vessels the firm intended to add.

During 1916 there was rising uncertainty about whether the United States could preserve her neutrality in the European war. The year before, when without prior warning the German submarine *U-20* torpedoed the unarmed British liner *Lusitania*, claiming she carried war supplies and was fair game, 1,198 passengers had died, including 128 Americans. This provocation raised the possibility of America's entry into the war, but Imperial Germany bowed to President

Left: The Frank M. Deering *(ex-*Jerome Jones, *1916), hauled out at an unidentified repair facility. Her bowsprit and jib boom loom high above the shipyard's telephone poles. Courtesy: Capts. Douglas K. and Linda J. Lee.*

Right: A solitary figure, probably a mate, gazes from the rail during a lapse in the superschooner Frank M. Deering*'s repairs. Courtesy: Capts. Douglas K. and Linda J. Lee.*

Woodrow Wilson's ultimatum, agreeing to exclude large passenger vessels from attack and indemnify U.S. citizens for their loss. America remained at peace.

In 1916 Wilson, a Democrat, stood for re-election with the slogan, "He Kept Us Out of War." The prevailing sentiment in the States was to preserve neutrality, which of course went hand-in-hand with prosperity. The Republican party was at pains to resolve the destructive factionalism that had handed the 1912 election to Wilson. To that end, future president Warren G. Harding, then Republican senator from Ohio, came to Bath in 1916 to confer with Harold M. Sewall, scion of the famous shipping family, former minister to the Hawaiian Islands (before their annexation), and one of Maine's most influential Republicans. During their discussions, which may have included Bath's war readiness, the talk must have gotten around to ships. According to the *Bath Daily Times*, Sewall insisted on taking Harding to Bath's South End, where "a veteran builder was superintending some of the work on a schooner then under construction." Sewall and Harding did indeed find Gard Deering overseeing work on the future *Maude M. Morey*, but willing to take a break under these unusual circumstances. Deering made a powerful impression on Harding, who was fascinated by the shipbuilder's vitality at his advanced age, and provided posterity with a rare close-up: "Harding frequently referred afterwards to his meeting with Mr. Deering and said that except for one thing he would never have realized that he had been talking with a man past 80 years of age. 'He is a most remarkable man, wonderfully vigorous and active,' said Senator Harding to Mr. Sewall. He said the only reason that would lead him to suspect that Mr. Deering had passed the allot[t]ed three score and ten years was his eyes. 'He has a de-

Kindred spirits: Sam Percy (left) and Gard Deering, chatting in the Percy & Small shipyard, June 1916. They are probably talking shop, for the European war has improved prospects for the schooner trade. Perhaps when things get brighter, Capt. Sam will attend to that broken windowpane. Courtesy: Douglas K. and Linda J. Lee Collection, Maine Maritime Museum.

lightful personality and I'm very glad you gave me the opportunity of meeting him' remarked Senator Harding."[123] What, exactly, they talked about during this brief meeting we shall never know. Judging from his future presidency, Harding could have used some advice from a man like Gard Deering, but that is another story.

Whether America went to war or not, it paid to be prepared, which is why in 1916 plans were made to strengthen the trolley tracks running north and south through Bath. Many of the vessels that once unloaded massive shipbuilding components were now making fortunes in other markets, so Deering and Percy & Small had become dependent upon supplies freighted in on railway cars. The components had been unloaded at the town center, loaded into wagons or trucks, driven down Washington Street, and unloaded at the yards. No more. New, heavier rails were laid that permitted loaded flatcars to be pulled along the old north-south trolley route to a siding at Percy & Small, right next door to Deering.[124] Beefing up the street railway tracks benefited all working shipyards in Bath and would soon be a crucial factor in the new Texas Company's production in the North End.

Woodrow Wilson narrowly won the 1916 presidential race and America continued to reap the benefits of neutrality. And also the problems: In January 1917, threatened by her enemies' transatlantic supply lines, Germany announced the resumption of unrestricted submarine warfare. Relations between Germany and the United States, worsened by German influence in Mexico and other international hassles, fell apart. On 6 April 1917 the Yanks went to war.

During the years of neutrality, Bath had made substantial adjustments to the times and to the resurgence of maritime prosperity. But after war was declared, the City of Ships entered a dizzying period of hyperactivity. Uncle Sam was determined to spare no effort or expense to win the war, and the war effort demanded ships. Therefore a newly established Emergency Fleet Corporation launched a campaign to establish shipyards to build, as quickly as possible, a vast U.S. merchant fleet. With its shipbuilding tradition and facilities, Bath immediately became a focal point of the Emergency Fleet strategy. In the North End, the new Texas Steamship Company, opened in 1916 as a shipyard for the Texas Oil Company, got busy and between 1917 and 1921 launched thirty-four merchant vessels, most of them requisitioned by the U.S.

government for war purposes. Bath Iron Works, back from the dead, and the old Kelley-Spear operation also had more work than they could handle. There were even wooden shipbuilding projects authorized; William Donnell's long-vacant yard came to life again under management of Bath's Pendleton Brothers.

By the end of 1921, when the war contracts expired and prewar conditions returned, Bath's overall output was 64 commercial vessels aggregating 155,539 tons, as well as 14 Navy destroyers. And then it was over.

But while it lasted, the City of Ships was transformed. The sudden labor shortage, accompanied by sky-high wages, brought thousands of new people into the city, doubling the population by late 1918 and necessitating ambitious housing projects that were hurriedly commenced. As historian Henry Wilson Owen vividly puts it, "What perhaps, more than anything else, makes the war period seem in retrospect so unreal, was the utter engrossment of the whole population in the war effort.... Housing facilities were hopelessly inadequate.... On the water front there grew up villages of houseboats. On the vacant lots people put up tents. Sheds, barns and other outbuildings were converted into temporary homes."[125] To Owen, Bath's war years were unimaginable to anyone who hadn't lived through them: a brief "delirium" of crowding, confusion, urgency, ready money, and reckless excess.

And what was Gardiner G. Deering doing during this delirium? Building schooners, losing schooners, selling schooners, and coining money.

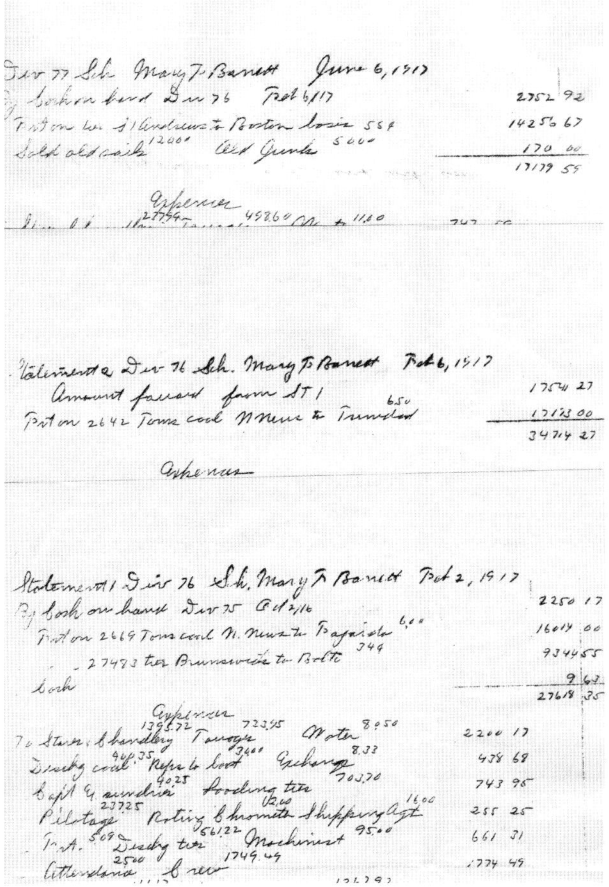

Boom times: A stack of dividend account sheets for the Mary F. Barrett, *1917. Courtesy: Maine Maritime Museum.*

Managing a schooner fleet in the war years was a delirium all its own, especially if one had spent half a century riding ups and downs to moderate success. Suddenly, after years in the doldrums, freight rates knew no limits, especially after the U.S. entry into the Great War. Take for example the case of the *Lydia McLellan Baxter*, one share of which had cost $1,155 in 1910. In 1911, when rates were low and schooners increasingly uncompetitive, she had earned $163 per share. This rose to $265 per share in 1915. In 1916 she earned $565; in 1917, $1,540. In 1918, although requisitioned for part of the year by the U.S. Shipping Board, she still earned $470 a

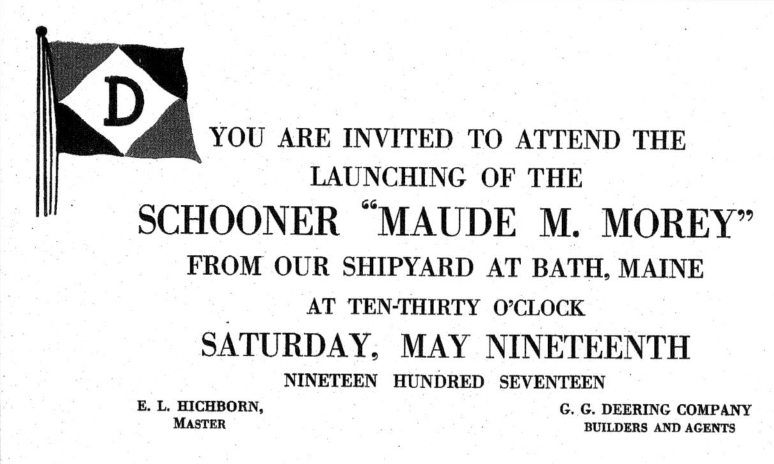

YOU ARE INVITED TO ATTEND THE
LAUNCHING OF THE
SCHOONER "MAUDE M. MOREY"
FROM OUR SHIPYARD AT BATH, MAINE
AT TEN-THIRTY O'CLOCK
SATURDAY, MAY NINETEENTH
NINETEEN HUNDRED SEVENTEEN
E. L. HICHBORN,
MASTER
G. G. DEERING COMPANY
BUILDERS AND AGENTS

Don't miss it: The debut of the four-master Maude M. Morey, *just after the United States has entered the Great War, will be marked by an honor guard of Boy Scouts to lend a sort of military touch. The new schooner takes her name from the wife of the mayor of Lewiston, Maine, an investor in G. G. Deering vessels. She will be an instant financial success. This invitation is the size of a business card. Courtesy: Capts. Douglas K. and Linda J. Lee.*

share. In 1919 her per-share dividends totaled $3,900. The *Jerome Jones/Frank M. Deering*, within two years of her 1916 debut at a cost of $1,500 per share, earned more than *twice* her building costs. In 1917 one *Jones* share earned $2,080, largely through a charter from Savannah to Montevideo with pipe. In 1918 the same share earned $3,030, mostly from a prepaid charter from Norfolk to Rio with coal.

Deering's next schooner, the four-masted, 1,364-ton *Maude M. Morey*, provides a dramatic example of the changing financial times brought on by the nation's war effort. Frank Deering was her master builder. She went overboard in May 1917, just weeks after America's entry into the war, with a local Boy Scout troop providing a paramilitary honor guard. The *Morey* was a near duplicate of 1911's *Lydia McLellan Baxter*. But whereas the *Baxter* had cost $74,000, the *Morey* ran Deering $135,000, enough perhaps to stay the hand of would-be investors. But those who ventured were those who gained. In 1917–1918 the *Morey* earned $214,000, better than one-and-a-half times her cost. Most of this was earned on three round-trip voyages to Brazil: coal out and, on at least one voyage, coffee back.

But G. G. Deering did not grow the fleet numerically. By 1916 everyone was buying schooners to get in on the shipping boom, so Deering of course sold. In 1916, the aging workhorse *Edwin R. Hunt* was bought by the Foreign & Domestic Transportation Corporation of New York. She had cost less than $52,100 to build in 1892. Now twenty-four years old and, judging by her logbook records, somewhat the worse for wear, she fetched $60,000. That figure, adjusted for inflation, indicates that after almost a quarter of a century's use, the *Hunt* brought about 60 percent of her original value. A shareholder who had paid $813.45 per sixty-fourth in 1892 (and had received dividends ever since) received $2,327.46 in sale proceeds and dividends in 1917.

The *Hunt's* buyers were eager to cash in on transatlantic freights such as coal to fuel-starved Greece despite the obvious risk of enemy attack. So it was that on 17 March 1917, sailing west from Crete in ballast, the *Hunt* was spotted and sunk by the German submarine *UC-25* forty miles off Cabo de Gata, Spain. As was usual in such cases, the *UC-25* did not waste a valuable torpedo on a wooden sailing vessel; her deck gun did the trick. The crew evacuated the *Hunt* with no casualties.

The loss of the *Edwin R. Hunt* provides an interesting example of the six-degrees-of-separation principle. Completing her Mediterranean patrol, the *UC-25* put into the Austrian naval base at Pula. There her command was given to Oberleutnant Karl Doenitz, who would rise to prominence in the postwar German navy, command the Third Reich's submarine force in the Second World War, and briefly assume the reins of the Nazi government after Adolf Hitler's suicide.

In 1917 Deering sold the *Henry O. Barrett* to New York interests from whom she was chartered to take case oil (canned petroleum in crates) to France at $135,000—almost enough to cover her purchase price. But life was becoming too dangerous in the war zone for sailing vessels, and by 1918 the U.S. government proscribed their participation in transatlantic trade. After her arrival at Le Havre, her new owners sold the *Barrett* to French interests.

Deering also disposed of the old Donnell four-master *Alice M. Colburn*, which he had bought during the prewar slump but which by 1917 had become a hot property. She went for $107,000.

These financial coups were offset somewhat by the loss of the *Edward E. Briry*. The *Briry* had been chartered for transatlantic trade and, in 1916, had freighted coal from Norfolk to Lisbon in twenty-five days, returning to Philadelphia in twenty-eight. But in December 1917 she was operating coastwise again, carrying 2,517 tons of coal from Norfolk for Portland. Her captain, William C. Elliot of Bath, had been delayed for two weeks as he tried to work the schooner around Nantucket Shoals in adverse weather. Elliot anchored to wait matters out, but the winds increased to seventy-five miles per hour, causing the *Briry* to drag both anchors and go aground on Stone Horse Shoal, Nantucket. She struck stern first, which drove her rudder post through the stern. Boarding surf swept away the cabin and midship houses, forcing all hands to seek shelter in the forward house where they managed to get a small fire going with oil from the donkey engine's drip pan. The *Briry* began to sink stern first, leaving only the bow above water.

Heroically, Capt. Leonard Oliver responded to the schooner's distress signal and, although striking the shoal once, maneuvered his tug *Paoli* close enough to the wreck to get the *Briry* crew safe aboard and landed in Vineyard Haven.[126] The *Edward E. Briry* was twenty-one at the time of her demise.

Thus, with sales and attrition, the Deering fleet numbered nine at the end of 1917.

Where did Deering profits go during Bath's Great War delirium? Company records indicate that thousands of dollars were diversified into long-term bonds in such companies as the Portland Water Works; Portland Railroad Company; the City of Portland, Oregon; Bloomington & Maine Railway and Light; Penn and Ohio Power and Light; Bell Telephone of Canada; and Remington Arms Co., Inc. Thousands more were invested in U.S. Liberty Loan Bonds. Harry Deering, business manager of the company, was presumably in charge of such investments. Because Harry's personal investment accounts are co-mingled with G. G. Deering Company's, it is barely possible that some of the above investments were his alone, although the large sums involved would seem to rule out that possibility. One investment, probably Harry's, stands out among the otherwise prudent roster: a $3,000 commitment to Imperial Russian War Bonds, purchased just weeks before the Imperial Russian government succumbed to revolution. Besides exemplifying one of the all-time classic bad bets, this investment suggests that the Deerings were out of touch with strategic changes in Europe, perhaps assuming that the Great War and its ironical home-front prosperity would continue indefinitely. For years the war had been a disastrous military stalemate, devouring people and resources with no decisive result, so such an attitude is understandable, even after the United States' entry. Many others in Bath were of the same mind. As Owen points out, although the city's entire resources were devoted to ending the war as quickly as possible, the prevailing assumption was that the boom times would go on forever. Delirium indeed.

But in the short run Gard Deering was a prudent realist who had learned not to count on good luck. His schooners carried war risk insurance in addition to the usual liability coverage.

Early in 1918, Kapitanleutnant Otto Droscher took command of one of the Imperial

German Navy's highest-tech vessels, the newly launched *U-117*, built at the Vulcan yard in Hamburg. The *U-117* was a mine-laying submarine capable of long-range cruising. In addition to mines she carried torpedoes and a mounted deck gun. In July 1918 she left Kiel, departed the Baltic for the North Sea, rounded the Shetland Islands, and headed for the eastern coast of the United States. Droscher's mission was to lay minefields off the U.S. coast and use the *U-117's* firepower to destroy enemy shipping in that area. His cruise was a dramatic success.

The sinister U-117, a major menace to American shipping in 1918 and the killer of Deering's Dorothy B. Barrett *in August of that year. Courtesy: Joe Hartwell, http://freepages.miliary.rootsweb.com/~cacunithistories/U_117.html.*

The *U-117* arrived off the northeast coast of the United States on 8 August. By 12 August the submarine had sunk nine American fishing vessels by gunfire and set charges and torpedoed two steamers: the armed Norwegian *Sommerstadt* (a kill), and the American tanker *Frederick R. Kellogg* (sunk but salvaged off Barnegat Lighthouse). While the *Kellogg* struggled for survival, losing seven men in the process, Droscher strewed mines that would later sink the U.S. freighter *San Saba*. Meanwhile, he resumed his cruise against American shipping. On 14 August, off the New Jersey coast, he spotted another alluring target: a deep-loaded northbound five-master.

In August 1918 Hungry Bill Merritt, with his sons Ray and Sewall aboard as mates, had taken the *Dorothy B. Barrett* out of Norfolk for Boston. This was the last leg of a long run for Merritt, who had sailed the *Barrett* from Santos, Brazil to Norfolk, where he had unloaded coffee and refilled with coal. Off Cape May the morning of 14 August, the seas were calm and the skies were clear. Suddenly, *Bam!* A 5.9-inch shell whistled past the *Barrett*. As Merritt recalled, "That was the first warning we had of a submarine." Merritt, who understood the international language of U-boats, neither needed nor received any further communication. "We went ahead and prepared to leave the vessel when the submarine appeared and fired four more shots. Then it submerged and came up again about 100 yards away and circled about us. We were not hailed and the U-boat apparently was waiting for us to leave." He and his crew clambered into the boats forthwith, leaving the *Barrett*, still under sail, to her fate. The *Barrett's* crew, now in no danger from enemy action, watched for a while as their schooner nosed down and began her death plunge. Sewall Merritt took a pair of remarkable photographs to remember

Left: Off Cape May New Jersey, 14 August 1918, the superschooner Dorothy B. Barrett *burns after being shelled by the* U-117. *The crew has abandoned ship but Capt. Merritt's son Sewall, a Barrett mate, snaps this photograph before rowing for shore. Alongside is a U.S. Navy SC-class patrol boat. Courtesy: The Merritt Family.*

Below: The last of the Dorothy B. Barrett. *The* U-117*'s latest victim takes her death plunge. Sewall Merritt photograph, courtesy: The Merritt Family.*

the occasion by—not that anyone on board was likely to forget. The *Barrett* sank in 100 feet of water, which meant that her topmasts would still have been visible on the surface as she hit bottom. But by that time all the *Barrett's* hands were pulling for Cape May. According to Capt. Merritt, the crew at first "continued to follow the periscope of the submersible, but the Germans apparently were not anxious for us to approach and really wanted us to get away. Finally we started to row toward shore.

"We rowed in about ten miles when we met a submarine destroyer [a 110-foot SC patrol boat] coming out, attracted by the shots." This vessel was apparently the second SC to investigate, for one of Sewall Merritt's photographs clearly shows such a vessel already on the scene before the *Barrett* went down. Merritt continued: "I sent the crew on in and returned on the destroyer to the spot where I had left my ship. When we got back to the place, there were no signs either of our boat or the submarine."[127] Knowing the *Barrett* was a goner, Droscher had not tarried to admire his handiwork—a wise move in view of the SCs' quick response. The *U-117* managed to evade an intense hunt by the U.S. Navy. A naval seaplane spotted the submarine on the surface, forcing her to submerge, but aerial bombs and depth charges from an SC failed to find their target.

Just one day after the *Barrett's* demise, the audacious Droscher laid another mine field off Fenwick Island, Delaware that would severely damage the U.S. battleship *Minnesota*, effectively knocking her out of the war, and sink the naval transport *Saetia* before the war's end. On the same day, after laying yet another minefield, Droscher repeated his tactic with the *Barrett*, stopping and sinking the powered schooner *Madrugada*. He was thwarted from further action by an alert naval aircraft. Droscher turned south and, on 16 August, off Cape Hatteras, torpedoed and sank the British steamer *Mirlo*. At this point, running low on fuel, he headed the *U-117* east for home, which he reached safely after wreaking further havoc and battling an armed merchantman in mid-Atlantic. Even after refueling en route, the submarine had to be towed the last few miles into Kiel—empty. By the time the last of her mines did their work, the *U-117* could claim twenty-four enemy vessels big and small, for her single cruise. But there would be no more cruises. In November 1918 Germany, in a state of economic and social collapse, signed an armistice.

FATHER AND SONS WHO OFFICERED SUNKEN SCHOONER

CAPT. WILLIAM MERRITT

Ray H. Merritt
First Mate

Sewall E. Merritt
Second Mate

Capt. William Merritt and his two sons, from a contemporaneous newspaper account of the vessel's sinking. Courtesy: The Merritt Family.

TREASURY DEPARTMENT,
BUREAU OF WAR RISK INSURANCE.
Form 1802.—F. C., Feb. 23-18.

ASSIGNMENT.
(SUBROGATION RECEIPT.)

Whereas, by a certain Policy of Insurance No. 17241 made and delivered in the City of Washington, D. C., the United States of America, through the Bureau of War Risk Insurance, became the insurers of G. G. Deering Co. for account of Gardiner G. Deering on Hull etc.,

From Hampton Roads, Va. to Prov. R.I. Boston, Mass: or Portland, Me.
On Sch. "DOROTHY B. BARRETT"

And Whereas, the said insured property has been lost or damaged;

And Whereas, the United States of America has paid the ~~sum of~~ proportionate part due me out of total of Seventy five thousand - - - - - Dollars ($75,000.00) in full settlement of any and all claims under the said policy;

Now in consideration of such payment, receipt whereof is hereby acknowledged, I hereby assign and transfer to the United States of America all my rights, title, and interest in respect of the said property, and any and all rights of action or claims against any princes, states, or persons whatsoever which I may have in respect thereof, the United States of America being hereby subrogated to all such rights;

And I hereby authorize the United States of America whenever it may deem proper to take any actions or proceedings whatsoever, or to enter into any agreements, in my name but at its expense, to recover the said property or the value thereof, for the use and benefit of the United States of America; and I further agree to make and execute all documents and to perform all such other acts as may be required of me to assist the United States of America;

And Finally I agree, if required to do so, to undertake in my own name such actions or proceedings on behalf of the United States of America, and at its expense, as it may direct.

In Witness Whereof, I have hereunto set my hand and seal, this ______ day of ______, A. D. 1918.

Signed, sealed, and delivered in presence of—

All is not lost: A subrogation agreement by which the Dorothy B. Barrett's *owners, having been compensated by the U.S. government for the schooner's loss, transfer all future claims to Washington. Uncle Sam expects to receive postwar reparations from defeated Germany. Courtesy: Maine Maritime Museum.*

The 1919 Versailles peace treaty banned submarines from the postwar German navy. The now useless *U-117* was requisitioned, sailed back across the Atlantic by Americans, and exhibited as a war prize in New York to promote a Victory Loan campaign. In June 1921 she was one of the designated targets for Col. Billy Mitchell's historic demonstration of aerial bombardment. Twelve bombs put an end to her off the Virginia coast.

Capt. Merritt was surely rankled by the *Dorothy B. Barrett's* loss, although his family has no recollection of this, remembering him as a jolly, salty character with a sea chest full of treasures.[128] The fourteen-year-old *Barrett*, which had cost $89,000 to build, had been insured for $75,000 (paid in full), and G. G. Deering Company bore Merritt no ill will for the mishap. On the contrary, in 1919 he was given command of Deering's last superschooner.

Four months before the *Dorothy B. Barrett* went down, G. G. Deering Company launched another vessel, the four-masted *Harry G. Deering* (1,342 tons, 208 feet). Although no giant, thanks to wartime inflation she cost a whopping $147,200—$12,000 more than the very similar *Maude M. Morey* of the previous year. Elisha Atkins was her master. As usual, a reporter was on hand to assure *Times* readers that Bath's latest schooner "presented a remarkably attractive picture…. 'She's as sound as a nut and as good as she looks,' said a grizzled old ship carpenter to a little group which had gathered to admire the graceful lines of the new craft which today is added to Uncle Sam's merchant marine."[129]

A later article about her in the *New York World* heaped praises upon her amenities, which were indeed impressive. In a possible allusion to the *Deering* crew's ethnicity, the *World* assured readers that the schooner was "better equipped then the average Harlem flat. She has electric lights, run by the donkey engine, hot and cold running water in her cabin and galley, and steam heat. Capt. Atkins has a double brass bed with bath." Added to the cabin luxuries was an interesting wrinkle: extra cabin berths "to be occupied by a passenger or two who wants a real sea voyage and hears of the Deering's doings." Obviously, going to sea aboard a sailing vessel, even a brand-new one, was to New Yorkers a whiff of bygone days.

"As sound as a nut and as good as she looks." That is the verdict of a veteran carpenter who helped build the Harry G. Deering *in 1918. A year later the schooner's mate will boast that "she went so fast the paint would not hold on." Courtesy: Maine Maritime Museum.*

What might have prompted dudes to go to sea aboard the *Harry G. Deering*, and what interested the *World* about her, was her combination of archaic and contemporary characteristics. "G.G. Deering of Bath, who built and owns the schooner, did not design her for speed, but for practical purposes. She can load 2,100 tons deadweight. Her speed already has been a great asset, however, in addition to her capabilities for rapid unloading and a quick turnaround. With cables strung from her peaks her cargo can be swung out of her in jig time."[130] Jig time was the name of the game for the *Deering*, which had just completed a passage from Norfolk to Para, Brazil with coal at $17.50 a ton. Ten years earlier, Gard Deering had admitted he could make money at $1.00 a ton—or, adjusting for inflation, $2.00 in 1918. In March 1919—postwar, but with astronomical wartime rates still in effect, she loaded 2,000 tons of raw rubber and 80 tons of butternuts and made it from Para to New York in *twenty days*, a record for sailing vessels and faster than steamers on the same route. Atkins, in a personal race with a competing steamer, had beaten the smoke yet again. His record-setting voyage, moreover, was achieved despite significant setbacks en route. It was this accomplishment that had prompted the *New York World* to investigate.

Determined to get a good story, a well-seasoned *World* journalist pumped Bill Struck, the *Deering's* equally well-seasoned mate, for details. He was well rewarded. Struck undoubtedly believed that as the practitioner of a dying art he was entitled to his fifteen minutes of fame.

"Bath, Maine, 1918": A builder's plate from one of the Harry G. Deering's *quarter bitts. Within a year the* Deering *will set a speed record: twenty days from Para, Brazil, to New York, beating a steamer on the same route. Courtesy: Capts. Douglas K. and Linda J. Lee.*

Accordingly, he eagerly obliged the reporter for posterity's sake, for which posterity owes him a debt of gratitude. Struck and the reporter produced a memorable account of the run from Para to New York, in which the *Harry G. Deering* "put to sea and headed around the Delta of the Amazon like a race horse taking the first turn.

"There was a fresh northeast breeze by which she could just fetch on her course to the north. She was close hauled and away with the bit in her teeth. For four days she was heeled to this and then the wind hauled to the east. Her sheets were eased and she picked up at ten knots, then thirteen. . . .

"Struck said a few whales were passed and that they ducked for shame at being outswam. He usually fishes when in the doldrums and like every complete sea trip, this record-breaking one had them too. After the easter there came a four day calm. One day the Deering was set back 27 miles by the current. But Struck did not mind that half as much as he did the fact that the fish were then in some other part of the ocean.

"When the breeze woke up again the Deering headed up east of Porto Rico. She skinned in this side of Bermuda and 'made' Cape Hatteras in the distance. During one spell of light wind and heavy sea her main sail ripped. Struck, the second mate and a seaman went aloft and spliced it without the Deering heaving to."

When she made New York, "all hands aboard were looking for the steamer that had been beaten on the run. She had not arrived. Capt. Atkins was pleased at this, particularly as he had been asked in Para if the Deering was fast enough to carry United States mail. All he said was 'Put it aboard.' Many a letter was read here yesterday that had been blown here from Brazil." Enough said. The *World* pronounced the *Harry G. Deering* "Queen of the Windjammer Fleet."[131]

It was probably the *Harry G. Deering* that returned from Brazil with a talking parrot. This exotic souvenir made quite a hit at the Deering yard, so the mate who owned her (Bill Struck?) presented her to Frank Deering as a surprise for his family. Frank's young sons were suitably delighted when the bird came home. But alas, the parrot was a bit too amusing, having picked up choice salty phrases during the long voyage from Brazil. When it opened its beak, the Frank

Cat. No. 1504 a
(Ed. Nov. 14-17—20,000.)

(TO BE RETAINED BY SEAMAN)

SEAMAN'S CERTIFICATE OF AMERICAN CITIZENSHIP OR INTENTION PAPERS

DEPARTMENT OF COMMERCE
BUREAU OF NAVIGATION

number 115
File E.

I, R.H.PADDISON
~~(a) Collector of the district of~~
(b) Shipping Commissioner of the port of NORFOLK VIRGINIA
do hereby certify, that E.D.ATKINS
an American seaman, aged 57 years, or thereabouts, of the height of 5 feet 9 inches, color of eyes Blue, of hair Black
complexion Fair, special characteristics
Gold bridgework on lower front teeth.

has, this day, produced to me proof and I do hereby certify that the said
E.D.ATKINS
(a) is a citizen of the United States of America.
~~(b) has taken out intention papers. (Former allegiance~~)

In witness whereof, I have hereunto set my hand and seal of office,
this 30 th day of January, 191 8

R.H. Paddison
~~(a) Collector of Customs.~~
(b) U. S. Shipping Commissioner.

E D Atkins

Left: Elisha Atkins's wartime seaman's certificate, issued shortly before taking command of the Harry G. Deering. By not saying cheese, Capt. Atkins has denied us a glimpse of his certified "special characteristics": gold bridgework. Courtesy: Parker Family Collection.

C Form 869.

SERIAL NUMBER
5772

ISSUE NUMBER 5

UNITED STATES DEPARTMENT OF COMMERCE
STEAMBOAT INSPECTION SERVICE

LICENSE

TO MASTER OF SAIL VESSELS OF OVER 700 GROSS TONS

This is to certify that Elisha D. Atkins has given satisfactory evidence to the undersigned United States Local Inspectors, Steamboat Inspection Service, for the district of New York that he is a skillful navigator and can be intrusted to perform the duties of Master upon Sail Vessels of over 700 gross tons, and is hereby licensed to act as such for the term of five years from this date, upon the waters of Any Oceans

Given under our hands this 1st day of August 1919

U.S. Local Inspector of Hulls.

U.S. Local Inspector of Boilers.

Right: "Master of Sail Vessels of over 700 Tons": Elisha Atkins's master's license, renewed in New York in August 1919 Courtesy: Parker Family Collection.

Deerings were scandalized—or at least embarrassed. Back went the parrot to its former owner.[132]

Early in her career, the Queen of the Windjammer Fleet earned royal dividends. By the end of 1919 she had netted 57 percent of her cost. But the war was now over, the urgency had passed, and the nation was beginning its futile search for what future president Warren G. Harding would call "normalcy." Bath's economic expansion would not continue; in fact the City of Ships would begin to slide back into the doldrums, left with empty shipyards and half-built housing projects.

But meanwhile, business continued as usual in the South End, where in April 1919 G. G. Deering Company launched its last vessel, the five-masted, 2,114-ton superschooner *Carroll A.*

LAUNCHING

OF THE SCHOONER

Carroll A. Deering

BATH, MAINE
APRIL THE FOURTH
1919

Left: A momentous occasion in more ways than one. The Carroll A. Deering *is the ninety-ninth and last in a fifty-three-year series of Gardiner Deering vessels. She is also the biggest, and will soon become the most notorious. The art nouveau motif surrounding the title forms an interesting contrast with the stolid Deering house flag. Courtesy: Maine Maritime Museum.*

Above: Where is everybody? On a cold, windy day in April 1919, with vestiges of snow lingering in the shipyard's ubiquitous clutter, the superschooner Carroll A. Deering *is ready to go overboard. Two lonely figures at the bow, dwarfed by the vessel's scale and her soaring bowsprit and jib boom, survey the empty yard. The expected spectators are probably waiting until the last minute before braving the wind. Courtesy: Capts. Douglas K. and Linda J. Lee.*

Right: With guests now gathered in her bow, the Carroll A. Deering *slides into the Kennebec in April 1919. Though this is a special occasion, the walk-in crowd is unusually light. Once the waiting tug has helped the* Deering *tie up, invitees will gather for dinner at downtown Bath's King Tavern. Courtesy: Maine Maritime Museum.*

Deering, with a capacity of 3,500 tons of coal. To eighty-five-year-old Gard Deering, optimism about the future was normalcy. He personally supervised the new vessel's construction.

The *Carroll A. Deering* was Gard Deering's ninety-ninth vessel. Her bowsprit and jib boom were probably longer than many of the little fishing schooners he and William Donnell had turned out half a century earlier. She had been conceived while Europe's Western Front was still using up men and supplies at an unimaginable rate. But by the time she went overboard, peace had at last broken out, raising uncertainties about the future. What would the world do with the oversupply of shipping tonnage cranked out in the heat of the crisis? More specifically, what use would the world have for oversize windjammers now that the crisis had passed?

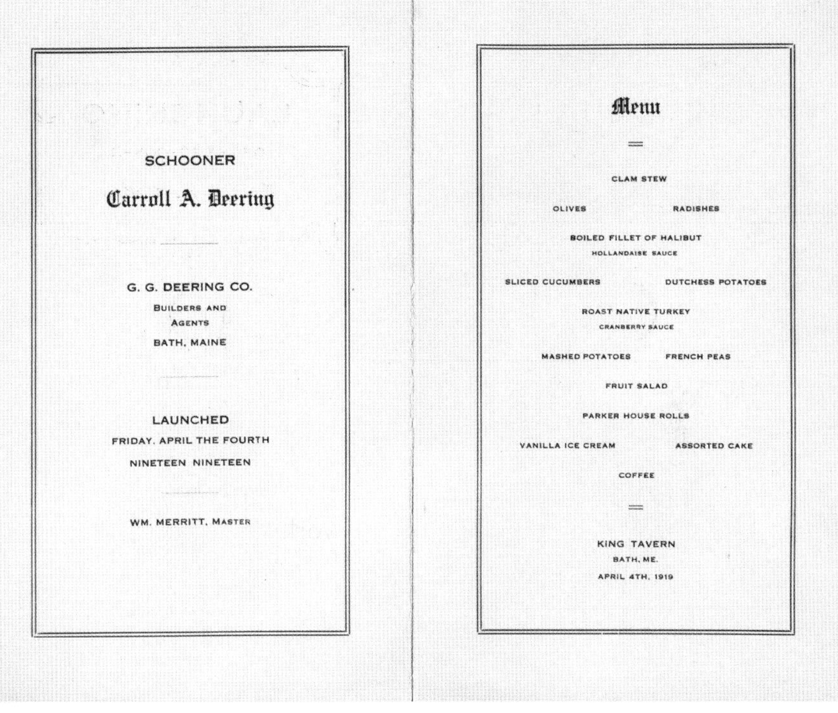
SCHOONER

Carroll A. Deering

G. G. DEERING CO.
BUILDERS AND
AGENTS
BATH, MAINE

LAUNCHED
FRIDAY, APRIL THE FOURTH
NINETEEN NINETEEN

WM. MERRITT, MASTER

Menu

CLAM STEW
OLIVES RADISHES
BOILED FILLET OF HALIBUT
HOLLANDAISE SAUCE
SLICED CUCUMBERS DUTCHESS POTATOES
ROAST NATIVE TURKEY
CRANBERRY SAUCE
MASHED POTATOES FRENCH PEAS
FRUIT SALAD
PARKER HOUSE ROLLS
VANILLA ICE CREAM ASSORTED CAKE
COFFEE

KING TAVERN
BATH, ME.
APRIL 4TH, 1919

One last cup of coffee, 4 April 1919. No VIP ever went home hungry from a Deering launching, but this will be the final festive gathering. Courtesy: Maine Maritime Museum.

The *Carroll A. Deering* was as well equipped as any windjammer to meet the postwar challenge of reduced demand. More than fifty years later her namesake, Gard's bookkeeping son, outlined her awesome proportions: "The Sch[ooner] Carroll A. Deering took about 8000 yards of duck to make the sails. The large lower sails weigh[ed] 700 to 1000 pounds. The masts were 110 feet long and 30 inches diameter. The top-mast[s] were about 16 inches in diameter.... She was 264 feet long and about 40 feet wide and around 25 feet deep.... She carried 110 fathoms of anchor chain on each side. The bar that the links of the chain were made of was two and one eighth inches in diameter.... The captain's cabin was all made of ash and mahogany and that was very nice. Nice as any home that I ever saw."[133] Her planking was five inches thick; her ceiling twelve inches. Although slightly more commodious, she approximated the size of the *Dorothy B. Barrett*, lost the previous year. Her captain, Hungry Bill Merritt, late of the *Barrett*, would presumably make a comfortable transition. Built at the top of the market, she cost $240,000 ($3,750 per share), more than two-and-a-half times the cost of the *Dorothy B. Barrett*.

At her celebratory launching the new schooner was florally christened by Carroll Deering's wife Annie. A pre-launch photograph of her depicts a wooden structure so improbably large that a row of animals marching two by two up her inclined ramp would not have looked out of place. Such enormity afforded her economy of scale, but the *Deering*, like her fleet mates, was small enough to trade in secondary seaports. And of course she had more than a half-century's expertise built into her. As for a possible postwar slump, there was reason to hope that wartime attrition, having far outstripped replacements, would make the world safe for surviving wooden schooners.[134] So off she went with coal to Rio at $19.50 per ton, returning from Buenos Aires to New York with grain. The next year, she freighted coal to Huelva, Spain, at $20.00 per ton. She was the last of a long and distinguished series, bringing the Deering fleet's total to ten working vessels. She also became the fleet's most famous, even notorious, vessel, generating an unsolved whodunit that bedevils maritime buffs and scholars to this day.

Although freight rates were softening, the *Carroll A. Deering* kept busy with long-range charters. In July 1920 she freighted coal from Baltimore to Guayanilla, Puerto Rico at $8.00 a ton; in September she was chartered for Rio at $10.90—still profitable although the delirium clearly was over. Outward bound on that voyage, Capt. Merritt became ill and put into Lewes, Delaware, where his son and first mate Sewall wired Deering for a replacement. Despite the short notice a competent replacement was found: William Wormwell of Portland. A well-known and accomplished schooner captain, Wormwell, sixty-six, had given up the sea full-time but was available as a relief skipper. He was taking life easy at a summer cottage in South Harpswell with his wife and daughter, but when asked to replace Merritt he immediately terminated his vacation and headed by train for Lewes. Both Merritts had left the *Deering*, so Wormwell sailed with a new mate, Charles McLellan. The rest of the crew stayed on: a Maine engineer, a West Indian steward-cook, and seven Scandinavians: a naturalized Finnish-American second mate and six Danish sailors.

The *Carroll A. Deering* discharged her coal at Rio. While in port Capt. Wormwell reportedly confided to a fellow captain his displeasure with his mate, a comment that in view of later events may have been more than griping shop-talk.[135] On 2 December 1920 the *Deering* left light for Barbados, where she was to receive orders for her next charter. Ashore at Bridgetown, Barbados, Mate McLellan, an insubordinate, heavy drinker, was jailed but Wormwell needed his services. Despite their incompatibility the captain bailed out McLellan, dried out the crew, and set sail for Norfolk to load coal.

On 29 January 1921, off the Carolina coast, the passing *Deering* hailed the lightship at Cape Lookout Shoals. Someone—not Capt. Wormwell, although his customarily private quarter-deck was uncharacteristically occupied by seamen—shouted that the *Deering* had lost both anchors in a gale and asked that that information be forwarded to Bath; then the schooner continued on her way north toward Hatteras. It was a somewhat puzzling incident, but it was nothing compared to what happened shortly afterward.

Early in the morning of 30 January, a lookout at the Cape Hatteras Coast Guard station spotted a huge five-master, sails still set, aground on Diamond Shoals. Her yawl boat seemed to be missing. The station launched a lifeboat to investigate but heavy seas kept it at a distance. When on 4 February the Norfolk salvage tug *Rescue* reached the vessel, still aground, she was breaking up. Capt. James Carlson and part of his crew were able to get aboard the wreck, which proved to be the *Carroll A. Deering*. Almost all of the *Deering's* sails were set although a few had been torn by wind. In the galley, food and coffee were ready for dinner. In the cabin, Capt. Wormwell's bed appeared to have been lately slept in. But, except for three hungry cats, there was not a soul aboard. The *Deering's* secondary boat, like the powered yawl boat, was gone. But where? Why?

Back home in Bath, the press closely followed these perplexing developments, probably by excerpting reports from nearer to the wreck site. On 7 February the *Times* related that "seagulls are perched in [the *Deering's*] rigging, waiting for an opportunity to pounce on the food she carries.... The vessel is said to be worth $270,000 but how much of her can be salvaged has not been determined.

"Coast guardsmen all along the coast are keeping a watch for bodies of the Carroll Deering's crew, in case they were drowned.... The trim, stately vessel presents a tragic but inspiring figure as she rests on the diamond shaped shoals, with her sails flying, puffed with wind, as if she were calmly sailing before the wind on a peaceful voyage.

THURSDAY EVENING, FEBRUARY 3, 1921.

NO NEWS RECEIVED OF MISSING CREW

Schooner Carroll A. Deering Remains on Sands Off Cape Hatteras

No news has come today concerning the Bath built schooner Carroll A. Deering which was driven on Diamond Shoals off Hatteras Monday night except that the vessel is lying there with all sails set but a rough sea has prevented reaching the craft, although the revenue cutter Seminole, and a boat with a representative of an insurance company, are lying off hoping to get more information as to the craft's condition when the seas, which are very rough, abate sufficiently.

The Deering was bound from Rio Janeiro to Norfolk, having called at Barbadoes and was in ballast. She was discovered abandoned by the coast guard crew at Beaufort, N. C., and the crew succeeded in getting within a quarter of a mile of the craft but owing to rough water could go no farther.

The fate of Capt. W. B. Wormell of Portland who was in charge of the craft temporarily, and the crew of 11 men who abandoned the schooner is unknown.

There were many Bath owners interested in this practically new Bath vessel, some of them insured and others not insured. One of the owners said that sixty-fourths in the Carroll cost each $3751. It was his opinion that the officers and crew were rescued by a passing vessel and that they will be heard from later. With heavy seas running on those dangerous shoals it was his belief that the schooner would prove a total loss.

The schooner is practically new having been built in 1918 by the G. G. Deering Co., and is 255.1 feet long, 44.3 feet beam, 25.3 feet deep. Gross tonnage 2114.

BATH DAILY TIMES, FRIDAY EVENING, FEBRUARY 4, 1921.

CAPTAIN'S WIFE DOUBTS SCHOONER IS DEERING

Mrs. Wormell Does Not Think Husband's Vessel is on Diamond Shoals

Some anxiety is felt in Portland for the safety of Capt. Willis B. Wormwell and crew of the five masted schooner Carroll A. Deering, bound from Rio Janeiro to Norfolk and reported as having been found in a derelict condition off Diamond Shoal. According to the report the vessel had been abandoned and was in grave danger of being pounded to pieces on the Diamond Shoal.

It has been reported that the derelict was discovered by the Coast Guard cutter Seminole and was identified as the Carroll A. Deering.

Mrs. Wormwell at her home, 61 Lawn avenue, this city, said today that she was not inclined to accept the report that this derelict reported by the Seminole was the Carroll A. Deering. She believes that had the vessel been abandoned Capt. Wormwell and the crew would have been heard from by this time as there are life saving coast guard crews all along the Diamond Shoal. She is anxiously awaiting some authentic word from Capt. Wormwell.

The Carroll A. Deering put into Barbadoes while bound from Rio Janeiro to Norfolk, Va., and sailed from Barbadoes for Norfolk on Jan. 9, according to the latest advice received by Mrs. Wormwell.

Capt. Wormwell is one of the best known skippers on the coast. For many years he commanded large five and six masted schooners in the J. S. Winslow & Co. fleet.—Portland Express.

SATURDAY EVENING, FEBRUARY 5, 1921.

DEERING WILL BE TOTAL LOSS

Firm Gets Message Saying Impossible to Save the Bath Craft

A telegram received this afternoon by the G. G. Deering Co., owners of the five masted schooner Carroll A. Deering, from Capt. William H. Merritt at Norfolk, Va., says that it is impossible to save the vessel. Capt. Merritt, whose home is in South Portland, and who was laying off for a trip and turned the vessel over to Capt. Wormwell, proceeded to Norfolk the middle of the week when news of the stranding of the schooner on Diamond Shoals was received.

A night letter was received by the Deerings this morning from Capt. Merritt stating that no trace of Capt. Wormwell or his crew of 11 had been found. It is feared by many that when the vessel went on the shoal the crew took to the small boats and were swamped in the surf.

The Carroll A. Deering was launched two year ago. She was valued at $200,000 and was on her way from Buenos Aires to Norfolk stopping at Barbadoes for orders, leaving there for Norfolk Jan. 9.

The wrecking tug Rescue of the Merritt & Chapman Co., had been sent from Norfolk by the Deering Co., through Crowell & Thurlow to the relief of the stranded vessel and is standing by now.

BATH DAILY TIMES, MONDAY EVENING, FEBRUARY 7,

MYSTERY SURROUNDS BATH BUILT VESSEL CARROLL A. DEERING

Some Seafaring Men are of Opinion Crew May Have Mutinied

A cloud of mystery surrounds the Bath built schooner, Carroll A. Deering, which went aground on Diamond Shoals, 80 miles south of Norfolk Jan. 30, with all her sails set and all rigging intact, but minus her crew. Members of the crew of the wrecking tug, Rescue, went aboard her Friday and found she was splitting to pieces and cannot be saved. They are preparing to strip her of all removable materials.

Capt. Merritt, of South Portland, Maine, who with G. G. Deering of Bath is part owner of the vessel, arrived Friday to determine what can be done to save her. Capt. Merritt up to last September was master of the schooner, being relieved because of illness, by Capt. Wormell. The schooner was bound from Barbadoes to Norfolk, light, when she went aground.

What has become of her crew is the question over which seafaring men are pondering. Many think the crew was lost in the sea in an attempt to get ashore when the schooner went aground. She lies on the southwest corner of Diamond Shoals about a mile and a half from shore, and for three days after she was first sighted she was covered with a heavy veil of mist.

The seagulls are perched in her rigging, waiting an opportunity to pounce on the food she carries. In her hold are nine feet of water and sand. The tide ebbs and flows through her split hull. No sign of any member of her crew has been found and no indication as to their fate has been received by coast guardsmen who have been standing by her since

The trim, stately vessel presents a tragic but imposing figure as he rests on the diamond shaped shoals, with her great sails flying, pulled with wind, as if she were calmly sailing before the breeze on a peaceful voyage.

One theory advanced is that the crew of the Carroll Deering mutinied while the vessel was at sea, and left her drifting with all sails set, and while this theory is a bare one, it is said by shipping men to afford as reasonable a cause for the condition of the schooner as any other speculation advanced up to this time.

Wrecking tugs from Norfolk are standing by the vessel, and will do everything possible to salvage the most valuable portions of her before she is beaten to pieces by the waves.

Dreamers.

Just before the World war Sir A. Conan Doyle wrote a fanciful tale in which he pictured the plight of England starved and almost subjected by enemy submarines. Fancy almost became fact when Germany made its desperate bid for victory. Between the imaginative deeds of the short story foe and the real deeds of the enemy obeying orders from Postdam there was little variance.

The United States has just read of the first practicable use of the telegraph for sending photographs. The same idea was used in a fiction plot ten years ago.

The world nearly always keeps faith in dreamers and prophets. An agile hand does not always go with an agile mind, but the world does not forget

WIFE OF CAPTAIN OF THE MYSTERY SHIP IS HOPEFUL

Due to Her Efforts the Government Takes up the Search

Starting from what seemed like a blank wall as far as any clues were concerned and undaunted by skepticism and discouragements that met her at every turn, Mrs. W. B. Wormell, wife of Capt. Wormell of the schooner Carroll A. Deering, worked persistently and untiringly to clear the mystery of the disappearance of her husband and his crew and the apparent abandonment of his vessel off Diamond shoals last January until she had obtained the evidence that has set the whole machinery of the United States government at work on the case.

It was Mrs. Wormell who directed the case from the first and it was she who did all the detective work that has resulted in the amazing developments which were given to the world Tuesday morning, nearly a month after the Government had been convinced and taken up the case.

During the time that she has been making her investigations, Mrs. Wormell has had the devoted assistance of her daughter, Miss Lulu Wormell, and except for the aid that has been given her by her pastor, Rev. A. B. Lorimer, of the Central Square Baptist church of Portland, this was about all the help she did have, until she had gotten her case in such shape that the most skeptical could not question its completeness.

It was a wonderful piece of work and speaks for itself of the courage and the mind of this Deering woman.

At her home at 61 Lawn avenue Tuesday, Mrs. Wormell told a representative of The Portland Press the story of the correspondence that she has conducted in her search for clues to the disappearance of her husband, of the investigations that she has made and the following up of the hundred and one clues that have come to her, that gave evidence of the slightest chance that they might lead to something definite.

Begins Work Next Day

It was with some slight show of indignation that she denied that it was the alleged message from the sulphur steamer Hewitt that started her off on her investigations.

"I began my work," she said, "the very next day after I learned that my husband's vessel had been found in an apparently abandoned condition and I did not rest until I had established the fact beyond any doubt that there was foul play on the Deering and that my husband and his men had either been made way with or had been carried away as prisoners.

"From the very first I encountered the disbelief and the skepticsim of the sea captains in this vicinity. I visited the owners of the vessel in Bath and found that they were disposed to do nothing and regarded the efforts I was making as a wild goose chase. But I continued my work and my investigations single-handed and with no help except what my daughter was able to give me.

"I wrote to all the sea captains of whom I knew who would be likely to have any knowledge of the crew or the conditions in South America from which the schooner sailed. These men I found had less skepticism of the foul play idea than those about here and this encouraged me to continue my work.

"But the first definite clue that I obtained was the picking up of the bottle

(Continued on Page Three)

WIFE OF CAPTAIN IS NOW HOPEFUI.

(Continued from Page One)

containing the message that was found off Buckstone, N. C. When I learned about that massage I obtained possession of the bottle and the writing from the Norfolk custom house in whose custody it was and with this I next set out to find if this message could have been written by any member of my husband's crew.

"I sent to Lewes where the crew was shipped and obtained the shipping commissioner's papers there. To make more certain I asked for and obtained the leaf of the hotel register in that place where the engineer, Henry Bates had signed his name.

Sure Bates' Writing

"When I compared Mr. Bates' writing with that note found in the bottle I was convinced that the note was written by him and then I set out to prove it. I wrote to his mother in Islesboro and asked her for letters from her son and es-

What could have happened? Accumulating press reports follow the deepening mystery of the Carroll A. Deering*'s loss and her crew's fate. Courtesy: Maine Maritime Museum.*

"One theory advanced is that the crew of the Carroll Deering mutinied while the vessel was at sea, and left her drifting with all sails set, and while this theory is a bare one, it is said by shipping men to afford as reasonable a cause for the condition of the schooner as any other speculation advanced to this time"[136] Perhaps time would tell. Or would it?

In the days that followed, no clues emerged about the *Deering* crew's fate. Meanwhile, the vessel was rapidly going to pieces. Capt. Merritt, sent by Deering to investigate the wreck, declared her a total loss. A few pitiful bits and pieces were saved. In the words of Carroll Deering, "all that they got off her as I remember now was four sails, two riding lights, some of the flags, four pieces of furniture and the big bell...."[137] Wormwell's Bible was retrieved and sent to his family in Portland. Part of the wreck soon broke away from the shoals and drifted off toward Okracoke. The rest was towed off and dynamited by the Coast Guard cutter *Seminole* in mid-March.

Over subsequent weeks, then months, then years, a few concerned people doggedly pursued the mystery of the crew's disappearance. Shortly after the disaster, Capt. Wormwell's daughter Lula and Merritt met with Harry and Carroll Deering to elicit the firm's help in solving the mystery. The Deerings begged off. For them the matter was closed. But Lula Wormwell refused to let the matter rest, following every rumor and clue about what had happened to her father and his men. There were plenty. For example, about the same time as the *Deering* piled up, the steamer *Hewitt*, loaded with a volatile cargo of sulphur, passed through the area but soon went missing off the New Jersey coast, probably because of an explosion. Had the ill-fated *Hewitt* perhaps picked up the *Deering's* crew? Then there was the Barbados connection: Could the crew of the *Deering* possibly have been rumrunning to the States behind Wormwell's back? There was also a message in a bottle purportedly found on nearby Buxton Beach that, in a hasty scrawl, described an attack on the *Deering* by another vessel. *Pirates?*

While the story was still national news, Lula Wormwell and associates elicited the U.S. government's help in solving the mystery. They convinced Secretary of Commerce Herbert Hoover that the case deserved thorough investigation. Hoover immediately pulled strings at the Department of State and the Secret Service. Considerable effort and taxpayers' money was spent on unraveling the mystery; reporting on suspicious sailors in foreign ports, for example, and chasing down clues along the U.S. coast. But aside from discrediting the bottled message as the work of a crackpot, no real headway was made. And there it stands. More than eighty-five years later, after repeated retellings in books, newspapers, and magazines, we are still in the dark about what happened, although the "bare" theory of Bath's "shipping men," ventured just days after the *Deering* wrecked, seems the most plausible. The truth about Capt. Wormwell and his crew will never be known.

By itself, the *Carroll A. Deering* disaster would have been more than enough trouble for G. G. Deering company in 1921. Unfortunately, other setbacks occurred. In May, while the *Carroll A. Deering* mystery was still news, there was trouble aboard the *Mary F. Barrett* as she idled at the Maine Central coal dock in Portland, waiting hopefully for a charter. As mentioned above in Chapter Four, a gang of waterfront toughs, probably motivated by racial and labor resentments, boarded the *Barrett* and attacked the black crew, murdering one sailor. But that misfortune was soon eclipsed by events on board the *Gardiner G. Deering*.

The accident-prone *Gardiner G. Deering* had continued to perform in character. In 1913, while carrying railroad ties from Mobile to Boston, she came out second best in a collision with the Holland-America Line steamer *Sloterdyk* off Nantucket, sustaining serious damage to her bow. On Christmas Day, 1920, at Santos, the *Deering's* coal cargo caught fire, doing $20,000 worth of damage and of course putting the schooner out of commission until repaired. By wire, Capt. Chester T. Wallace was instructed to bring the vessel to Bath for repairs at the Deering yard. Accordingly, the *Deering* started for home. After calling at Barbados, she deadheaded for Maine. In June 1921 she arrived in Portland, but without her skipper. Capt. Wallace of the *Gardiner G. Deering* had been shot dead by the vessel's cook during an altercation at sea. After duly filing a report of the killing with the U.S. consul in Nassau, the vessel proceeded to Portland, where she was boarded by federal officers who directed her to proceed under tow directly to the Deering yard in Bath. It is possible, in the aftermath of the *Mary F. Barrett* killing, that Portland was considered too hot a spot for the *Deering's* all-black sailors. Upon her arrival in Bath, a waiting U.S. marshal arrested Wilmot, charging him with murder.

The *Gardiner G. Deering* was towed up the Kennebec by the tug *Cumberland* to the wharf from

Out of commission: The accident-prone Gardiner G. Deering*'s pumps hard at work after her frontal collision with the Holland-America steamer* Sloterdyk *off Nantucket in 1913. Seven years later she will again be disabled when her coal cargo catches fire at Santos, Brazil. Courtesy: Capts. Douglas K. and Linda J. Lee.*

which she had commenced her first sail. The *Times* correctly noted that as the superschooner slowly rounded Fiddlers Reach and approached the Deering yard, she passed "the pretty little home of Capt. Wallace at 218 Washington street from which Mrs. Wallace is able to look directly at the big, powerful hull of the ship upon which her husband sailed to his doom."[138]

Capt. Wallace's killing was copiously reported: "'I've been a praying man for eight years and I've regretted the day I ever came aboard this vessel,' said Harry Wilmot, 46, colored cook aboard the five masted schooner Gardiner G. Deering when he was placed under arrest...to answer a charge of murder in shooting and killing the well known commander of the vessel, Capt. Chester T. Wallace of Bath on April 25th last. The cook made no objection to accompanying the officer, in fact he said he was glad to go to court where he could explain the whole affair." Wilmot, a family man from Virginia with thirty years at sea, pleaded self-defense.[139] He told a bizarre story and the crew backed him up.

Somewhere north of Barbados Capt. Wallace had begun to act abnormally, obsessing about an imagined stowaway. (His behavior begs the question of whether Wallace had heard the fanciful tales of trouble aboard the ill-fated *Carroll A. Deering*.) According to the *Deering's* mate, the skipper, armed with a pistol, began pacing the deck "in a highly strong mood," ordering Wilmot to produce the nonexistent stowaway, and punctuating his demand with potshots at the masthead. He went forward to the engine room and, standing at the companionway, fired three shots at the engineer without effect because the mate, by his own account, "was able to beckon the engineer how to dodge. The latter was able to circle about the mast and escaped being hit by the bullets." Wallace returned to the mess room and fired twice at Wilmot, who escaped through a small port with a flesh wound. "Whipping from his own pocket a revolver the cook...fired two shots at his captain. 'I didn't want to kill him,' he is alleged to have said, 'but I wanted to wound him to save my own life.' One of Wilmot's bullets struck Wallace in the chest and down he went. 'I'm sorry I had to shoot him but it was a case of his life or mine.' The mate concurred. Why was Wilmot packing a pistol? He had bought it several years before, he said, expecting to sell it "in a southern port," but had been unable to get a good price. Charges were dropped.

Repair work commenced on the *Gardiner G. Deering*. The *Times* provided one last interesting detail: "Foremost among those at the Deering yard while the schooner was being docked was Gardiner G. Deering himself, the aged head of the G. G. Deering Co., for whom the five masted schooner is named. An enlarged likeness of Mr. Deering hangs from a partition in the main cabin of the vessel."[140] And as the vessel was nudged to the wharf, "it was the aged builder who took general supervision of her docking, walking along the edge of the wharf with the same elastic step as in his youth, when he gave directions where to fasten the lines."[141] Gardiner G. Deering was eighty-seven; *Gardiner G. Deering* was seventeen—no spring chicken in schooner years. True to form, the old man would personally supervise his namesake's restoration. He probably jumped at the challenge, for, in the midst of the postwar shipping glut, G. G. Deering Company had no plans for new vessels.

As he busied himself repairing the superschooner that bore his name, Gard Deering probably worked with a heavy heart. Even a hardcore optimist like himself had to admit by mid-1921 that building more schooners was out of the question. At Percy & Small next door, all was quiet. Work there on a vessel had halted a year ago at the framing stage and would not resume. Uptown, the high-tech yards were growing quiet as wartime contracts expired. In 1920, G. G. Deering had sold the creaky *Lewis H. Goward* to a New York firm, a move that, whatever the price, had been prescient. In April 1921 came the news that the *Goward* had been lost to fire near Key West. In that year the *Elisha Atkins* was sold to New York. She would be wrecked at Cape Lookout, North Carolina, in 1924.

Shipbuilding? Why bother? In May, just days before the *Gardiner G Deering's* arrival, Gard had undoubtedly read the *Times's* doleful news that "sailing vessels, which were bringing fabulous prices three or four years ago are now selling at figures that must stagger their owners," in some cases one-sixth of their construction costs. Capt. Pierce Lewis, formerly of Bath, who had lately delivered a now-redundant steamer to Uncle Sam in Newport News, told the *Times* that more than 500 decommissioned steamers were anchored in the James River, "while 25 miles further up the river are approximately 300 wooden boats. These are tied together head to tail in bunches of nine, one mother ship carrying a crew of 30 men at Shipping Board wages being assigned to look after the other eight ships."[142] Between excess vessels and reduced demand, freight rates were plummeting. The question was not whether to build more schooners. The question was how—or if—to manage the eight that remained in the family fleet.

Finishing up work on the *Gardiner G. Deering*, Gard could take some satisfaction that under his sons' management the family firm had diversified its assets. The Deerings, in fact, were wealthy. But building schooners had never been just about money.

Shipshape again after a few weeks' refit, the *Gardiner G. Deering* cast off from the shipyard wharf and took a tow out of the Kennebec to a Portland dry-dock where she would be scraped and repainted. Gard Deering went home.

A few weeks later, Bath residents noticed that Deering was no longer seen sitting on his porch, as was his habit when off work. The old man had complained of a slight indisposition and stayed indoors. In mid-October he felt no better and took to his bed. On 21 October 1921 he died peacefully. In death as in life, Gardiner Deering's timing was impeccable.

For Lydia Deering, Gard's eighty-three-year-old widow, grief had exacerbated longstanding mental problems diagnosed as Alzheimer's disease and depression. For years she had been under a local doctor's care and had received "Christian Science treatment" for her disorder in Massachusetts, to no apparent avail. Out of consideration for her, Gard's funeral on the 23rd was a brief one, held at home on Washington Street. The spacious house was filled with floral tributes described as "beautiful and abundant, there being many large set pieces from organizations with which Mr. Deering had been identified, personal friends and business associates...." These tributes were supplemented by numerous condolence letters and telegrams "from far and near for Mr. Deering was well known up and down the Atlantic seaboard."[143] The house was crowded with mourners including bankers, local politicians, lodge brothers, and congregants of the Corliss Street Baptist Church. Borne by six grandsons, Deering's body was interred in the North End's Oak Grove Cemetery.

The funereal tributes were no greater than a man of Deering's local reputation deserved. More surprising, and of course more enduring, were eulogies provided by the press which, avoiding mawkishness and platitudes, admirably captured what it was about the man that had so engaged people for decades. "Papers in all parts of New England are commenting upon the death of Bath's veteran shipbuilder," wrote the *Bath Daily Times* on 27 October, "and holding him up as one of the finest examples of this race of old time builders and owners, who have done so much for the American merchant marine. The Portland Evening Express of last night says: 'The coming generation will do well indeed, if it maintains the reputation of the shipbuilders of the past half century in Maine.' These old timers in the industry have about all gone. Mr. Deering was the oldest active builder of the lot. He saw many changes in ship construction in his day, inaugurated some of them, and took advantage of the various changed conditions as they came along, winning success in his work and the respect of his fellow men."

"The oldest active Maine shipbuilder": Gardiner G. Deering near the end of his life. F. V. Moody photograph, courtesy: Maine Maritime Museum.

Well said. But it was the *Boston Globe's* tribute that deserves the last word: "On the west bank of the Kennebec at Bath, which was once almost continuous shipyards from the north of the city to far south of it, wooden schooners have continued to grow their graceful contours to the musical chink of chisel and caulking iron long after most of the other yards gave up the fight. Until the war gave an impetus to shipbuilding, the story went that an apple tree had grown up and borne fruit where the keel of the last tall ship was laid in the Sewall yard; but the Deerings went on building. Gardiner Deering was the patriarch of Maine shipbuilding. Your steel ship has to have a steel works to build it. Old Mr. Deering's wooden vessels seemed to sprout from the chip-strewn yard as naturally as the fabled apple tree above mentioned, and with no more machine shop visible than a smithy in a wooden shed. The offices of the yard were in another wooden shed, a one or two-roomed affair. His vessels plowed our coastal seas carrying the family name long after most Maine ships had been cut down into coal barges. The others might give up. Not he!... Something of the dignity which clings round the whole New England maritime tradition invested the figure of this sturdy old man. He went on building good wooden vessels when few others could or dared.

"At the hale age of 88 his sail has finally dipped over the great horizon. New England is the poorer for the loss of him and his kind."[144]

Three days after Deering was laid to rest, his namesake, whose repair had been his last act as a shipbuilder, cleared Portland for Norfolk to load coal.

CHAPTER SIX

We Don't Talk About the Family

More than a generation after his father's death, in a hastily typed letter, Carroll Deering explained the challenges he and his brothers faced in the early 1920s. Business, he said, dropped overnight. "We stop[ped] at the right time."[145] Carroll was referring to shipbuilding, not fleet management; for after their father's death, the three sons continued for a while to seek charters for the company vessels. It was not as if they needed the money. The company no longer depended on charter dividends. And Gard, having provided financial resources for his wife during his lifetime, had left almost all of his $420,000 personal estate (not including shipyard stock) to his four children in equal proportions. Perhaps family tradition impelled them to persist at a business that would probably never revive. More likely, however, family problems distracted them from reality. If it is true that the blessings of one generation can be a curse for the next, the Deerings fit the pattern. The blessings Gard enjoyed had been earned through hard work and keen timing—not good luck. When it came to luck, Frank, Harry, and Carroll Deering were their father's sons.

Ominous distractions took form just months after the old man's death. In February 1922 Frank Deering, an indulgent father of five, suffered a severe horse bite and died from its complications. For some time before his death, relations between Frank's wife Lulu and his siblings Harry and Emma had been hostile. The day after Frank's funeral, his mother Lydia revised her will, leaving the bulk of her personal estate to Emma. Eight days later she added a codicil to her will dividing her inheritance from Gard—about $120,000—between Emma, Harry, and Carroll, and specifically disinheriting Frank's children. At the time of his unexpected death, Frank's children stood eventually to inherit from their grandparents' estates about $22,000 apiece. The revisions of Lydia's will changed that. The financial details were complicated but their gist was that upon Lydia's death, Frank's children would inherit far less of the Deering fortune while Harry, Carroll, and especially Emma would inherit far more. Meanwhile Lydia, whose mental incapacity had rendered her incapable of managing her affairs, also transferred her substantial bank accounts and stocks to Emma, on whose management she now depended.

Lydia's last days were listless, melancholy, and uncommunicative. Such had been her lot since about 1914, but before his death Gard had been able to coax her to perform basic tasks. She had long since given up attending church, her sole outside pleasure being occasional rides in Gard's car. She had lost interest in her children, grandchildren, and great-grandchildren. Now, convalescing from a hip fracture, she was housebound, utterly dependent upon Emma even for meals, and almost completely withdrawn. On 18 December 1922, fourteen months after Gard's death and ten months after Frank's, Lydia died.

Considering her longstanding mental disorder, which had worsened in her last days, the recent changes to her will were disallowed by the probate court, but Emma and her siblings successfully appealed. For her part Lulu Deering took legal action to defend her chidren's rights under Lydia's previous will. When the case was heard the key issues of course were Lydia's degree of mental competence and, Lulu Deering contended, Emma's undue influence upon her helpless mother, exacerbated by personal enmity toward Lulu. Harry and Carroll, who had evidently objected to the size of Emma's benefits, withdrew objections after the three siblings made a private arrangement more beneficial to the brothers.

In a beautifully written, candid brief, attorneys W. S. Pattangall and William Glidden provided a painful litany of Lydia Deering's joyless old age, in which she "had become as helpless mentally as a little child and could not summon sufficient mental energy to wash, to dress or undress herself," hardly a woman to indulge in family intrigue, much less complex, split-second revisions of her will.[146] The case was eventually settled out of court, with Frank Deering's children receiving proceeds from the estate. But negotiations dragged on so long, and so much legal expense was involved, that Frank's children ended up with only $4,850 apiece, about six years after the dispute had begun.[147]

Relations between Deering descendants had understandably deteriorated over these painful years, and they never recovered. By general agreement, various Deerings lost touch with each other. "We don't talk about the family," became the unofficial maxim.[148] The family fragmented further. By the time inheritance issues were, so to speak, settled, Lulu had married Capt. Elisha Atkins, and Harry Deering had died after closing out the business that was the source of the family's much-disputed wealth.

When the shipyard closed, Carroll recalled, "there was still work to be done in the office, handling books for several of the vessels that we managed for the shareholders. We had some tails ahanging and I stayed on to wind things up."[149] Eight long tails ahanging, to be exact.

Except for the rebuilt *Gardiner G. Deering* and the hard-working *Mary F. Barrett*, the remaining Deering vessels were their newest and, Gard would have said, their best: four four-masters and four five-masters. They stayed in service in the early 1920s but their earnings dropped precipitously. For example, the *Lydia McLellan Baxter*, which had earned $3,900 per share in 1919 from three long-range trips, earned $500 per share in 1921 and nothing at all in 1921. The *Harry G. Deering*, after netting $2,120 per share in 1919, slipped to $760 in 1920 and $80 in 1921. It is easy to see why Harry and Carroll elected to downsize the company as quickly as possible. By 1922, their shareholders undoubtedly concurred. Easier said than done. Deering vessels were in top shape and highly regarded for performance, but finding willing buyers at any price was chancy.

Once again Mother Nature stepped in to simplify the process. The *Frank M. Deering*, which had earned only $70 per share in 1922, went ashore near Cobb Island, Virginia on 6 February 1923 although she was under way in fair weather. Her crew's distress signal was readily spotted and all hands were removed by the Coast Guard cutter *Manning*. The vessel was a total loss.[150] In 1924, G.G. Deering sold the *Lydia McLellan Baxter* to John C. Roney. Three years later she was ignominiously cut down to a barge. She lasted until 1937.

Back home again: The Courtney C. Houck *on a rare visit to the Deering yard in 1920. Courtesy: Capts. Douglas K. and Linda J. Lee.*

Holding up well: The Mary F. Barrett, *hauled out for repairs in September 1920. Courtesy: Capts. Douglas K. and Linda J. Lee.*

The Deerings' good connections eased the process of further reductions. For years, Peter H. Crowell and Luther K. Thurlow, close associates of Gard Deering, had owned in the company's vessels. Crowell & Thurlow of Boston managed an impressive merchant fleet. Although they had invested heavily in steam freighters, the partners continued to believe that schooners still had a place in American commerce. Accordingly, they stepped in to purchase some of G. G. Deering's inventory at a time when buyers were few and far between. In 1924 the *Mary L. Baxter* changed hands. In 1926, the *Courtney C. Houck*, *Maude M. Morey*, and *Harry G. Deering* joined the Crowell & Thurlow fleet. Things did not work out as rosily as Crowell & Thurlow hoped, however, so the vessels changed hands again and eventually became useless to their owners.

Schooners found a momentary shipping niche in the mid 1920s when Florida's real estate boom created a need for construction lumber. In 1925, the *Mary F. Barrett* and *Gardiner G. Deering* were taken over by the Boston Ship Brokerage Company and put into that trade. After Crowell & Thurlow had taken the last of the Deering vessels, G. G. Deering Company sold its silent shipyard to the Standard Oil Company. In 1926, the family quit the maritime trades. In 1927, Harry Deering died.

The last Deering schooners did not go quietly despite the changing times; so a few final anecdotes about them are in order. Renamed *John Hildebrand*, the ex-*Mary L. Baxter* stayed active until March 1928 when, carrying coal from Norfolk to Eastport, Maine, she was disabled off the New Jersey coast and became a derelict after a fishing boat had rescued her crew.

The *Gardiner G. Deering* had one last mishap left in her. In October

Left: Still working: The Maude M. Morey, *now owned by Crowell & Thurlow, in 1924. Courtesy: Capts. Douglas K. and Linda J. Lee.*

Above: A white elephant? The Maude M. Morey *in her last years of service. Courtesy: Capts. Douglas K. and Linda J. Lee.*

1926, full of coal for Bangor, Maine, she got into trouble off Matinicus Rock, lost her sails, and took on water. Her old Hyde Windlass pumps malfunctioned as coal dust in the water clogged their mechanisms, and the vessel seemed doomed. Persisting against the worst of conditions, a *Deering* sailor saved the distressed vessel by lying prone for hours, clearing one pump's valves while the second worked, then reversing the tortuous process as needed to keep the vessel afloat. The wretched *Deering* was towed into Rockland by the lighthouse tender *Ilex*.

Incidents like this one had become novel, so the *Deering's* close call was widely reported in Maine, although no journalist bothered to learn the identity of the heroic "colored seaman"

No further use: The Gardiner G. Deering, *listing from a shift in her residual coal cargo, at Belfast, Maine, in 1927. She will soon be auctioned off for $525, less than 1 percent of her original cost. Courtesy: Capts. Douglas K. and Linda J. Lee.*

who had saved the vessel.[151] The helpless *Deering* was then towed to Stockton Springs and then to Belfast where, listing from the shifting of her residual coal, she was sold at a marshal's auction for $525 (⁶⁄₁₀ of 1 percent of her original cost) in December 1927. Towed again, this time to Castine, she moved no more. On the Fourth of July 1930 she was destroyed when holiday celebrants set her afire.

In September 1929, the *Harry G. Deering*, still working, delivered coal to Bath. It was her first visit to the City of Ships since her 1918 launching. Although described by the *Bath Daily Times* as a "trim little schooner," the 211-footer had to unstep her topmasts to clear the new Carlton Bridge spanning the Kennebec. Carroll Deering, who came to the riverside to look her over, recalled that the schooner, under the late Elisha Atkins's command, "was paying dividends when many other schooners were losing money."[152] But the *Harry G. Deering's* dividend days were about over. She soon joined the *Courtney C. Houck* and *Maude M. Morey* in Boothbay Harbor's Mill Cove to wait further developments, if any.

The *Courtney C. Houck's* last years in the coal trade were interrupted in 1921 when she became a movie star. Hollywood had decided to make a six-reel movie of the comic maritime novel, *Cappy Ricks*, by Peter Kyne. The plot called for a large sailing vessel (the barkentine *Retriever* in the original story), and the *Houck* seemed to fill the bill. She rented for several hundred dollars per day. To satisfy Coast Guard requirements, the superschooner's name had to be officially changed to *Retriever*, then changed back to *Courtney C. Houck* when filming was completed.[153] Most of the original *Cappy Ricks* reels have been lost, but the 1915 novel is still readily available. Readers with a sense of humor are apt to find it delightful; those with a bent toward political correctness may not. After her brief moment of glory, the five-master, once again *Courtney C. Houck*, went back to the coal trade. In 1930 her career was over and she joined the idle *Harry G. Deering* and *Maude M. Morey* in Mill Cove, Boothbay Harbor.

And there the three windjammers sat for years along with a few other white elephants. If you had visited Boothbay Harbor in the 1930s, and were a camera buff, you would surely have taken photographs of these and other large schooners lashed together in the small cove, slowly succumbing to wind and weather. And if you were in town on 9 October 1937, you could have attended a wharfside marshal's auction with a few other bystanders and salvagers at which sev-

Left: Out of work: The Maude M. Morey *idles at Boothbay Harbor. Courtesy: Capts. Douglas K. and Linda J. Lee.*

Above: What will she bring? Looking forward on the deck of the Maude M. Morey *at Boothbay Harbor. She is about to be auctioned to the highest bidder and will go for a song. Charles S. Morgan photograph, courtesy: Capts. Douglas K. and Linda J. Lee.*

Below: Looking for a bargain? The Maude M. Morey *in October 1937, just before being sold at auction. There will not be much bidding competition. Alongside to the left is the* Harry G. Deering. *Charles S. Morgan photograph, courtesy: Capts. Douglas K. and Linda J. Lee.*

Left: The retired superschooner Courtney C. Houck *idling at Boothbay Harbor. Courtesy: Capts. Douglas K. and Linda J. Lee.*

Right: The ravages of time: The Courtney C. Houck *in October 1937, looking somewhat the worse for her long retirement. Charles S. Morgan photograph, courtesy: Capts. Douglas K. and Linda J. Lee.*

Above: Past saving: The deck of the bedraggled Courtney C. Houck *at the time of her auction. Her building costs were $240,000. She will sell for $255. Charles S. Morgan photograph, courtesy: Capts. Douglas K. and Linda J. Lee.*

Going, going.... The Maude M. Morey *is knocked down to a buyer for $320 at Boothbay Harbor, October 1937. The stone-faced bidders on the wharf have literally kept their hands in their pockets. Charles S. Morgan photograph, courtesy: Capts. Douglas K. and Linda J. Lee.*

eral aging schooners were knocked down to the highest bidder. The sparsely attended event was a far, far cry from the festive launching ceremonies that commenced these vessels' careers. But if your dream was to own a schooner, however briefly, you should have raised your hand. The *Maude M. Morey,* which had cost more than $135,000 to build, opened on a $50 bid and closed at a princely $320. Moments later, as if to prove that size wasn't everything, the "trim little schooner" *Harry G. Deering* opened at $200 and closed at $800. Her building cost had been $147,200. Sometimes, though, it pays to wait. The *Courtney C. Houck,* third in the sale, opened at $50 and closed at $255. She had cost $240,000, which made her something of a bargain, even to a salvage company.

The *Harry G. Deering* was converted to a barge. The *Maude C. Morey* stayed at her moorings until 1942, when she was towed to Casco Bay to serve as a wartime breakwater. A generation later her hull was still visible at low tide.[154] The *Courtney C. Houck* never escaped the confines of Mill Cove. On 4 August 1945, to celebrate the end of the Second World War, she was made into a victory bonfire. The remnants of her blackened hulk still rest in Mill Cove.

On 14 December 1925, the *Portland Press Herald,* still in the thrall of the endangered superschooners, reported the Boston Ship Brokerage Company's acquisition of the *Gardiner G. Deering* and *Mary F. Barrett*: "Tradition wills that a Bath built ship must die with her boots on. The Deering and the Barrett [have] successfully bucked gale and hurricane over a score of years and their adventurous keels are to have another opportunity to ride the treacherous ocean currents.... The Gardiner G. Deering and the Mary F. Barrett are the last of a long line of thoroughbreds of the sea put together on the shores of the broad Kennebec and dipped from the ways into the river's strong waters." Less than a year later the *Gardiner G. Deering* had become permanently disabled off Matinicus Rock, as described above. The *Mary F. Barrett*, however, soldiered on until October 1927, when she reappeared in Bath and was tied up at the old Percy & Small wharf. The aging superschooner had become an interesting curiosity. But was she, like other old vessels, apt to overstay her welcome, idling and decomposing into an eyesore? No. For one thing, she did not stay tied up but broke loose, drifting to the Kennebec's west shore before being re-secured. For another, liens against her had forced her sale to anyone who could find a proper use for her. Her five sticks were cut off in hope of making her into a barge, but that plan fell through. In 1928, Joe Totman of Five Islands, a village on Georgetown Island southeast of Bath, acquired her for salvage. Totman's plan was to beach her in a spot convenient to his home and break her apart at his convenience. Not so fast! When the *Mary F. Barrett* was towed over from Bath by the tug *Seguin*, aroused neighbors in boats put up such a protest that Totman had her hauled to a secluded cove in nearby Robinhood, where she was beached. There she stayed, and there she still is, after a fashion. On a July 4th in the early 1950s she, in the tradition of her old partners *Gardiner G. Deering* and *Courtney C. Houck*, was

The still-recognizable hull of the Mary F. Barrett *ca. 1957, almost thirty years after she was beached at Robinhood, Maine. She is still an evocative, alluring presence. Courtesy: Capts. Douglas K. and Linda J. Lee.*

Left: The Mary F. Barrett*'s rotting stem, still held together by stem irons in 1985. Courtesy: Capts. Douglas K. and Linda J. Lee.*

Below: Exposed: Visitors to the Mary F. Barrett *hulk in 1985 observe her exposed deck beam bracing, which Gardiner Deering had devised to eliminate hanging knees in schooner construction. Courtesy: Capts. Douglas K. and Linda J. Lee.*

set afire. But despite the damage she held together recognizably as a superschooner. As tourism grew in mid-coast Maine, the old, secluded behemoth became a popular site for boaters and visiting tour boats out of Boothbay Harbor. By the 1970s, however, time had done its work, remodeling the hull into a nondescript hulk, albeit an impressive one. By the turn of the new century nonboaters could catch a distant view of her by standing on tiptoe at the Robinhood Marina parking lot and looking east. Binoculars, helped. So did a little imagination.

The 1920s were a watershed in the history of the Bath Deerings. Selling the fleet severed the family's longstanding connection to the sea. Squabbling about inheritance fragmented the family internally. Soon Black Friday and the Great Depression would dissipate much of that fortune. An era had truly ended with Gard Deering's passing.

Two factors kept memories of the Deering schooner fleet alive during the decades after the company folded. One was Carroll Deering, who retained memorabilia of the years that had been the apex of his career. The other was the unsolved case of the "Mystery Ship of the Diamond Shoals," which continued to fascinate saltwater buffs.

Carroll, who took no other job after the company closed, seemed a bit of a lost soul, living on his maritime memories while admitting wistfully that he had not once been to sea. He was receptive and helpful to interested visitors, with whom he swapped stories over a libation or two in his barn, where he kept a few artifacts from the old vessels. These included the 32-foot name pennant of the *Carroll A. Deering*, which she had flown only on her launching day, and her bell, which was one of the handful of items salvaged from her wreck on Diamond Shoals. Over the years Carroll took to making ship models of all sorts from kits, which he added to his nautical collection. He also kept a scrapbook of "pictures of boats and schooners, that I have cut out of the papers from time to time. Nothing special."[155]

"Nothing special": An aging Carroll A. Deering, with his ship models and memories. Courtesy: Maine Maritime Museum.

One visitor of note to Carroll Deering's barn was Edward Rowe Snow, a prolific writer of popular books about maritime New England, with special emphasis on storms, shipwrecks, ghosts, pirates, and mysteries. He was at work on such a book in 1948 and, seeking a new wrinkle on the persistent *Carroll A. Deering* mystery, he sought out the vessel's namesake in

Bath. Snow spent time with Carroll Deering in the barn and in a tiny building on the edge of what was once the Deering shipyard, a sort of office in which Deering kept his models, clippings, and a few pieces of furniture from the old days. Conferring at length about the *Deering* mystery, the two enthusiasts made no breakthrough, but the visit gave an interesting immediacy to Snow's *Mysteries and Adventures along the New England Coast*, published later that year by Dodd, Mead & Company.

About the same time, Carroll Deering was also sought out by Lt. W. J. Lewis Parker, a Nova Scotia-born officer in the U.S. Coast Guard. Lew Parker, a serious scholar, was the first to focus attention on the recent history of American schooners. In sharp contrast to Snow, whose books emphasized melodrama, Parker was a "rivet counter" preoccupied with the most punctilious details of schooner history and commerce. For decades he photographed, gathered information, and wrote about these vanishing windjammers, amassing an enormous, comprehensive, unique archive on the subject. Schooners were a lifelong passion to Lew Parker, so a visit to the home of the erstwhile Deering fleet was inevitable. He was warmly received. In his seminal book *The Great Coal Schooners of New England* (1948) Parker praised Gardiner Deering's vessels, pointing out that the five-masters *Henry O. Barrett*, *Mary F. Barrett*, and *Gardiner G. Deering* "must have been very staunch vessels, for they remained in the register an average of twenty-six years which was well over twice the life span of their contemporaries from other yards."[156] Publicity from a man like Edward Rowe Snow undoubtedly sustained interest in the old vessels, but Gard Deering would have especially appreciated Parker's approval.

Carroll Deering died in 1967. By then, other Bath maritime buffs had chartered the Bath Marine Museum (later renamed Maine Maritime Museum) to exhibit, publish, and keep alive the City of Ships' rich maritime history. One of the new museum's early acquisitions was Carroll's pride and joy, the huge pennant his namesake had flown from her jigger mast when she slid into the Kennebec years before.

Thirty years after Carroll's death, the tiny building that was his retreat slowly succumbed to neglect near the site where his namesake was launched. Inside the locked, debris-strewn building nothing remained but an antique safe, a broken, emptied oak desk minus its roll-top, and a small, framed image of the once-famous Deering house flag.

Another link to the old days was Miriam Stover Thomas of South Harpswell, who as a five-year-old had summered in a cottage near William Wormwell's family in 1920 and had watched as Capt. Wormwell aborted his vacation, said goodbye, and left to take command of the *Carroll A. Deering*. Forty-eight years later, to resolve her longstanding interest in the "Mystery Ship's" case, Thomas made a pilgrimage to North Carolina's outer banks where, standing atop a sand dune, she glimpsed distant Diamond Shoals. "I felt like a White Russian meeting Anastasia," she wrote in 1973. "Something which I had heard so much about but never expected to see." Another sight awaited her: At a nearby filling station she was able to gaze upon the capstan and a few cabin timbers that had been part of the *Carroll A. Deering*. These relics, buried in beach sand after they had drifted to Okracoke Island in 1921, had been uncovered by a 1955 hurricane. They were now being exhibited as an enticement to tourists.[157] Waste not, want not.

A few unrecognizable hulks, a few museum artifacts, and a few memorable stories: By the 1970s little remained of Deering's maritime enterprise.

If you drove down Washington Street in Bath in the 1990s (no more trolleys, their tracks had been torn up in 1937), you might be astonished at the degree of heavy industry extending along the waterfront from the downtown well into the South End. All of it belonged to the Bath Iron Works, the only shipbuilding operation left in the City of Ships. The Iron Works, locally called BIW, having revived before the Great War's delirium, had somehow survived postwar hard times to grow exponentially during the Second World War. Despite severe competition the company was still going strong in the 1990s. As in wartime, its stock in trade was U.S. Navy destroyers. It had become legendary for quality and speed of output and was now Maine's largest private employer. Since earliest times, Bath had always been a one-industry town. In the 1990s she was also a one-company town.

How the riverscape had changed! North of the old ferry landing Bath's shipyards had all but disappeared, leaving a few pilings and assorted rubble amongst the woodsy overgrowth. Part of Bath's downtown had been flattened into parking lots for commuting BIW workers. Just south of the business district and the Carlton Bridge the shipyard's 400-foot-tall level-luffing crane, of its type the "biggest in the Western Hemisphere," towered over the river. Farther south, BIW's "Green Monster," an enormous, windowless, green-painted assembly building, ran for blocks, cutting off Washington Street's view of the Kennebec. At 606 Washington, the now-blinded classical white house that had been home to the Gardiner Deering family had been taken over for Iron Works offices. As in the North End, there was scarcely a trace of Bath's wooden shipbuilding days—until you got a mile below town to the site of the expanded Maine Maritime Museum.

If you, as a bona fide schooner buff, had come to town to visit the museum, you would be gratified by what you saw. A large new building housing exhibits, storage, and office space literally overlooked the old Percy & Small shipyard. Somehow, Percy & Small's property had survived changing times and changing uses with almost all of its original buildings intact. It was in fact the sole remaining American wooden shipyard in such a condition. Sam Percy's famous, noisy, high-tech mill and joiner shop looked very much as it had at the turn of the century, and the Maine Maritime Museum's ongoing goal was to restore and re-equip the yard as in days of yore—without the wood chips and clutter, of course. Just north of Percy & Small was William T. Donnell's Victorian trophy house, also undergoing museum restoration. Between the museum's exhibits and the shipyard buildings, you did not need much imagination to invoke some of the sights, sounds, and smells of the superschooner heyday.

Dedication of the Deering Pier
Sunday, June 26, 1994

Maine Maritime Museum & Shipyard

A reminder of the Good Old Days: Part of an invitation to attend the christening of the Maine Maritime Museum's Deering Pier, built at the site of the old Deering shipyard. Courtesy: Parker Family Collection.

Ever since its founding in 1962, the museum, like Tennessee Williams's Blanche DuBois, had always depended on the kindness of strangers. Starting from scratch and perpetually short of funds, it nonetheless benefited repeatedly from local and regional generosity. The Percy & Small property, for example, had been donated by Mr. and Mrs. Lawrence M. C. Smith, visionary philanthropists who, despite its shabbiness, saw the historical importance of the old shipyard, bought it in 1968 and held it until 1971, when the Maine Maritime Museum board was up to the job of taking it as a gift. Percy & Small's shipyard, refurbished with grant assistance, soon became a National Historic Site.[158] Donnell House, acquired in 1981, was also a Smith gift to the museum.

Just south of the Percy & Small yard, of course, was the old G. G. Deering shipyard site, although virtually nothing remained there to suggest its historical importance. In contrast with Percy & Small, not a single Deering-era building had survived. Standard Oil, which had bought the yard from the Deerings, later sold the property to the Gibbons Company, a local oil distributor. When Gibbons relocated, the property came onto the market. It was obviously just right for the museum (location, location, location!) but once again the question of money arose. And once again a benefactor came forward: Elizabeth Noyce, Maine's greatest living philanthropist, who had made the Maine Maritime Museum one of her most favored charitable projects. In 1986, thanks to Betty Noyce, the old Deering yard was added to the museum complex.

What goes around, comes around: On 25 June 1994, Gard Deering's great-great-great-grandson Gardiner Parker snips the tape, opening the Maine Maritime Museum's new Deering Pier. Courtesy: Parker Family Collection.

If you visited Maine Maritime Museum on Sunday, 26 June 1994, you witnessed another gratifying site: the dedication of a newly constructed wharf named Deering Pier. The new structure, part of the museum's long-rang plan to redevelop its waterfront, had been built in the old Deering yard at a cost of $163,000 by two favorably disposed local contractors, Harry C. Crooker & Sons of Topsham and Reed & Reed of Woolwich. If you joined the crowd attending the opening ceremony on that sunny afternoon you stood where the last fourteen Deering vessels had gone down the ways. Furthermore, you stood with some of Gard Deering's direct descendants, for whom this was indeed a happy event.

Other participants included the Maine Maritime Museum's board chairman and the chairman of Bath's city council. After the assembled guests were welcomed, Nathan Lipfert, the Maine Maritime Museum's library director, gave a brief history of the shipyard from its earliest days. A U.S. Navy chaplain offered a prayer. Then, at about six p.m., seven-year-old Gardiner Reed Parker, great-great-great-grandson of Gardiner Deering, did the ribbon-cutting honors, a gesture pleasingly reminiscent of earlier moments when Dorothy Barrett, Helen Atkins, the Baxter sisters, and other youngsters had christened new vessels and sent them down the ways to hopeful applause. Perhaps the new pier would serve to refresh memories of an era not long passed yet utterly vanished.

The Deering Pier's stated purpose was to serve as a docking site for "tall ships" (as surviving windjammers were now called) that might visit the Kennebec. Located south of town, the pier could play host to vessels that, like the *Harry G. Deering*, were too tall to fit under the Carlton Bridge. Tall, of course, is a relative term. No windjammer the size of, say, the *Mary F. Barrett* or *Carroll A. Deering* would ever again visit the Kennebec. Like a glimpse of a wolly mammoth, or a zeppelin droning just overhead, the astonishing sight of a superschooner looming through a mist would have to be imagined by future generations. Imagined but not forgotten.

"There has been a shipyard outfitting wharf on this site since at least 1854 . . . . Gardiner G. Deering constructed schooners here from 1901 to 1919." A commemorative plaque and granite monument at the Maine Maritime Museum's Deering wharf. Courtesy: Parker Family Collection.

Notes

1. *Bath Daily Times* (hereafter cited as *BDT*), 9 September 1889.

2. "A Branch of the Deering Family of Maine" (typescript [copy], Parker Family Papers, Woolwich, ME, hereafter cited as PFP).

3. Sagadahoc Preservation Survey, 2001 (Sagadahoc History and Genealogy Room, Patten Free Library, Bath, ME, hereafter cited as SHGR/PFL).

4. *BDT*, 9 September 1889.

5. Ibid., 29 June 1911.

6. *Weekly Mirror* (Bath), 18 June 1853, quoted in William Avery Baker, *A Maritime History of Bath, Maine and the Kennebec River Region* (2 vols., Bath, ME: Marine Research Society of Bath, 1973), p. 424.

7. William R. Donnell, untitled lecture on William T. Donnell (typed transcript [copy], 1984, Reference Collection [MS-54], Maine Maritime Museum, Bath, ME, hereafter cited as RC/MMM).

8. Ibid.

9. *BDT*, 24 October 1910.

10. Donnell House Docent Manual (typescript [copy], MMM).

11. William R. Donnell, "William T. Donnell—Shipbuilder" (typescript [copy], 1961, PFP).

12. Tonnages cited in this narrative are gross tons: vessels' internal capacity measured at 100 cubic feet per ton. Lengths measure distances bow to stern between perpendiculars (stem post to stern post), and exclude overhanging elements beyond those points such as bowsprits or rudders. A completed schooner would thus be substantially longer overall than indicated by her registered length. Readers may find such dimensions useful for comparing the relative sizes of vessels.

13. "A Group of Fishing Vessels Built by Deering and Donnell of Bath Maine, 1866 to 1886" (undated manuscript, RC/ MMM).

14. City of Bath real estate records (SPSES/PFL); William R. Donnell lecture (RC/.MMM).

15. Donnell, "William T. Donnell" (PFP).

16. For a lucid, detailed explanation of this and other aspects of schooner construction, see Ralph Linwood Snow and Captain Douglas K. Lee, *A Shipyard in Maine: Percy & Small and the Great Schooners* (Gardiner, ME: Tilbury House; and Bath, ME: Maine Maritime Museum, 1999), a volume that is essential reading for anyone interested in Maine maritime history.
17. Excerpt from *Bath Commercial*, 22 September 1877, in Mark W. Hennessy Research Papers (MS-52, hereafter cited as MHRP/ MMM).
18. *BDT*, 25 March 1882.
19. MHRP/MMM.
20. Nathan R. Lipfert, "Death in the Shipyard: Occupational Injury among Shipwrights at Bath, Maine, in he 1890s" (*The Log of Mystic Seaport*, Spring 2001), pp. 79–85.
21. *Bath Anvil*, hereafter cited as *BA*, 11 April 1908.
22. Ibid.
23. Baker, pp. 841–868 *passim*; "A Group of Fishing Vessels Built by Deering & Donell" (RC/MMM).
24. Baker, p. 612.
25. Donnell lecture transcript (RC/MMM).
26. "A Group of Fishing Vessels Built by Deering and Donnell" (RC/MMM).
27. Ibid; Henry Wilson Owen, *The Edward Clarence Plummer History of Bath, Maine* (1926; reprinted Bath: Bath Area Bicentennial Committee, 1976), p. 244.
28. *BDT*, 13 March 1885, quoted in Baker, p. 629.
29. Hennessy, notes on schooner *Oliver S. Barrett* (MHRP/MMM).
30. Snow and Lee, p. 108.
31. Undated newspaper quotation (ca. 7 May 1886), in MHRP/MMM
32. Hennessy, notes on schooner *William T. Donnell* (MHRP/MMM).
33. A complete list of Deering & Donnell vessels comprises Appendix A of this book.
34. These and other pertinent *BDT* have been collated in Robin A.S. Haynes, comp. "Donnell Family —Bath Daily Times—'Local News Columns'" (typescript [copy], RC/MMM).
35. City of Bath real estate Records (SHGR/PFL).
36. Parker McCobb Reed, *History of Bath and Environs, Sagadahoc County, Maine, 1604–1894* (Portland, ME; Lakeside Press, 1894), pp. 242–243.

37. Ibid., p. 245.

38. *BA*, 11 April 1908.

39. Donnell House Docent Manual (MMM).

40. Donnell lecture transcript (RC/MMM).

41. Ibid.

42. "Donnell House Docent Manual (MMM), pp. 16, 18.

43. Ibid.

44. Reed, p. 265.

45. "A Group of Fishing Vessels Built by Deering and Donnell" (RC/MMM)..

46. Ibid.

47. Ibid.; Reginald B. Hegarty, comp.,*Returns of Whaling Vessels Sailing from American Ports: A Continuation of Alexander Starbuck's "History of the American Whale Fishery," 1876–1928* (New Bedford: Old Dartmouth Historical Society and Whaling Museum, 1959, pp. 38–43).

48. Snow and Lee, p. 39.

49. Unidentified newspaper quotation (MHRP/MMM).

50. Dividend details here and elsewhere are taken from records in Deering Family Papers [MS-235], hereafter cited as DFP/MMM.

51. Ibid.; Unidentified newspaper quotation (MHRP/MMM).

52. Baker, p. 681.

53. Unidentified quotation in MHRP/MM.

54. Hennessy, notes on schooner *Horatio L. Baker* (MHRP/MMM).

55. Hennessy, notes on schooner *John S. Deering* (MHRP/MMM).

56. For a pleasantly detailed account of the ice trade see Jennie C. Everson, *Tidewater Ice of the Kennebec River* (Freeport, ME: Published for the Maine State Museum by Bond Wheelwright Co., 1970).

57. W. H. Bunting, *A Day's Work: A Sampler of Historic Maine Photographs, 1860–1920* (Gardiner, ME: Tilbury House; and Portland, ME: Maine Preservation, 1997), p. 304.

58. Baker, p. 585.

59. Everson, p. 176–177.

60. Wayne E. Reilly, "Maine Man Was 'Napoleon of Commerce"

(http://bangordailynewsws.com/news/columnist).

61.Logbook of schooner *Samuel Dillaway* of Bath, 1893–1895 (Small Manuscript Collection 54/03/MMM). Quoted remarks about the *Dillaway's* trips of the period are from this logbook.

62. Discussed briefly in Bunting, p. 304.

63. Capt. Douglas K. Lee, interview with the author, May 2007.

64. Ibid.

65. The *Wesley M. Oler's* brush with disaster is detailed in William A. Hill, "At Sea in the Blizzard of '98" (*The Rudder*, June 1951, pp. 18–19, 63).

66. Ibid., p. 19.

67. *BDT*, 6 December 1902.

68. Hennessy, notes on schooner *David P. Davis* (MHRP/MMM).

69. Ibid.

70. *BA*, 11 April 1911.

71. Hennessy, notes on schooner *David P. Davis* (MRFP/MMM).

72. *Bath Enterprise*, hereafter cited as *BE*, 8 February 1902.

73. *BDT*, 29 March 1902.

74. Ibid., 8 May 1899.

75. Ibid., 13 November 1900.

76. Hennessy note in MHRP/MMM.

77. *BDT*, 27 October 1899.

78. Nathan Lipfert, "A Brief History of the Piece of Bath, Maine, Property Acquired by Maine Maritime Museum, Previously Owned by the Gibbons Company" (typescript [copy], PFP).

79. Capt. Samuel Percy, interview with Mark Hennessy, 1924 (typescript, Mark H. Hennessy Collection, 1784–1954 [MS-18], hereafter cited as MHC/MMM).

80. Snow and Lee, pp. 74–75, 346.

81. *BA*, 11 April 1908.

82. *BDT*, 20 October 1903.

83. Ibid., 25 August 1921.

84. *BI*, 15 October 1910.

85. *BDT*, 29 June 1911.

86. Bill of sale, 1/64, schooner *Malcolm B. Seavey*, to Margaret Shorey (Small Manuscript Collection, hereafter cited as SMC/MMM).

87. Ledger, 1896–1901 (DFP/MMM). Wherever possible, cost figures are derived from Deering business records in this collection.

88. *BE*, 27 November 1901.

89. George E. Smith, "A Brooksville Mariner Recalls the *Gardiner G. Deering*" (Supplement to the *Ellsworth* [ME] *American*, 9 March 1989), p. 3.

90. *BDT*, 8 March 1904.

91. *BI*, 8 August 1906.

92. "Articles of Agreement" (typescript document loosely filed in Ledger, 1896–1919 [DFP/MMM]); W. L. Pattangal and W. S. Glidden, "Emma H. Rogers et al., Appellants, in the Matter of Lydia M. Deering's Will" (legal brief, May 1923, PFP).

93. Harrie B. Coe, *Maine; Resources, Attractions, and Its People* (5 vols.; New York: Lewis Historical Publishing Company, Inc., 1928–1931), V, p. 186.

94. *BI*, 15 October 1910; *BA*, 26 August 1907, quoted in Snow and Lee, p. 121.

95. *BI*, 15 October 1910.

96. Ibid.

97. Snow and Lee, p. 255.

98. Ibid.

99. Logbook of schooner *Samuel Dillaway* (MMM), 27 August 1894.

100. *BDT*, 21 and 22 May 1921.

101. Logbook of schooner *Samuel Dillaway* (MMM), 30 May 1895.

102. *Boston Post*, 5 February 1904; Hennessy, notes on schooner *Edward E. Briry* (MHRP/MMM).

103. *Courier-Gazette* (Rockland, ME), 2 January 1906.

104. Ibid., 2 and 9 January 1906.

105. *BDT*, 7 March 1910.

106. Ibid., 1 May 1911.
107. Owen, p. 307.
108. *BI*, 15 October 1910.
109. *BDT*, 31 August 1909.
110. Hennessy, notes on schooner *Montrose W. Houck* (MHRP/MMM).
111. *BI*, 15 October 1910.
112. Unidentified clipping, 5 December 1911 (*Lydia McLellan Baxter* folder, RC/MMM).
113. Hennessy, notes on schooner *Malcolm B. Seavey* (MHRP/MMM).
114. Hennessy, notes on schooner *William R. Wilson* (ibid.); *William R. Wilson* file (Frank Mason Collection, hereafter cited as FMC/MMM).
115. *Virginian Pilot*, 19 February 1913.
116. *New York World*, ca. 13 February 1919, reprinted in *BI*, 15 February 1919.
117. Logbook of schooner *Edwin L. Hunt* of Bath, 1913–1914 (DFP/MMM). Quoted remarks about the *Hunt*'s trips of the period are from this logbook.
118. Snow and Lee, pp. 287–188.
119. Hennessy, notes on schooner *Lydia M. Deering* (MHRP/MMM).
120. *BDT*, 31 March 1916.
121. Harold G. Foss to W. J. L. Lewis Parker, Hancock, ME, 24 September 1956 (Capts. Douglas K. and Linda J. Lee Collection).
122. Pattangal and Glidden brief (PFP).
123. *BDT*, 25 October 1921.
124. Snow and Lee, p. 326.
125. Owen, p. 323.
126. Hennessy, notes on schooner *Edward E. Briry* (MHRP/MMM); *Edward E. Briry* file (FMC/MMM).
127. *New York Times*, 15 August 1918.
128. Katherine Jensen (William Merritt's great-granddaughter) to Ken Martin, 14 April 2007.
129. *BDT*, 10 April 1918.
130. *New York World*, ca. 13 February 1919, reprinted in *BI*, 15 February 1919.

131. Ibid.

132. Barbara Parker (Frank Deering's granddaughter), interview with Ken Martin, April 2007.

133. Carroll A. Deering to Leila H. Chamberlain, 2 November 1954 (Small Manuscript Collection 01/04/MMM).

134. *BDT*, 20 February 1919.

135. George Edwin Smith "The History of the Carol[l] A. Deering" (typescript, 1968, *Carroll A. Deering* folder, RC/MMM).

136. *BDT*, 7 February 1921.

137. Carroll A. Deering to Leila H. Chamberlain, 2 November 1954 (Small Manuscript Collection 01/04/MMM).

138. *BDT*, 14 June 1921.

139. Ibid.

140. Ibid.

141. Ibid., 24 Octoer 1921.

142. Ibid., 24 May 1921.

143. Ibid., 25 October 1921.

144. *Boston Globe,* ca. 25 October 1921, reprinted in *BDT*, 26 October 1921.

145. Carroll A. Deering to Leila N. Chamberlain, 4 October 1954 (Small Manuscript Collection 01/04/MMM).

146. Pattangal and Glidden brief (PFP)

147. Walter S. Glidden to Lulu D. Atkins, 14 November 1927 (PFP).

148. Barbara Parker interview.

149. *BDT*, 22 April 1965.

150. *Virginian Pilot and The Norfolk Landmark*, 7 February 1923.

151. *Portland Press Herald*, 29 September 1926.

152. *BDT*, 6 September 1928.

153. Nathan R. Lipfert, "Bath Ships Scored Big in Hollywood," *Times Record* (Brunswick, ME), 5 July, 1978.

154. Paul C. Morris, *Four Masted Schooners of the East Coast* (Orleans, MA: Lower Cape Publishing, 1975), p. 167.
155. Carroll A. Deering to Leila H. Chamberlain, 4 October 1954 (Small Manuscript Collection 01/04/MMM).
156. Lt. W. J. Lewis Parker, U.S.C.G., *The Great Coal Schooners of New England, 1870–1909* ([Mystic, CT]: Marine Historical Association, 1948), p. 83.
157. Miriam Stover Thomas, *Flotsam and Jetsam* (n.p.: By the Author, 1973), p. 109–111; or see ibid., "The Mystery of the Carroll A. Deering," *Down East*, July 1972, p. 128.
158. Snow and Lee, p. 342.

Appendix A

VESSELS BUILT BY DEERING & DONNELL, 1866–1886

NOTE: All vessels are schooners unless specified otherwise. Three-masted schooners are indicated by (3) following their names.

DATE	NAME	GROSS TONNAGE	LENGTH	BREADTH	DEPTH
1866	*Hattie J. Hamlin*	32	55.9	17.0	6.7
1866	*R. B. Gangloff* (boat)	9			
1867	*Lizzie D. Saunders*	44	62.4	20.3	6.55
1867	*Willliam Walworth*	44	79.1	20.2	6.5
1868	*Glenwood*	62	73.4	21.3	7.4
1868	*Josephine*	39	60.5	19.4	6.35
1868	*Sea Queen*	61	73.3	21.2	7.3
1869	*J. H. Orne*	68	74.1	21.8	7.4
1869	*Ocean Belle*	67	74.1	26.5	7.6
1869	*White Eagle*	70	74.2	21.8	7.7
1870	*Dauntless*	70	74.3	21.8	7.5
1870	*Oceanus*	47	70.8	20.2	6.9
1870	*E. L. Rowe*	69	73.2	21.5	7.5
1871	*William H. Foye*	70	72.6	21.5	7.8
1872	*Mary O. Dell*	48	71.4	20.2	7.0
1872	*Walter B. Chester* (3)	421	132.5	32.0	14.8
1873	*Ajax* (3)	319	133.6	32.6	8.2
1873	*Georgie Shepard* (3)	586	147.5	33.2	16.0
1874	*Uncle Joe*	63	73.8	21.6	7.0
1874	*Willis E. Shepard* (3)	475	141.4	32.5	15.1

DATE	NAME	GROSS TONNAGE	LENGTH	BREADTH	DEPTH
1875	*George A. Upton*	56	75.6	20.6	7.3
1875	*Henry Friend*	67	74.2	21.9	8.0
1875	*Herbert M.Rogers*	78	78.7	22.2	8.0
1875	*Lizzie*	72	76.5	22.0	7.8
1875	*Martha C.*	79	77.9	22.1	7.9
1876	*Alice*	90	83.9	22.6	8.2
1876	*Gatherer*	96	84.1	22.6	8.6
1876	*Winifred J. King*	64	77.6	21.0	7.4
1877	*Golden Hind*	75	77.1	22.0	7.7
1877	*Marion*	82	79.3	22.0	8.1
1877	*Nimbus*	60	77.4	21.1	7.2
1877	*Willie M. Stevens*	81	78.8	22.0	7.9
1879	*Reuben S. Hunt*	183	95.3	26.4	11.8
1879	*Sarah M. Jacobs*	80	79.2	22.0	8.0
1880	*Electric Light* (3)	565	146.6	33.6	16.3
1880	*Frank C. Pettis*	30	53.0	16.5	5.3
1880	*Horace Albert*	69	73.1	21.5	7.6
1881	*David W. Hunt* (3)	349	135.4	32.3	10.4
1881	*E. H. Cornell* (3)	356	137.4	33.0	10.3
1881	*Ethel*	72	74.8	21.9	7.9
1881	*James A. Garfield*	74	74.5	22.0	8.0
1882	*Alice Montgomery* (3)	732	163.6	35.4	15.6
1882	*Carrie E. Laine*	73	75.6	22.0	8.2
1882	*Charles H. Haskell* (3)	476	145.8	34.0	12.4
1882	*Eliza R.*	72	74.9	22.0	8.0
1882	*Lizzie B. Morse* (3)	333	126.4	32.9	10.3
1882	*Matthew Kearney*	79	74.2	22.1	7.9
1882	*Maude M. Story*	76	77.5	22.0	8.0
1882	*William C. Greene* (3)	368	130.6	32.6	11.3
1883	*Emma*	81	80.7	22.1	8.3

DATE	NAME	GROSS TONNAGE	LENGTH	BREADTH	DEPTH
1883	*James Dyer*	81	82.6	22.3	8.1
1883	*Josiah R. Smith* (3)	704	166.8	35.3	15.0
1883	*Maude S.*	79	79.6	23.0	8.2
1883	*Samoset* (sloop)	49	67.0	20.9	4.85
1883	*Solitaire*	86	84.8	23.1	8.5
1883	*Vesta*	76	79.2	22.1	8.2
1883	*William T. Donnell* (3)	511	149.1	34.2	14.65
1884	*Gardiner G. Deering* (3)	718	161.2	34.8	18.0
1884	*Laura Bell*	82	82.5	22.5	7.8
1884	*Lucy W. Dyer*	82	82.5	22.5	7.9
1884	*Oliver S. Barrett* (3)	635	153.0	35.4	13.4
1885	*Christina Ellsworth*	97	84.2	23.6	8.8
1885	*Eliza A. Thomas*	93	83.0	23.4	8.8
1885	*Grover Cleveland*	92	81.8	23.8	8.8
1885	*Henry Morganthau*	90	82.2	23.3	8.3
1885	*Mabel Kenniston*	83	80.5	22.1	8.3
1885	*Melissa D. Robbins*	91	84.0	23.1	8.3
1886	*Carleton Belle*	139	93.7	24.5	9.3
1886	*John C. Whittier*	104	84.3	23.6	8.9
1886	*Samuel Dillaway* (3)	811	170.4	35.2	17.9

Appendix B

VESSELS BUILT BY G. G. DEERING, 1887–1919

NOTE: All vessels are schooners. Three-, four-, and five-masted schooners are indicated by (3), (4), and (5), respectively, following their names.

DATE	NAME	GROSS TONNAGE	LENGTH	BREADTH	DEPTH
1887	*John C. Haynes* (3)	720	171.3	35.1	17.8
1888	*Ellen Lincoln*	97	179.4	35.8	18.25
1888	*Horatio L. Baker* (3)	828	180.1	35.8	18.1
1888	*Reuben L. Richardson*	97	84.8	23.6	8.8
1889	*John S. Ames* (4)	916	188.2	38.3	18.7
1889	*Lydia M. Deering* (4)	1225	204.7	41.1	21.1
1890	*William C. Tanner* (4)	1034	191.4	38.3	19.3
1891	*John S. Deering* (3)	479	147.0	34.0	12.2
1891	*Wesley M. Oler* (4)	1061	191.1	39.0	19.2
1892	*Edwin R. Hunt* (4)	1132	196.6	38.9	19.4
1893	*David P. Davis* (4)	1231	203.8	39.0	21.4
1895	*Lewis H. Goward* (4)	1199	205.6	39.4	19.6
1896	*Edward E. Briry* (4)	1613	228.5	42.9	20.3
1899	*Henry O. Barrett* (5)	1807	244.7	42.9	24.0
1901	*Malcolm B. Seavey* (4)	1247	203.2	40.0	21.5
1901	*Mary F. Barrett* (5)	1833	241.4	43.3	24.7
1902	*Fairfield* (3)	564	155.6	35.3	13.0
1903	*Gardiner G. Deering* (5)	1982	251.6	44.4	25.1
1905	*Dorothy B. Barrett* (5)	2088	259.5	45.4	25.1

DATE	NAME	GROSS TONNAGE	LENGTH	BREADTH	DEPTH
1906	*Elisha Atkins* (4)	1259	202.0	40.9	21.1
1908	*William R. Wilson* (4)	1385	214.3	41.2	21.8
1909	*Mary L. Baxter* (4)	1036	188.4	38.0	18.6
1911	*Lydia McLellan Baxter* (4)	1352	209.2	40.3	21.8
1911	*Montrose W. Houck* (4)	1104	191.1	39.0	19.0
1913	*Courtney C. Houck* (5)	1627	212.9	42.7	24.6
1916	*Jerome Jones** (5)	1891	249.6	43.1	24.9
1917	*Maude M. Morey* (4)	1364	207.7	40.1	22.1
1918	*Harry G. Deering* (4)	1342	207.7	40.1	22.1
1919	*Carroll A. Deering* (5)	2114	255.1	44.3	25.3

* Renamed *Frank M. Deering* in 1918.

Bibliography

[Badger, Barber]. *The Naval Temple: Containing A Complete History of the Battles Fought by the Navy of the United States*. Boston: Barber Badger, 1816.

Baker, William Avery. *A Maritime History of Bath, Maine, and the Kennebec River Region*. 2 vols. Bath, ME: Marine Research Society of Bath, 1973.

Bath Anvil, 1908.

Bath Daily Times, 1865–1919, 1965.

Bath Independent, 1889–1921.

Berman, Bruce D. *Encyclopedia of American Shipwrecks*. Boston: The Mariners Press, 1972.

Bunting, W. H. *A Day's Work: A Sampler of Historic Maine Photographs, 1860–1920. Part I*. Gardiner, ME: Tilbury House; and Portland, ME: Maine Preservation, 1997.

Bunting, W. H. *A Day's Work: A Sampler of Historic Maine Photographs, 1860–1920. Part II*. Gardiner, ME: Tilbury House; and Portland, ME: Maine Preservation, 2000.

Cahill, Robert Ellis. *Haunted Ships of the North Atlantic*. Salem, MA: Old Saltbox Publishing House, 1997.

Caniff, Milton. *Terry Lee, Flight Officer, USA*. Racine, WI: Whitman Publishing Co., 1944.

Chapelle, Howard I. *The American Fishing Schooners*. New York: W. W. Norton Company, Inc., 1973.

Coe, Harrie B. *Maine: Resources, Attractions, and its People*. 5 vols. New York: Lewis Historical Publishing Company, Inc., 1928–1931.

Davis' City of Bath Directory, August 1902. Bath, ME: City Directory Company, 1902.

Deering Family Papers (MS-235). Maine Maritime Museum, Bath, ME.

G. G. Deering Co. Occasional Correspondence, 1907–1914. Parker Family Papers, Woolwich ME.

Donnell, William R. "William T. Donnell—Shipbuilder." Typescript (copy), 1961. Parker Family Papers, Woolwich, ME.

Fred T. Drake Collection (MS-8). Maine Maritime Museum, Bath, ME.

Everson, Jennie G. *Tidewater Ice of the Kennebec River*. Maine Heritage Series No. 1. Freeport, ME: Bond Wheelwright Co. for the Maine State Museum, 1970.

Fairburn, William Armstrong. *Merchant Sail*. Ed. by Ethel M. Ritchie. 6 vols. Center Lovell, ME: Fairburn Marine Education Foundation, 1954–1955.

Frost, Wesley. *German Submarine Warfare: A Study of its Methods and Spirit*. New York and London: D. Appleton and Company, 1918.

Greenhill, Basil. *The Merchant Schooners*. 1951. Reprint, Annapolis: Naval Institute Press, 1988.

Hegarty, Reginald B., comp. *Returns of Whaling Vessels Sailing from American Ports: A Continuation of Alexander Starbuck's "History of the American Whale Fishery."* New Bedford: Old Dartmouth Historical Society and Whaling Museum, 1959.

Mark W. Hennessy Collection, 1784–1954 (MS-18). Maine Maritime Museum, Bath, ME.

Mark W. Hennessy Research Papers (MS-53). Maine Maritime Museum, Bath, ME.

Hewitt, Charles E. *A Backward Glance: A Selection of Photographs of Bath in the 1890's*. Ed. by John Gaffney. Brunswick, ME: Brunswick Publishing Co., 1976.

Hill, William H. "At Sea in the Blizzard of '98." *The Rudder*, June 1951, pp. 18–19, 63.

Illustrated Historical Souvenir of the City of Bath, Maine, containing Half-tone Engravings of the Mayors, Ship-builders, Business and Professional Men, 1800–1899. N.p.: Walter Frye Turner, 1899.

Jane's Fighting Ships of World War I. 1919. Reprint, New York: Military Press, 1990.

Kaiser, Frederick F. *Built on Honor, Sailed with Skill: The American Coasting Schooner*. Ann Arbor: Sarah Jennings Press, 1989.

Kilfoil, Fred. "Portland's Double Mystery: The Crews That Vanished." *Maine Sunday Telegram* (Portland), 23 December 1973.

Kyne, Peter B. *Cappy Ricks, or The Subjugation of Matt Peasley*. 1915. Reprint, New York: Grosset & Dunlap, 1916.

Laurence, Frederick Sturgis. *Coasting Passage*. 2nd Ed. Concord, MA: Charles S. Morgan, Publisher, for the Bath Marine Museum, 1968.

Leavitt, John F. *Wake of the Coasters*. Middletown, CT: Wesleyan University Press, 1970.

Lee, Capt. Douglas K. Interview with Ken Martin, Rockland, ME, March 2007.

Lee, Captains Douglas K. and Linda J., comp. Historical Schooner Archive and Collection. Rockland, ME.

Douglas K. and Linda J. Lee Collection (PC-69). Maine Maritime Museum, Bath, ME.

Lipfert, Nathan. R. "Bath Ships Scored Big in Hollywood." *Times Record* (Brunswick, ME), 5 July 1978.

Lipfert, Nathan R "A Brief History of the Piece of Bath, Maine, Property Acquired by the Maine Maritime Museum, Previously Owned by the Gibbons Company, Currently Leased in Part by S.A.I.L., Inc." Typescript (copy), Parker Family Papers, Woolwich, ME.

Lipfert, Nathan R. "Death in the Shipyard: Occupational Injury among Shipwrights at Bath, Maine, in the 1890s." *The Log of Mystic Seaport*, Spring 2001, pp. 78–87.

Lipfert, Nathan R. "The Shipyard Worker and the Iron Shipyard." *The Log of Mystic Seaport*, Fall 1983, pp. 75–82.

List of Merchant Vessels of the United States. Published annually. Washington, D.C.: Government Printing Office, 1886–1929.

Lloyd's Register of Shipping. Published annually in single or multiple volumes. London: Lloyd's Register of Shipping, 1855–1925.

Logbook of Schooner *Edwin R. Hunt* of Bath, 1913–1914 (filed in Deering Family Papers [MS-235]). Maine Maritime Museum, Bath.

Logbook of Schooner *Samuel Dillaway* of Bath, 1893–1895. Maine Maritime Museum, Bath, ME.

Martin, Kenneth R., and Ralph Linwood Snow. *The Pattens of Bath: A Seagoing Dynasty*. Bath, ME: Maine Maritime Museum and Patten Free Library, 1996.

Frank Mason Reference Collection (MS 296). Maine Maritime Museum, Bath, ME.

Merritt Family Collection, South Portland, ME.

Morris, Paul C. *American Sailing Coasters of the North Atlantic*. Chardon, OH: Block and Osborn Publishing Company, 1973.

Morris, Paul C. *Captain from Cape Cod: The Merchant Fleets of Crowell & Thurlow*. Orleans, MA: Lower Cape Publishing, 2002.

Morris, Paul C. *Four-Masted Schooners of the East Coast*. Orleans, MA: Lower Cape Publishing, 1975.

Morris, Paul C. *Schooners and Schooner Barges*. Orleans, MA: Lower Cape Publishing, 1984.

New York Maritime Register, 1908–1911, 1927.

O'Leary, Wayne M. *Maine Sea Fisheries: The Rise and Fall of a Native Industry, 1830–1890*. Boston: Northeastern University Press, 1996.

Owen, Henry Wilson. *The Edward Clarence Plummer History of Bath, Maine*. 1936. Reprint, Bath, ME: Bath Area Bicentennial Committee, 1976.

Paine, Lincoln. *Down East: A Maritime History of Maine*. Gardiner, ME: Tilbury House; and Portland: OpSail Maine 2000, 2000.

Parker, Barbara, and Sally Jackson. Interview with Ken Martin, Woolwich, ME, April 2007.

Parker, Jackson. "Deering & Donnell Shipbuilders, Bath, Maine, 1866–1919." Typescript (copy), 1968. Parker Family Papers, Woolwich, ME.

Pattangall, W.R., and W.S. Glidden. "Emma A. Rogers et al., Appellants, in the matter of Lydia M. Deering's Will" (Sagadahoc SS., Supreme Court of Probate, May Term, 1923.) Typescript (copy), 1923. Parker Family Collection.

Pert, P.L., Jr. *A Summary History of Bath, Maine 1850 to 1900*. [Bath, ME]: By the author, 1995.

Photograph File. Maine Maritime Museum, Bath, ME.

Real Estate Records, City of Bath. Sagadahoc History and Genealogy Room, Patten Free Library, Bath, ME.

Record of American and Foreign Shipping. Published annually. New York: American Bureau of Shipping, 1867–1925.

Reed, Parker McCobb. *History of Bath and Environs, Sagadahoc County, Maine, 1604–1894*. Portland, ME: Lakeside Press, 1894.

Reference Collection (MS-54). Maine Maritime Museum, Bath, ME.

Reynolds, Erminie S., and Kenneth R. Martin. *"A Singleness of Purpose": The Skolfields and Their Ships*. Bath, ME: Maine Maritime Museum, 1987.

Rogers, John C. *Origins of Sea Terms*. American Maritime Library, Vol. XI. Mystic, CT: Mystic Seaport Museum, 1984.

Rowe, William Hutchinson. *The Maritime History of Maine: Three Centuries of Shipbuilding and Seafaring*. Freeport, ME: Bond Wheelwright Company, 1948.

Sagadahoc Preservation, Inc. City of Bath South End Street Survey, 2001. Sagadahoc History and Genealogy Room, Patten Free Library, Bath, ME.

The Sesquicentennial of Bath, Maine, 1847–1997. Bath, ME: Bath Historical Society, 1997.

Shaw, William E., comp. *William E. Shaw's Directory of Bath and Surrounding Towns, 1900–1901*. Boston: W.E. Shaw, 1900.

Showell, Jak Millmann. *The U-Boat Century: German Submarine Warfare, 1906–2006*. Annapolis: Naval Institute Press, 2006.

Simpson, Bland. *Ghost Ship of the Diamond Shoals: The Mystery of the* Carrol A. Deering. Chapel Hill and London: University of North Carolina Press, 2002.

Singer, Stephen D. *Shipwrecks of Florida*. Sarasota: Pineapple Press, Inc., 1992.

Small Manuscript Collection. Maine Maritime Museum, Bath, ME.

Smith, George E. "A Brooksville Mariner Recalls the *Gardiner G. Deering*." Supplement to the *Ellsworth* [Maine] *American*, 9 March 1989, p. 3.

Snow, Edward Rowe. *Mysteries and Adventures along the Atlantic Coast*. New York: Dodd, Mead & Company, 1948.

Snow, Ralph Linwood. *Bath Iron Works: The First Hundred Years*. Bath, ME: Maine Maritime Museum, 1987.

Snow, Ralph Linwood. Interviews with Ken Martin, Richmond, ME, March–April 2007.

Snow, Ralph Linwood, and Captain Douglas K. Lee. *A Shipyard in Maine: Percy & Small and the Great Schooners*. Gardiner, ME: Tilbury House; and Bath, ME: Maine Maritime Museum, 1999.

Stick, David. *Graveyard of the Atlantic: Shipwrecks of the North Carolina Coast*. Chapel Hill: University of North Carolina Press, 1952.

Thomas, Miriam Stover. *Flotsam and Jetsam*. N.p.: By the author, 1973.

Thomas, Miriam Stover. "The Mystery of the Carroll A. Deering." *Down East,* July 1972, pp. 121–24.

Tod, Giles M.S. *The Last Sail Down East*. Barre, MA: Barre Publishers, 1965.

Wilder, Joe, at http://freepages.military.rootsweb.com/~cacunithistories/U_117.html.

Wood, Richard G. *A History of Lumbering in Maine, 1820–1861*. University of Maine Studies, Second Series, No. 33. Orono, ME: University of Maine, 1961.

Index